Foundations
of the Metaphysics
of Morals
with Critical
Essays

Foundations of the Metaphysics of Morals

Immanuel Kant

TRANSLATED BY LEWIS WHITE BECK

with Critical Essays

Edited by

Robert Paul Wolff

THE BOBBS-MERRILL COMPANY, INC.

INDIANAPOLIS   NEW YORK

The Bobbs-Merrill
Text and Commentary
Series / Harold Weisberg,
General Editor

171
K16g Eb

Contents

v

Introduction

There is probably no piece of philosophical writing whose greatness is more widely acknowledged, and whose meaning is more widely disputed, than Kant's *Foundations of the Metaphysics of Morals*. Since it first appeared in 1785, four years after the great *Critique of Pure Reason*, it has provoked thousands of pages of argument, interpretation, and discussion. Ironically, despite Kant's insistence that he had nothing new to say about morality and sought merely to make explicit the deepest convictions of the ordinary man of conscience, philosophers are unanimous in acknowledging the *Foundations* as one of the very small number of genuinely original works on moral philosophy.

Part of the difficulty of Kant's essay derives from the complexity of the subject itself. It would be strange indeed if a work which explored the foundations of man's duties and rights should succeed in being both important and easy. But Kant himself must be held responsible for at least some of the obscurity of this difficult work. The bare outline of his argument is not at all apparent. Even after close study, the reader is still somewhat at a loss to say just what Kant takes as premises, and what exactly he seeks to prove. Then too, much of the argument is couched in a psychological terminology which was not even universal in the philosophy of Kant's day, and which since has quite passed from the customary vocabulary of western philosophy. More legitimately, but no less forbiddingly, Kant presupposes the conclusions of his analysis of cognition in the *Critique of Pure Reason*. An author has a right to require that his readers master his first book before tackling the second, but when that first book is the *Critique*, there will be many indeed who never survive the ordeal.

And yet, when all the warnings are issued and the qualifications expressed, the *Foundations* remains as an independent work of genius, capable of seizing the mind and moving the heart. In its dry, forbidding way, it utters some of the most beautiful words ever written about the moral life. In any abridgment of the moral wisdom of mankind, there must surely appear Kant's great formulation of the highest command of morality: Act so that you treat humanity, whether in your own person or in that of another, always as an end and never as a means only.

II

According to Kant, cognition of whatever sort involves two elements: an object of thought which is present to the mind, and a thought directed to it. The given object is called by Kant the *matter* of cognition, and the thought directed to it is called the *form* of cognition. For example, in experience we are presented with objects through our capacity to be affected, or our "sensibility," and the result of the effect of the objects upon our senses is the variety of perceptions which pass before our consciousness. These are the matter of our empirical knowledge. We then organize and interpret the perceptions and make judgments based upon them, employing for this purpose concepts lying ready in the mind. These concepts, and the thought processes in which they are employed, are the form of empirical knowledge.

The formal element in cognition, since it arises in the mind, can be characterized as *a priori*. Sometimes it is merely relatively a priori, as is the concept "horse," for example. When we approach any particular experience, the concept "horse" lies ready in the mind, and is employed by us to characterize the experience if our perceptions fit the concept. But of course if we trace the concept back far enough, we find that it has ultimately been derived from earlier perceptions of horses, and hence is, strictly or absolutely, *a posteriori*. It is Kant's principal contention in the *Critique of Pure Reason* that among our concepts there are some which are not merely relatively, or proximately, a priori, but absolutely and ultimately a priori, such as the concept of a cause, or of a substance. These are prior to and in no sense derived from particular experiences.[1] The mark of the truly a priori in cognition is *necessity*, for no con-

---

[1] It might be worthwhile to clear up a persistent misunderstanding concerning Kant's use of the terms a priori and a posteriori. Strictly speaking, these terms are adverbs, and they modify such verbs as "to know" or "to judge." Thus, Kant never actually speaks of "synthetic a priori judgments." He speaks only of "synthetic judgments a priori," and this is merely an elliptical way of saying "synthetic judgments *known* a priori." It follows that one cannot tell whether a judgment "is a priori," which is to say "can be known a priori," merely by inspecting it; the reason is that a priority is not a quality of judgments, but a quality of the way in which judgments are known, and hence of the relation between the judgments and the mind. It is, in Kantian terms, perfectly proper to speak of a priori cognition, but not of a priori judgments.

cept or knowledge of necessity can be abstracted from given perceptions (in this respect, Kant accepted Hume's skeptical argument); conversely, any knowledge which is known a priori will, as universally valid, be necessary.

Since cognition involves form and matter, it would appear that there could be three kinds of knowledge: that which concerns itself solely with the form of thought, without any attention to the matter or objects of thought; that which concerns itself with the form of thought in its application to some object; and that which concerns itself only with the matter of thought, without the employment of, or attention to, conceptual form. The first kind of knowledge, Kant says, comprises what the ancients called logic. It deals with the laws of thought. The second comprises theoretical knowledge, or science, and practical philosophy, or ethics. There can be no knowledge of the third sort, for knowledge involves thought and seeks laws; a knowledge of matter alone, if such could exist, would involve neither. (The contemporary doctrine of sense-datum reports or a language of the pure given is, on a Kantian view, simply a confusion.)

In the second category of knowledge, we can distinguish two major branches according to whether the aim of the cognitive process is to determine the object of cognition, in the sense of finding out what it is and what is true about it, or to determine the object of cognition, in the sense of bringing it into existence. In the first case, the cognition is theoretical, in the second case it is practical.

Material knowledge, although directed to objects, may yet have a purely a priori or formal part, concerned with what can be known independently of the experience of the objects. Kant calls this pure theoretical or pure practical philosophy. Now logic is possible a priori because it abstracts from all objects of thought and merely explicates the laws of any correct thinking. Hence logic tells us nothing about objects—it contains only analytic judgments. But it is not at all clear how material philosophy—science and ethics—could yield a priori cognition, nor indeed is it clear that it can. The function of the Critical Philosophy is precisely to explain *how* we can gain substantive rational knowledge a priori, to prove *that* we can, and then to discover *what* it is.

The a priori cognition that we seek may be either conditionally or unconditionally a priori. This distinction lies at the heart of Kant's ethical theory, and in its terms we can specify precisely how he differs from such moral philosophers as Hume. If a cognition is a priori relative only to the particular instance to which it applies, we may call it *relatively* a priori. As we have seen, all empirical concepts which we carry about with us as we observe the world are, in this sense, relatively a priori. But according to Kant, some cognition is prior to all the instances to which it applies, and is relative only to the most general conditions under which any objects at all can be given to us. These cognitions we may call *conditionally* a priori, and the Critical Philosophy with regard to them becomes a search for the "a priori conditions of the possibility of experience in general," as Kant frequently puts it. For example, the law of cause and effect is valid for all objects of experience. We can know this a priori because the conditions under which anything can be given as an object of experience for us include precisely the condition that it stand in the sorts of relations to other objects of experience that we call causal.

In the *Critique of Pure Reason*, Kant offers a theory of the conditionally a priori character of all theoretical knowledge. Such knowledge, he concludes, is possible only of objects under the conditions of their being given to us as appearances and only under the further condition of their being thought by us according to those fundamental concepts, lying ready in the mind, which he calls categories. In a complicated and difficult argument, Kant shows that we could only have a priori knowledge of such a conditional sort, and that we actually do have such knowledge.

Previous rationalist philosophers had sought a different kind of a priori cognition, which Kant calls *unconditioned*. Such knowledge is *not* limited by the conditions under which something is given to the mind, and hence purports to be valid with absolute universality. Unconditionally a priori cognition, if such there were, would be valid of everything whatever, not merely of everything insofar as it could be an object of human experience. However, in the section of the *Critique* known as the Transcendental Dialectic, Kant decisively refutes all pretentions to knowledge of that sort.

When we turn from theoretical to practical philosophy, what sense can we give to the term "object"? Since in the practical use of our reason we seek to make the object of our thought actual—to bring it into existence—the term "object" must refer to the end or goal that we are attempting to realize by our action. In order for something to be an object of our practical reason, it must be capable of moving us to try to bring it into existence. (More precisely, the object must be such that the concept of it is capable of moving us to bring it into existence.) For example, if I desire shelter from the rain, the concept of a lean-to is capable of moving me to cut branches, tie them together, and set them at an angle to the ground.

Theoretical cognition tells me what the objects of my thoughts are; it tells me what the world *is*. Practical cognition tells me what the objects of my actions are, which is to say, it tells me what the world *ought to be*. Exactly as in the case of theoretical cognition, we can distinguish practical judgments which can be known relatively a priori, conditionally a priori, and (perhaps) unconditionally a priori. A relatively a priori practical judgment is one which tells me what I must do in order to bring about ends of a certain type; it tells me this prior to any particular instance of that type, but not absolutely independently of that thing's being an end for me. Such judgments are rules for action in pursuit of ends which I happen to have; they are called by Kant Rules of Skill.

A conditionally a priori practical judgment is one which tells me what I must do in order to bring about ends which, because of my nature as a human being, I cannot help but set for myself. Such judgments are absolutely binding upon me under the condition that I am in fact the sort of being it assumes, and hence under the condition that I do pursue the end which it posits. According to Kant, happiness is such a universally posited end, and hence conditionally a priori practical judgments are called Counsels of Prudence. Aristotle's *Nicomachean Ethics*, for example, is entirely devoted to just such conditionally a priori practical judgments.

Kant might have undertaken to develop a moral theory along the lines of his theory of knowledge, by demonstrating that certain practical principles are embedded in the structure of human nature and hence conditionally a priori. Hume, for example, offers just such a theory in his *Treatise of Human Nature* and *Enquiry Concerning the Principles of Morals*. He argues that our mind is so constituted that we are disposed to feel a natural sentiment of approval for actions, persons, and objects which are useful or agreeable to ourselves or others. Moral judgments, which express that sentiment of approbation, are thus a priori conditional upon human nature actually possessing such a disposition. If the basic character of human nature were to change over night, so that we came to feel a sentiment of approbation for what is painful rather than for what is agreeable, it would be the case that what had yesterday been bad was today good, and what yesterday was good would today be bad.

Kant espouses just such a theory of the conditionally a priori in his theory of knowledge, for he freely admits that the human mind might have been created with different forms of sensibility, and even perhaps with different categories of thought. But he utterly repudiates the suggestion that our moral judgments might be similarly conditioned upon human nature. He insists that if moral discourse is acknowledged to have any significance at all, we must suppose its judgments to be universally valid and binding no matter how our tastes, inclinations, sentiments, and dispositions might alter. In short, Kant insists that Ethics, like Logic, must discover unconditionally a priori cognitions, or moral laws. As we have seen, Logic accomplishes this task by abstracting from all matter of thought whatsoever and concerning itself with the bare form of thought in general. As a result, its judgments are one and all analytic, and hence tell us nothing new about the world. Ethics, however, lies under the obligation of producing equally unconditioned judgments which yet are substantively significant and tell us what we absolutely are bound to do. It too must abstract from all matter, which in the case of practical reason means from all ends or purposes of action; hence, Ethics must seek the principles which would guide a *pure* reason in its practical employment. We may summarize the tasks of Ethics under three headings: first, to explain *how* pure reason can be practical, second, to show *that* pure reason is practical, and third, to discover the laws of pure practical reason.

The search for unconditionally a priori cognition proved fruitless in theoretical philosophy, and the manifest difficulty of the analogous enterprise in practical philosophy is the real source of the complexity and obscurity of Kant's ethical writings. Prima facie, he is seeking precisely what he insisted in the first *Critique* could not be found, namely substantive knowledge of the absolutely unconditioned. And yet, Kant is surely right in insisting that nothing less will serve to ground moral judgments if they are to be valid in any ordinary sense. Consider what it could mean to say that man's moral obligations are conditioned upon his having a certain human nature. This might mean simply that the characteristics of the persons involved determine *which* valid moral principles apply to a given situation. For example, if the method of communication among men were such as to make lying impossible (such as thought transference), so that men either communicated truthfully or not at all, then the obligation to tell the truth would be irrelevant. It would not be false that rational agents should be truthful with one another; it would simply make no sense to command a human to tell the truth. Similarly, among angels, if there are any, the imperative "Do not kill!" is superfluous, for angels are immortal. In this trivial sense, therefore, the nature of human nature is a relevant consideration in moral deliberation, and if human nature should change, men's obligations would also change.

But suppose someone were to assert that *whether* a moral principle is valid depends upon the nature of human nature, and in particular upon the characteristics of the agent. This would mean, as Hume actually acknowledged, that a valid moral principle could become invalid merely because something changed in the moral agent. But this is manifestly absurd. It may perhaps be merely an illusion that men have moral obligations, but if they do, then the obligations are not conditioned upon some facet of men's character. Moral philosophy has seen many attempts to derive moral imperatives from a consideration of human nature, but all of them are necessarily incomplete. For example, many philosophers argue that human beings have need N or capacity C, and that we therefore have an obligation to assist men in satisfying need N or in developing capacity C. But always there is an unstated assumption that we stand under an absolute obligation to assist others in satisfying their (true) needs or in developing their (genuine) capacities. And this obligation is independent of the particular nature of those needs and capacities. Hence if it is valid at all, it is universally valid, no matter what human nature may be, and the moral principle which articulates it must be an unconditionally a priori cognition.

III

The difference in the ways Kant approaches his task in the *Critique of Pure Reason* and the *Foundations* can be traced to the difference in the aims of the two works. In the *Critique*, it is Kant's purpose to lay a foundation for the relatively esoteric knowledge of mathematics and physics, but in the end, as we have seen, he thinks it possible to assign only conditional necessity and validity to them. In the *Foundations*, on the other hand, he deals with moral principles which he firmly believes to be known, in some sense, by every decent man, however untutored. And yet he seeks to show that these principles have an absolutely unconditioned necessity of the sort possessed only by the laws of logic. The argument of the *Foundations*, as a consequence, is both more popular and more difficult than that of the *Critique*. The use of examples and the frequent appeals to common-sense morality give the argument an appearance of familiarity, but as we read past the opening section, we ascend to more and more abstruse considerations, until in the last section Kant presents us with a discussion of the very nature of the noumenal moral agent himself. Since it is easy enough to lose sight of the line of argument, I shall try briefly to sketch what Kant is trying to achieve in each section of the *Foundations*.

Kant begins, in section one, with ordinary moral consciousness, and proceeds in the manner that he calls "analytic exposition." That is, he *assumes* that our moral consciousness is essentially correct, and asks what principles are contained implicitly within it. By this procedure he seeks to *persuade* us that we all in fact assent to a certain very general principle of action, which Kant calls the highest moral law. He states it as: "I should never act in such a way that I could not also will that my maxim should be a universal law." The first section is not intended to *prove* anything. Even if it is correct, it merely analyzes what we seem to believe, assuming that our moral consciousness agrees with that of Kant. It would be quite open to any reader, as far as anything Kant says in the first section is concerned, to reject the conclusions of the section on the grounds that his own pre-systematic moral convictions simply differ from Kant's. Thus far no arguments of a genuinely valid sort have been presented.

In section two, Kant begins again, this time taking as his starting point the notion of a will that is rational. By analyzing this notion (that is, the *concept* of a rational will, not any particular principles or judgments concerning such a will), he seeks to prove that a rational will must have the obligation to adopt the highest moral law as its principle of action. The remainder of the section explores the law, demonstrates alternatives and (supposedly) equivalent formulations of it, gives examples of its application, and introduces the concepts of a moral person, an end-in-itself, autonomy, and a kingdom of ends. The chapter, if successful, proves that *if* reason can be practical—i.e., if there can be a will guided by reason alone—then its highest principle must be the moral law.

One might suppose that in section three Kant would complete the argument by proving that man does indeed have a reason that can be practical. However, the *Critique of Pure Reason* has shown that we could not have knowledge of man as a noumenal reality, or thing-in-himself, and it is as such, if at all, that he would possess a pure practical reason. Kant is

forced, therefore, to confine himself to proving two less powerful propositions which, taken together, define the limit of our
theoretical knowledge of the foundations of morality. The two
propositions are: first, that there is no logical contradiction between the assumption that our reason can be practical and the
knowledge that all the events in the world are causally determined; and second, that a rational agent must assume that his
reason can be practical, even though he can never have theoretical knowledge that it is.

If Kant's arguments in sections two and three are successful, then any person who thinks of himself as a rational agent
must in all consistency acknowledge the validity of the law, or
Categorical Imperative, as the highest normative principle of
his action. This is still not a perfectly airtight proof, of course,
for it is theoretically open to someone to deny that he is a rational moral agent. Nevertheless, the power of Kant's argument
can be measured by the extremity of the skepticism which one
would have to espouse in order to reject it.

IV

In this edition of the *Foundations*, Lewis White Beck's fine
translation has been brought together with a group of essays
by contemporary students of Kant's ethical theory. The purpose of thus combining text with commentary is to provide a
number of suggestions for interpreting and arguing with
Kant's theory. The several essays are in no sense a definitive
key to the *Foundations*. The student will find, very possibly to
his dismay, that even the experts disagree vigorously on how
to interpret central passages. Nevertheless, a careful reading
of the text in conjunction with the essays should raise the level
of understanding of even the most advanced student of Kant's
philosophy.

The opening essay by Professor Julius Ebbinghaus is both

a many-sided discussion of the conflicting interpretations which have been put on Kant's Categorical Imperative and also a testament to Professor Ebbinghaus' conviction that Kant's moral philosophy, correctly understood, can never serve as a justification for blind obedience to authority. Since the *Foundations* is in a sense a defense of a single proposition, namely the Categorical Imperative, it is fitting that the commentary should begin with this essay.

The next two essays are broader discussions of concepts which play a central role in the argument of the *Foundations*. Professor Schrader explores the contrast between autonomy and heteronomy and connects these notions to the nature of moral imperatives. Professor Beck, whose translation of the *Foundations* appears in this edition, contributes an analysis of the nature of apodictic imperatives. Since Kant's argument turns on the distinction between hypothetical and apodictic or "categorical" imperatives, Professor Beck's essay is central to an understanding of this argument. (Professor Beck is also the author of a definitive commentary on the second of Kant's great ethical treatises, the *Critique of Practical Judgment*, University of Chicago Press, 1960. In addition, a number of his papers are collected in *Studies in the Philosophy of Kant*, Bobbs-Merrill: Indianapolis, 1965.)

Professor Dietrichson's essay continues the discussion with an exploration of the notion of universalizability. This contribution by Kant to the vocabulary of moral philosophy has recently been the object of a vigorous debate in books and journal articles. A number of philosophers in England and America have found in the concept of universalizability the key to the distinctive unconditionality which moral commands are felt to exhibit. (Students may wish to pursue the subject further by reading Professor Marcus G. Singer's recent book, *Generalization in Ethics*, New York: Alfred Knopf, 1961.)

Following these discussions of the Categorical Imperative

and its logical form, we have a spirited debate between Messrs. Harrison and Kemp of England on the correct interpretation of the famous four examples of the Categorical Imperative which Kant offers in section two of the *Foundations*. The statement, criticism, and rebuttal make it quite clear that the last word has not yet been written about even this relatively simple portion of Kant's argument.

Professor Robert Shope brings many of the insights and techniques of modern philosophical analysis to bear on the problems discussed by Schrader, Beck, Dietrichson, Harrison, and Kemp. His essay, like the essay by Professor Ebbinghaus with which we begin, may be seen as a complete interpretation of the *Foundations* rather than a commentary on one part of it only.

The technical complexities of Kant's moral philosophy are important, after all, only insofar as they help us understand the moral condition in the broadest sense. It is fitting therefore that we end the commentary with an essay by the late Mrs. Pepita Haezrahi on Kant's seminal notion of man as an end in himself. Kant is not the first philosopher to speak of the intrinsic value of man's humanity, of course, but his treatment of the subject near the end of section two is justly famous. Mrs. Haezrahi builds on that notion a rounded interpretation of Kant's view of the moral condition.

These are only nine of the scores of essays devoted to Kant's moral philosophy that have appeared in journals of philosophy over the years. It cannot too often be repeated that they are contributions to a continuing discussion. The importance of Kant's moral philosophy is measured not by the numbers of his disciples but by the vigor with which his arguments are contested and his doctrines debated. It is to be hoped that some of the readers of this volume will in time add their voices to the conversation.

Selected bibliography

German editions

Kants gesammelte Schriften. Königliche Preussische Akademie der Wissenschaften edition. Berlin: G. Reimer, 1902–1942.

Kants sämmtliche Werke. Ed. Karl Vorländer. 10 vols. Leipzig: Felix Meiner, 1921–1940.

Immanuel Kants Werke. Ed. Ernst Cassirer, with Herman Cohen, Artur Buchenau, Otto Buek, Albert Görland, and B. Kellermann. 11 vols. Berlin: Bruno Cassirer, 1912–1922.

Commentaries and secondary works on the Foundations

Beck, Lewis White. *A Commentary on Kant's Critique of Practical Reason.* Chicago: University of Chicago Press, 1960.

Duncan, A. R. C. *Practical Reason and Morality. A Study of Immanuel Kant's Foundations for the Metaphysics of Morals.* Edinburgh: Thomas Nelson & Sons, 1957.

Paton, H. J. *The Categorical Imperative. A Study in Kant's Moral Philosophy.* London: Hutchinson, 1946. Chicago: University of Chicago Press, 1948.

Ross, Sir William David. *Kant's Ethical Theory. A Commentary on the Grundlegung zur Metaphysik der Sitten.* Oxford: Clarendon Press, 1954.

Translations of other Kantian works

AVAILABLE IN LIBRARY OF LIBERAL ARTS PAPERBACK

Analytic of the Beautiful: from The Critique of Judgment. Trans. Walter Cerf. 1963.

Critique of Practical Reason. Trans. Lewis White Beck. 1956.

First Introduction to the Critique of Judgment. Trans. James Haden. 1965.

The Metaphysical Elements of Justice: Part I of The Metaphysics of Morals. Trans. John Ladd. 1965.

The Metaphysical Principles of Virtue: Part II of the Metaphysics of Morals. Trans. James Ellington. 1964.

Perpetual Peace. Trans. Lewis White Beck. 1957.

Prolegomena to Any Future Metaphysics. Trans. Lewis White Beck, 1950.

OTHER AVAILABLE PAPERBACKS

Critique of Pure Reason. Trans. Norman Kemp Smith. New York: St. Martin's Press, 1963.

Lectures on Ethics. Trans. Louis Infield. Foreword by L. W. Beck. New York: Harper Torchbooks, 1949.

Religion Within the Limits of Reason Alone. Trans. T. M. Greene and H. H. Hudson. New York: Harper Torchbooks, 1960.

Textual Note

The FOUNDATIONS OF THE METAPHYSICS OF MORALS is reprinted from the *Library of Liberal Arts* edition (*New York: Bobbs-Merrill, 1959*), which in turn was a slightly revised version, by Lewis White Beck, of this work as it appeared in his volume KANT'S CRITIQUE OF PRACTICAL REASON AND OTHER WRITINGS IN MORAL PHILOSOPHY (*Chicago: University of Chicago Press, 1949*). The page numbers of the Königliche Preussische Akademie der Wissenschaft edition (*Berlin, 1902–1938*), the standard reference for Kantian works, appear in brackets in the text within the first line of each Akademie page. Professor Beck's footnotes are in brackets; the rest are Kant's own.

The commentary consists of articles reprinted from journals, with the exception of Robert K. Shope's article, printed here for the first time, and that by Paul Dietrichson, which he has extensively revised. Errors were corrected in the reprinted articles, and minor changes made for consistency in footnote styling; other slight editorial additions are in brackets.

Foundations

of the metaphysics

of morals

Preface

Ancient Greek philosophy was divided into three [387] sciences: physics, ethics, and logic. This division conforms perfectly to the nature of the subject, and one can improve on it
perhaps only by supplying its principle in order both to insure
its exhaustiveness and to define correctly the necessary sub-
divisions.

All rational knowledge is either material, and concerns
some object, or formal, and is occupied merely with the form
of understanding and reason itself and with the universal rules
of thinking without regard to distinctions between objects.
Formal philosophy is called logic. Material philosophy, however, which has to do with definite objects and the laws to
which they are subject, is itself divided into two parts. This is
because these laws are either laws of nature or laws of free-

dom. The science of the former is called physics and that of the latter ethics. The former is also called theory of nature and the latter theory of morals.

Logic can have no empirical part—a part in which universal and necessary laws of thinking would rest upon grounds taken from experience. For in that case it would not be logic, i.e., a canon for understanding or reason which is valid for all thinking and which must be demonstrated. But, on the other hand, natural and moral philosophy can each have its empirical part. The former must do so, for it must determine the laws of nature as an object of experience, and the latter because it must determine the human will so far as it is affected by nature. The laws of the former are laws according to which everything happens; those of the latter are laws according [388] to which everything should happen, but allow for conditions under which what should happen often does not.

All philosophy, so far as it is based on experience, may be called empirical; but, so far as it presents its doctrines solely on the basis of a priori principles, it may be called pure philosophy. The latter, when merely formal, is logic; when limited to definite objects of understanding, it is metaphysics.

In this way there arises the idea of a twofold metaphysics—a metaphysics of nature and a metaphysics of morals. Physics, therefore, will have an empirical and also a rational part, and ethics likewise. In ethics, however, the empirical part may be called more specifically practical anthropology; the rational part, morals proper.

All crafts, handiworks, and arts have gained by the division of labor, for when one person does not do everything, but each limits himself to a particular job which is distinguished from all the others by the treatment it requires, he can do it with greater perfection and with more facility. Where work is not thus differentiated and divided, where everyone is a jack-of-all-trades, the crafts remain at a barbaric level. It might be worth considering whether pure philosophy in each of its parts does not require a man particularly devoted to it, and whether it would not be better for the learned profession as a whole to warn those who are in the habit of catering to the taste of the public by mixing up the empirical with the rational in all sorts of proportions which they do not themselves know and who call themselves independent thinkers (giving the name of speculator to those who apply themselves to the merely rational part). This warning would be that they should not at one and the same time carry on two employments which differ widely in the treatment they require, and for each of which perhaps a special talent is needed since the combination of these talents in one person produces only bunglers. I ask only whether the nature of the science does not require that a careful separation of the empirical from the rational part be made, with a metaphysics of nature put before real (empirical) physics and a metaphysics of morals before practical anthropology. These prior sciences[1] must be carefully purified of everything empirical so that we can know how much pure reason can accomplish in each case and from [389] what sources it creates its a priori teaching, whether the latter inquiry be conducted by all moralists (whose name is legion) or only by some who feel a calling to it.

Since my purpose here is directed to moral philosophy, I narrow the proposed question to this: Is it not of the utmost necessity to construct a pure moral philosophy which is completely freed from everything which may be only empirical and thus belong to anthropology? That there must be such a philosophy is self-evident from the common idea of duty and moral laws. Everyone must admit that a law, if it is to hold morally, i.e., as a ground of obligation, must imply absolute

[1] [Reading the plural with the Academy ed.]

necessity; he must admit that the command, "Thou shalt not lie," does not apply to men only, as if other rational beings had no need to observe it. The same is true for all other moral laws properly so called. He must concede that the ground of obligation here must not be sought in the nature of man or in the circumstances in which he is placed, but sought a priori solely in the concepts of pure reason, and that every other precept which rests on principles of mere experience, even a precept which is in certain respects universal, so far as it leans in the least on empirical grounds (perhaps only in regard to the motive involved), may be called a practical rule but never a moral law.

Thus not only are moral laws together with their principles essentially different from all practical knowledge in which there is anything empirical, but all moral philosophy rests solely on its pure part. Applied to man, it borrows nothing from knowledge of him (anthropology) but gives him, as a rational being, a priori laws. No doubt these laws require a power of judgment sharpened by experience, partly in order to decide in what cases they apply and partly to procure for them an access to man's will and an impetus to their practice. For man is affected by so many inclinations that, though he is capable of the idea of a practical pure reason, he is not so easily able to make it concretely effective in the conduct of his life.

A metaphysics of morals is therefore indispensable, not merely because of motives to speculate on the source of the a priori practical principles which lie in our reason, but [390] also because morals themselves remain subject to all kinds of corruption so long as the guide and supreme norm for their correct estimation is lacking. For it is not sufficient to that which should be morally good that it conform to the law; it must be done for the sake of the law. Otherwise the conformity is merely contingent and spurious, because, though the unmoral ground may indeed now and then produce lawful actions, more often it brings forth unlawful ones. But the moral law can be found in its purity and genuineness (which is the central concern in the practical) nowhere else than in a pure philosophy; therefore, this (i.e., metaphysics) must lead the way, and without it there can be no moral philosophy. Philosophy which mixes pure principles with empirical ones does not deserve the name, for what distinguishes philosophy from common rational knowledge is its treatment in separate sciences of what is confusedly comprehended in such knowledge. Much less does it deserve the name of moral philosophy, since by this confusion it spoils the purity of morals themselves and works contrary to its own end.

It should not be thought that what is here required is already present in the celebrated Wolff's propaedeutic to his moral philosophy, i.e., in what he calls universal practical philosophy, and that it is not an entirely new field that is to be opened. Precisely because his work was to be universal practical philosophy, it deduced no will of any particular kind, such as one determined without any empirical motives but completely by a priori principles; in a word, it had nothing which could be called a pure will, since it considered only volition in general with all the actions and conditions which pertain to it in this general sense. Thus his propaedeutic differs from a metaphysics of morals in the same way that general logic is distinguished from transcendental philosophy, the former expounding the actions and rules of thinking in general, and the latter presenting the particular actions and rules of pure thinking, i.e., of thinking by which objects are known completely a priori. For the metaphysics of morals is meant to investigate the idea and principles of a possible pure will and not the actions and conditions of the human volition as such, which are for the most part drawn from psychology.

That in general practical philosophy laws and duty are [391] discussed (though improperly) is no objection to my assertion. For the authors of this science remain even here true to their idea of it. They do not distinguish the motives which are presented completely a priori by reason alone, and which are thus moral in the proper sense of the word, from the empirical motives which the understanding, by comparing experiences, elevates to universal concepts. Rather, they consider motives without regard to the difference in their source but only with reference to their greater or smaller number (as they are considered to be all of the same kind); they thus formulate their concept of obligation, which is anything but moral, but which is all that can be desired in a philosophy that does not decide whether the origin of all possible practical concepts is a priori or only a posteriori.

As a preliminary to a metaphysics of morals which I intend some day to publish, I issue these *Foundations*. There is, to be sure, no other foundation for such a metaphysics than a critical examination of a pure practical reason, just as there is no other foundation for metaphysics than the already published critical examination of the pure speculative reason. But, in the first place, a critical examination of pure practical reason is not of such extreme importance as that of speculative reason, because human reason, even in the commonest mind, can easily be brought to a high degree of correctness and completeness in moral matters, while, on the other hand, in its theoretical but pure use it is entirely dialectical. In the second place, I require of a critical examination of a pure practical reason, if it is to be complete, that its unity with the speculative be subject to presentation under a common principle, because in the final analysis there can be but one and the same reason which must be differentiated only in application. But I could not bring this to such a completeness without bringing in observations of an altogether different kind and without thereby confusing the reader. For these reasons I have employed the title, *Foundations of the Metaphysics of Morals*, instead of *Critique of Pure Practical Reason*.

Because, in the third place, a metaphysics of morals, in spite of its forbidding title, is capable of a high degree of popularity and adaptation to common understanding, I find it useful to separate this preliminary work of laying the foundation in order not to have to introduce unavoidable subtleties [392] into the later, more comprehensive, work.

The present foundations, however, are nothing more than the search for and establishment of the supreme principle of morality. This constitutes a task altogether complete in its intention and one which should be kept separate from all other moral inquiry.

My conclusions concerning this important question, which has not yet been discussed nearly enough, would, of course, be clarified by application of the principle to the whole system of morality, and it would receive much confirmation by the adequacy which it would everywhere show. But I must forego this advantage, which would in the final analysis be more privately gratifying than commonly useful, because ease of use and apparent adequacy of a principle are not any sure proof of its correctness, but rather awaken a certain partiality which prevents a rigorous investigation and evaluation of it for itself without regard to consequences.

I have adopted in this writing the method which is, I think, most suitable if one wishes to proceed analytically from common knowledge to the determination of its supreme principle, and then synthetically from the examination of this principle and its sources back to common knowledge where it finds its application. The division is therefore as follows:

1. First Section. Transition from the Common Rational Knowledge of Morals to the Philosophical.
2. Second Section. Transition from the Popular Moral Philosophy to the Metaphysics of Morals.
3. Third Section. Final Step from the Metaphysics of Morals to the Critical Examination of Pure Practical Reason.

First section / Transition from

the common rational knowledge of

morals to the philosophical

Nothing in the world—indeed nothing even beyond the [393] world—can possibly be conceived which could be called good without qualification except a *good will*. Intelligence, wit, judgment, and the other talents of the mind, however they may be named, or courage, resoluteness, and perseverance as qualities of temperament, are doubtless in many respects good and desirable. But they can become extremely bad and harmful if the will, which is to make use of these gifts of nature and which in its special constitution is called character, is not good. It is the same with the gifts of fortune. Power, riches, honor, even health, general well-being, and the contentment with one's condition which is called happiness, make for pride and even arrogance if there is not a good will to correct their influence on the mind and on its principles of action so as to make it universally conformable to its end. It need hardly be mentioned that the sight of a being adorned with no feature of a pure and good will, yet enjoying uninterrupted prosperity, can never give pleasure to a rational impartial observer. Thus the good will seems to constitute the indispensable condition even of worthiness to be happy.

Some qualities seem to be conducive to this good will and can facilitate its action, but, in spite of that, they have no intrinsic unconditional worth. They rather presuppose a [394] good will, which limits the high esteem which one otherwise rightly has for them and prevents their being held to be absolutely good. Moderation in emotions and passions, self-control, and calm deliberation not only are good in many respects but even seem to constitute a part of the inner worth of the person. But however unconditionally they were esteemed by the ancients, they are far from being good without qualification. For without the principle of a good will they can become extremely bad, and the coolness of a villain makes him not only far more dangerous but also more directly abominable in our eyes than he would have seemed without it.

The good will is not good because of what it effects or accomplishes or because of its adequacy to achieve some proposed end; it is good only because of its willing, i.e., it is good of itself. And, regarded for itself, it is to be esteemed incomparably higher than anything which could be brought about by it in favor of any inclination or even of the sum total of all inclinations. Even if it should happen that, by a particularly unfortunate fate or by the niggardly provision of a stepmotherly nature, this will should be wholly lacking in power to accomplish its purpose, and if even the greatest effort should not avail it to achieve anything of its end, and if there remained only the good will (not as a mere wish but as the summoning of all the means in our power), it would sparkle like a jewel in its own right, as something that had its full worth in itself. Usefulness or fruitlessness can neither diminish nor augment this worth. Its usefulness would be only its setting, as it were, so as to enable us to handle it more conveniently in commerce or to attract the attention of those who are not yet connoisseurs, but not to recommend it to those who are experts or to determine its worth.

But there is something so strange in this idea of the absolute worth of the will alone, in which no account is taken of any use, that, notwithstanding the agreement even of common sense, the suspicion must arise that perhaps only high-flown fancy is its hidden basis, and that we may have misunderstood the purpose of nature in its appointment of reason [395] as the ruler of our will. We shall therefore examine this idea from this point of view.

In the natural constitution of an organized being, i.e., one suitably adapted to life, we assume as an axiom that no organ will be found for any purpose which is not the fittest and best adapted to that purpose. Now if its preservation, its welfare —in a word, its happiness—were the real end of nature in a being having reason and will, then nature would have hit upon a very poor arrangement in appointing the reason of the creature to be the executor of this purpose. For all the actions which the creature has to perform with this intention, and the entire rule of its conduct, would be dictated much more exactly by instinct, and that end would be far more certainly attained by instinct than it ever could be by reason. And if, over and above this, reason should have been granted to the favored creature, it would have served only to let it contemplate the happy constitution of its nature, to admire it, to rejoice in it, and to be grateful for it to its beneficent cause. But reason would not have been given in order that the being should subject its faculty of desire to that weak and delusive guidance and to meddle with the purpose of nature. In a word, nature would have taken care that reason did not break forth into practical use nor have the presumption, with its weak insight, to think out for itself the plan of happiness and the means of attaining it. Nature would have taken over not only the choice of ends but also that of the means, and with wise foresight she would have entrusted both to instinct alone.

And, in fact, we find that the more a cultivated reason deliberately devotes itself to the enjoyment of life and happiness, the more the man falls short of true contentment. From this fact there arises in many persons, if only they are candid enough to admit it, a certain degree of misology, hatred of reason. This is particularly the case with those who are most experienced in its use. After counting all the advantages which they draw—I will not say from the invention of the arts of common luxury—from the sciences (which in the end seem to them to be also a luxury of the understanding), they nevertheless find that they have actually brought more trouble on their shoulders instead of gaining in happiness; they [396] finally envy, rather than despise, the common run of men who are better guided by mere natural instinct and who do not permit their reason much influence on their conduct. And we must at least admit that a morose attitude or ingratitude to the goodness with which the world is governed is by no means found always among those who temper or refute the boasting eulogies which are given of the advantages of happiness and contentment with which reason is supposed to supply us. Rather their judgment is based on the idea of another and far more worthy purpose of their existence for which, instead of happiness, their reason is properly intended, this purpose, therefore, being the supreme condition to which the private purposes of men must for the most part defer.

Reason is not, however, competent to guide the will safely

with regard to its objects and the satisfaction of all our needs (which it in part multiplies), and to this end an innate instinct would have led with far more certainty. But reason is given to us as a practical faculty, i.e., one which is meant to have an influence on the will. As nature has elsewhere distributed capacities suitable to the functions they are to perform, reason's proper function must be to produce a will good in itself and not only good merely as a means, for to the former reason is absolutely essential. This will must indeed not be the sole and complete good but the highest good and the condition of all others, even of the desire for happiness. In this case it is entirely compatible with the wisdom of nature that the cultivation of reason, which is required for the former unconditional purpose, at least in this life restricts in many ways—indeed can reduce to less than nothing—the achievement of the latter conditional purpose, happiness. For one perceives that nature here does not proceed unsuitably to its purpose, because reason, which recognizes its highest practical vocation in the establishment of a good will, is capable only of a contentment of its own kind, i.e., one that springs from the attainment of a purpose which is determined by reason, even though this injures the ends of inclination.

We have, then, to develop the concept of a will which [397] is to be esteemed as good of itself without regard to anything else. It dwells already in the natural sound understanding and does not need so much to be taught as only to be brought to light. In the estimation of the total worth of our actions it always takes first place and is the condition of everything else. In order to show this, we shall take the concept of duty. It contains that of a good will, though with certain subjective restrictions and hindrances; but these are far from concealing it and making it unrecognizable, for they rather bring it out by contrast and make it shine forth all the brighter.

I here omit all actions which are recognized as opposed to duty, even though they may be useful in one respect or another, for with these the question does not arise at all as to whether they may be carried out *from* duty, since they conflict with it. I also pass over the actions which are really in accordance with duty and to which one has no direct inclination, rather executing them because impelled to do so by another inclination. For it is easily decided whether an action in accord with duty is performed from duty or for some selfish purpose. It is far more difficult to note this difference when the action is in accordance with duty and, in addition, the subject has a direct inclination to do it. For example, it is in fact in accordance with duty that a dealer should not overcharge an inexperienced customer, and wherever there is much business the prudent merchant does not do so, having a fixed price for everyone, so that a child may buy of him as cheaply as any other. Thus the customer is honestly served. But this is far from sufficient to justify the belief that the merchant has behaved in this way from duty and principles of honesty. His own advantage required this behavior; but it cannot be assumed that over and above that he had a direct inclination to the purchaser and that, out of love, as it were, he gave none an advantage in price over another. Therefore the action was done neither from duty nor from direct inclination but only for a selfish purpose.

On the other hand, it is a duty to preserve one's life, and moreover everyone has a direct inclination to do so. But for that reason the often anxious care which most men take of it has no intrinsic worth, and the maxim of doing so has no moral import. They preserve their lives according to duty, but [398] not from duty. But if adversities and hopeless sorrow completely take away the relish for life, if an unfortunate man, strong in soul, is indignant rather than despondent or dejected over his fate and wishes for death, and yet preserves his life without loving it and from neither inclination nor fear but from duty—then his maxim has a moral import.

To be kind where one can is duty, and there are, moreover, many persons so sympathetically constituted that without any motive of vanity or selfishness they find an inner satisfaction in spreading joy, and rejoice in the contentment of others which they have made possible. But I say that, however dutiful and amiable it may be, that kind of action has no true moral worth. It is on a level with [actions arising from] other inclinations, such as the inclination to honor, which, if fortunately directed to what in fact accords with duty and is generally useful and thus honorable, deserve praise and encouragement but no esteem. For the maxim lacks the moral import of an action done not from inclination but from duty. But assume that the mind of that friend to mankind was clouded by a sorrow of his own which extinguished all sympathy with the lot of others and that he still had the power to benefit others in distress, but that their need left him untouched because he was preoccupied with his own need. And now suppose him to tear himself, unsolicited by inclination, out of this dead insensibility and to perform this action only from duty and without any inclination—then for the first time his action has genuine moral worth. Furthermore, if nature has put little sympathy in the heart of a man, and if he, though an honest man, is by temperament cold and indifferent to the sufferings of others, perhaps because he is provided with special gifts of patience and fortitude and expects or even requires that others should have the same—and such a man would certainly not be the meanest product of nature—would not he find in himself a source from which to give himself a far higher worth than he could have got by having a good-natured temperament? This is unquestionably true even though nature did not make him philanthropic, for it is just here that the worth of the character is brought out, which is morally and incomparably [399] the highest of all: he is beneficent not from inclination but from duty.

To secure one's own happiness is at least indirectly a duty, for discontent with one's condition under pressure from many cares and amid unsatisfied wants could easily become a great temptation to transgress duties. But without any view to duty all men have the strongest and deepest inclination to happiness, because in this idea all inclinations are summed up. But the precept of happiness is often so formulated that it definitely thwarts some inclinations, and men can make no definite and certain concept of the sum of satisfaction of all inclinations which goes under the name of happiness. It is not to be wondered at, therefore, that a single inclination, definite as to what it promises and as to the time at which it can be satisfied, can outweigh a fluctuating idea, and that, for example, a man with the gout can choose to enjoy what he likes and to suffer what he may, because according to his calculations at least on this occasion he has not sacrificed the enjoyment of the present moment to a perhaps groundless expectation of a happiness supposed to lie in health. But even in this case, if the universal inclination to happiness did not determine his will, and if health were not at least for him a necessary factor in these calculations, there yet would remain, as in all other cases, a law that he ought to promote his happiness, not from inclination but from duty. Only from this law would his conduct have true moral worth.

It is in this way, undoubtedly, that we should understand those passages of Scripture which command us to love our neighbor and even our enemy, for love as an inclination cannot be commanded. But beneficence from duty, when no inclination impels it and even when it is opposed by a natural and unconquerable aversion, is practical love, not pathological love; it resides in the will and not in the propensities of feeling, in principles of action and not in tender sympathy; and it alone can be commanded.

[Thus the first proposition of morality is that to have moral worth an action must be done from duty.] The second proposition is: An action performed from duty does not have its moral worth in the purpose which is to be achieved through it but in the maxim by which it is determined. Its moral value, therefore, does not depend on the realization of the object of the action but merely on the principle of volition by which the action is done without any regard to the objects of [400] the faculty of desire. From the preceding discussion it is clear that the purposes we may have for our actions and their effects as ends and incentives of the will cannot give the actions any unconditional and moral worth. Wherein, then, can this worth lie, if it is not in the will in relation to its hoped-for effect? It can lie nowhere else than in the principle of the will, irrespective of the ends which can be realized by such action. For the will stands, as it were, at the crossroads halfway between its a priori principle which is formal and its a posteriori incentive which is material. Since it must be determined by something, if it is done from duty it must be determined by the formal principle of volition as such since every material principle has been withdrawn from it.

The third principle, as a consequence of the two preceding, I would express as follows: Duty is the necessity of an action executed from respect for law. I can certainly have an inclination to the object as an effect of the proposed action, but I can never have respect for it precisely because it is a mere effect and not an activity of a will. Similarly, I can have no respect for any inclination whatsoever, whether my own or that of another; in the former case I can at most approve of it and in the latter I can even love it, i.e., see it as favorable to my own advantage. But that which is connected with my will merely as ground and not as consequence, that which does not serve my inclination but overpowers it or at least excludes it from being considered in making a choice—in a word, law itself—can be an object of respect and thus a command. Now as an act from duty wholly excludes the influence of inclination and therewith every object of the will, nothing remains which can determine the will objectively except the law, and nothing subjectively except pure respect for this practical law. This subjective element is the maxim[1] that I ought to follow such a law even if it thwarts all my inclinations. [401]

Thus the moral worth of an action does not lie in the effect which is expected from it or in any principle of action which has to borrow its motive from this expected effect. For all these effects (agreeableness of my own condition, indeed even the promotion of the happiness of others) could be brought about through other causes and would not require the will of a rational being, while the highest and unconditional good can be found only in such a will. Therefore, the pre-eminent good can consist only in the conception of the law in itself (which can be present only in a rational being) so far as this conception and not the hoped-for effect is the determining ground of the will. This pre-eminent good, which we call moral, is already present in the person who acts according to this conception, and we do not have to look for it first in the result.[2]

[1] A maxim is the subjective principle of volition. The objective principle (i.e., that which would serve all rational beings also subjectively as a practical principle if reason had full power over the faculty of desire) is the practical law.

[2] It might be objected that I seek to take refuge in an obscure feeling behind the word "respect," instead of clearly resolving the question with a concept of reason. But though respect is a feeling, it is not one received through any [outer] influence but is self-wrought by a rational concept;

But what kind of a law can that be, the conception [402] of which must determine the will without reference to the expected result? Under this condition alone the will can be called absolutely good without qualification. Since I have robbed the will of all impulses which could come to it from obedience to any law, nothing remains to serve as a principle of the will except universal conformity of its action to law as such. That is, I should never act in such a way that I could not also will that my maxim should be a universal law. Mere conformity to law as such (without assuming any particular law applicable to certain actions) serves as the principle of the will, and it must serve as such a principle if duty is not to be a vain delusion and chimerical concept. The common reason of mankind in its practical judgments is in perfect agreement with this and has this principle constantly in view.

Let the question, for example, be: May I, when in distress, make a promise with the intention not to keep it? I easily

---

thus it differs specifically from all feelings of the former kind which may be referred to inclination or fear. What I recognize directly as a law for myself I recognize with respect, which means merely the consciousness of the submission of my will to a law without the intervention of other influences on my mind. The direct determination of the will by the law and the consciousness of this determination is respect; thus respect can be regarded as the effect of the law on the subject and not as the cause of the law. Respect is properly the conception of a worth which thwarts my self-love. Thus it is regarded as an object neither of inclination nor of fear, though it has something analogous to both. The only object of respect is the law, and indeed only the law which we impose on ourselves and yet recognize as necessary in itself. As a law, we are subject to it without consulting self-love; as imposed on us by ourselves, it is a consequence of our will. In the former respect it is analogous to fear and in the latter to inclination. All respect for a person is only respect for the law (of righteousness, etc.) of which the person provides an example. Because we see the improvement of our talents as a duty, we think of a person of talents as the example of a law, as it were (the law that we should by practice become like him in his talents), and that constitutes our respect. All so-called moral interest consists solely in respect for the law.

distinguish the two meanings which the question can have, viz., whether it is prudent to make a false promise, or whether it conforms to my duty. Undoubtedly the former can often be the case, though I do see clearly that it is not sufficient merely to escape from the present difficulty by this expedient, but that I must consider whether inconveniences much greater than the present on may not later spring from this lie. Even with all my supposed cunning, the consequences cannot be so easily foreseen. Loss of credit might be far more disadvantageous than the misfortune I now seek to avoid, and it is hard to tell whether it might not be more prudent to act according to a universal maxim and to make it a habit not to promise any-thing without intending to fulfill it. But it is soon clear to me that such a maxim is based only on an apprehensive concern with consequences.

To be truthful from duty, however, is an entirely different thing from being truthful out of fear of disadvantageous con-sequences, for in the former case the concept of the action it-self contains a law for me, while in the latter I must first look about to see what results for me may be connected with it. For to deviate from the principle of duty is certainly bad, but to be unfaithful to my maxim of prudence can sometimes be very [403] advantageous to me, though it is certainly safer to abide by it. The shortest but most infallible way to find the answer to the question as to whether a deceitful promise is consistent with duty is to ask myself: Would I be content that my maxim (of extricating myself from difficulty by a false promise) should hold as a universal law for myself as well as for others? And could I say to myself that everyone may make a false promise when he is in difficulty from which he otherwise can-not escape? I immediately see that I could will the lie but not a universal law to lie. For with such a law there would be no promises at all, inasmuch as it would be futile to make a pretense of my intention in regard to future actions to those who would not believe this pretense or—if they overhastily did so—who would pay me back in my own coin. Thus my maxim would necessarily destroy itself as soon as it was made a universal law.

I do not, therefore, need any penetrating acuteness in order to discern what I have to do in order that my volition may be morally good. Inexperienced in the course of the world, incapable of being prepared for all its contingencies, I ask myself only: Can I will that my maxim becomes a universal law? If not, it must be rejected, not because of any disadvantage accruing to myself or even to others, but because it cannot enter as a principle into a possible universal legislation, and reason extorts from me an immediate respect for such legislation. I do not as yet discern on what it is grounded (a question the philosopher may investigate), but I at least understand that it is an estimation of the worth which far outweighs all the worth of whatever is recommended by the inclinations, and that the necessity of my actions from pure respect for the practical law constitutes duty. To duty every other motive must give place, because duty is the condition of a will good in itself, whose worth transcends everything.

Thus within the moral knowledge of common human reason we have attained its principle. To be sure, common human reason does not think of it abstractly in such a universal form, but it always has it in view and uses it as the standard of its judgments. It would be easy to show how common human [404] reason, with this compass, knows well how to distinguish what is good, what is bad, and what is consistent or inconsistent with duty. Without in the least teaching common reason anything new, we need only to draw its attention to its own principle, in the manner of Socrates, thus showing that neither science nor philosophy is needed in order to know what one has to do in order to be honest and good, and even wise and virtuous. We might have conjectured beforehand that the knowledge of what everyone is obliged to do and thus also to know would be within the reach of everyone, even the most ordinary man. Here we cannot but admire the great advantages which the practical faculty of judgment has over the theoretical in ordinary human understanding. In the theoretical, if ordinary reason ventures to go beyond the laws of experience and perceptions of the senses, it falls into sheer inconceivabilities and self-contradictions, or at least into a chaos of uncertainty, obscurity, and instability. In the practical, on the other hand, the power of judgment first shows itself to advantage when common understanding excludes all sensuous incentives from practical laws. It then becomes even subtle, quibbling with its own conscience or with other claims to what should be called right, or wishing to determine correctly for its own instruction the worth of certain actions. But the most remarkable thing about ordinary reason in its practical concern is that it may have as much hope as any philosopher of hitting the mark. In fact, it is almost more certain to do so than the philosopher, because he has no principle which the common understanding lacks, while his judgment is easily confused by a mass of irrelevant considerations, so that it easily turns aside from the correct way. Would it not, therefore, be wiser in moral matters to acquiesce in the common rational judgment, or at most to call in philosophy in order to make the system of morals more complete and comprehensible and its rules more convenient for use (especially in disputation) than to steer the common understanding from its happy simplicity in practical matters and to lead it through philosophy into a new path of inquiry and instruction?

Innocence is indeed a glorious thing, but, on the other hand, it is very sad that it cannot well maintain itself, being [405] easily led astray. For this reason, even wisdom—which consists more in acting than in knowing—needs science, not to learn from it but to secure admission and permanence to its precepts. Man feels in himself a powerful counterpoise against all commands of duty which reason presents to him as so deserving of respect; this counterpoise is his needs and inclinations, the complete satisfaction of which he sums up under the name of happiness. Now reason issues inexorable commands without promising anything to the inclinations. It disregards, as it were, and holds in contempt those claims which are so impetuous and yet so plausible, and which will not allow themselves to be abolished by any command. From this a natural dialectic arises, i.e., a propensity to argue against the stern laws of duty and their validity, or at least to place their purity and strictness in doubt and, where possible, to make them more accordant with our wishes and inclinations. This is equivalent to corrupting them in their very foundations and destroying their dignity—a thing which even common practical reason cannot ultimately call good.

In this way common human reason is impelled to go outside its sphere and to take a step into the field of practical philosophy. But it is forced to do so not by any speculative need, which never occurs to it so long as it is satisfied to remain merely healthy reason; rather, it is so impelled on practical grounds in order to obtain information and clear instruction respecting the source of its principle and the correct determination of this principle in its opposition to the maxims which are based on need and inclination. It seeks this information in order to escape from the perplexity of opposing claims and to avoid the danger of losing all genuine moral principles through the equivocation in which it is easily involved. Thus, when practical common reason cultivates itself, a dialectic surreptitiously ensues which forces it to seek aid in philosophy, just as the same thing happens in the theoretical use of reason. In this case, as in the theoretical, it will find rest only in a thorough critical examination of our reason.

Second section / Transition from

the popular moral philosophy

to the metaphysics of morals

If we have derived our earlier concept of duty from the [406] common use of our practical reason, it is by no means to be inferred that we have treated it as an empirical concept. On the contrary, if we attend to our experience of the way men act, we meet frequent and, as we ourselves confess, justified complaints that we cannot cite a single sure example of the disposition to act from pure duty. There are also justified complaints that, though much may be done that accords with what duty commands, it is nevertheless always doubtful whether it is done from duty, and thus whether it has moral worth. There have always been philosophers who for this reason have absolutely denied the reality of this disposition in human actions, attributing everything to more or less refined self-love. They have done so without questioning the correctness of the concept of morality. Rather they have spoken with sincere regret of the frailty and corruption of human nature, which is noble enough to take as its precept an idea so worthy of respect but which at the same time is too weak to follow it, employing reason, which should legislate for human nature, only to provide for the interest of the inclinations either singly or, at best, in their greatest possible harmony with one another.

It is in fact absolutely impossible by experience to discern [407] with complete certainty a single case in which the maxim of an action, however much it may conform to duty, rested solely on moral grounds and on the conception of one's duty. It sometimes happens that in the most searching self-examination we can find nothing except the moral ground of duty which could have been powerful enough to move us to this or that good action and to such great sacrifice. But from this we cannot by any means conclude with certainty that a secret impulse of self-love, falsely appearing as the idea of duty, was not actually the true determining cause of the will. For we like to flatter ourselves with a pretended nobler motive, while in fact even the strictest examination can never lead us entirely behind the secret incentives, for, when moral worth is in question, it is not a matter of actions which one sees but of their inner principles which one does not see.

Moreover, one cannot better serve the wishes of those who ridicule all morality as a mere phantom of human imagination overreaching itself through self-conceit than by conceding to them that the concepts of duty must be derived only from experience (for they are ready to believe from indolence that this is true of all other concepts too). For, by this concession, a sure triumph is prepared for them. Out of love for humanity I am willing to admit that most of our actions are in accordance with duty; but, if we look more closely at our thoughts and aspirations, we everywhere come upon the dear self, which is always there, and it is this instead of the stern command of duty (which would often require self-denial) which supports our plans. One need not be an enemy of virtue, but only a cool observer who does not confuse even the liveliest aspiration for the good with its reality, to be doubtful sometimes whether true virtue can really be found anywhere in the world. This is especially true as one's years increase and one's power of judgment is made wiser by experience and more acute in observation. This being so, nothing can secure us against the complete abandonment of our ideas of duty and preserve in us a well-founded respect for its law except the clear conviction that, even if there never were actions springing from such pure sources, our concern is not whether this or [408] that was done but that reason of itself and independently of all appearances commands what ought to be done. Our concern is with actions of which perhaps the world has never had an example, with actions whose feasibility might be seriously doubted by those who base everything on experience, and yet with actions inexorably commanded by reason. For example, pure sincerity in friendship can be demanded of every man, and this demand is not in the least diminished if a sincere friend has never existed, because this duty, as duty in general, prior to all experience, lies in the idea of a reason which determines the will by a priori grounds.

It is clear that no experience can give occasion for inferring the possibility of such apodictic laws. This is especially clear when we add that, unless we wish to deny all truth to the concept of morality and renounce its application to any possible object, we cannot refuse to admit that the law of this concept is of such broad significance that it holds not merely for men but for all rational beings as such; we must grant that it must be valid with absolute necessity and not merely under contingent conditions and with exceptions. For with what right could we bring into unlimited respect something that might be valid only under contingent human conditions? And how could laws of the determination of our will be held to be laws of the determination of the will of a rational being in general and of ourselves in so far as we are rational beings, if they were merely empirical and did not have their origin completely a priori in pure, but practical, reason?

Nor could one give poorer counsel to morality than to attempt to derive it from examples. For each example of morality which is exhibited to me must itself have been previously judged according to principles of morality to see whether it is worthy to serve as an original example, i.e., as a model. By no means could it authoritatively furnish the concept of morality. Even the Holy One of the Gospel must be compared with our ideal of moral perfection before He is recognized as such; even He says of Himself, "Why call ye Me (whom you see) good? None is good (the archetype of the good) except God only (whom you do not see)." But whence do we have the concept of God as the highest good? Solely from the idea [409] of moral perfection which reason formulates a priori and which it inseparably connects with the concept of a free will. Imitation has no place in moral matters, and examples serve only for encouragement. That is, they put beyond question the practicability of what the law commands, and they make visible that which the practical rule expresses more generally. But they can never justify our guiding ourselves by examples and our setting aside their true original which lies in reason.

If there is thus no genuine supreme principle of morality which does not rest merely on pure reason independently of all experience, I do not believe it is necessary even to ask whether it is well to exhibit these concepts generally (*in abstracto*), which, together with the principles belonging to them, are established a priori. At any rate, this question need not be asked if knowledge which establishes this is to be distinguished from ordinary knowledge and called philosophical. But in our times this question may perhaps be necessary. For if we collected votes as to whether pure rational knowledge separated from all experience, i.e., metaphysics of morals, or popular practical philosophy is to be preferred, it is easily guessed on which side the majority would stand.

This condescension to popular notions is certainly very commendable once the ascent to the principles of pure reason has been satisfactorily accomplished. That would mean the prior establishment of the doctrine of morals on metaphysics and then, when it is established, to procure a hearing for it through popularization. But it is extremely absurd to want to achieve popularity in the first investigation, where everything depends on the correctness of the fundamental principles. Not only can this procedure never make claim to that rarest merit of true philosophical popularity, since there is really no art in being generally comprehensible if one thereby renounces all basic insight, but it produces a disgusting jumble of patched-up observations and half-reasoned principles. Shallowpates enjoy this, for it is very useful in everyday chitchat, while the more sensible feel confused and dissatisfied without being able to help themselves. They turn their eyes away, even though philosophers, who see very well through the delusion, find little audience when they call men away for a time from this pretended popularization in order that they may [410] rightly appear popular after they have attained a definite insight.

One need only look at the essays on morality which that popular taste favors. One will sometimes meet with the particular vocation of human nature (but occasionally also the idea of a rational nature in general), sometimes perfection, and sometimes happiness, here moral feeling, there fear of God, a little of this and a little of that in a marvelous mixture.

However, it never occurs to the authors to ask whether the principles of morality are, after all, to be sought anywhere in knowledge of human nature (which we can derive only from experience). And if this is not the case, if the principles are completely a priori, free from everything empirical, and found exclusively in pure rational concepts and not at all in any other place, they never ask whether they should undertake this investigation as a separate inquiry, i.e., as pure practical philosophy or (if one may use a name so decried) a metaphysics[1] of morals. They never think of dealing with it alone and bringing it by itself to completeness, and of requiring the public, which desires popularization, to await the outcome of this undertaking.

But a completely isolated metaphysics of morals, mixed with no anthropology, no theology, no physics or hyperphysics, and even less with occult qualities (which might be called hypophysical), is not only an indispensable substrate of all theoretically sound and definite knowledge of duties; it is also a desideratum of the highest importance to the actual fulfillment of its precepts. For the pure conception of duty and of the moral law generally, with no admixture of empirical inducements, has an influence on the human heart so much more powerful than all other incentives[2] which may be [411]

[1] If one wishes, the pure philosophy of morals (metaphysics) can be distinguished from the applied (i.e., applied to human nature), just as pure mathematics and pure logic are distinguished from applied mathematics and applied logic. By this designation one is immediately reminded that moral principles are not founded on the peculiarities of human nature but must stand of themselves a priori, and that from such principles practical rules for every rational nature, and accordingly for man, must be derivable.

[2] I have a letter from the late excellent Sulzer* in which he asks me why the theories of virtue accomplish so little even though they contain so much that is convincing to reason. My answer was delayed in order that

* [Johann Georg Sulzer (1720–79), an important figure at the court and in literary circles in Berlin. Cf. *Allgemeine deutsche Biographie*, XXXVII, 144–147.]

derived from the empirical field that reason, in the consciousness of its dignity, despises them and gradually becomes master over them. It has this influence only through reason, which thereby first realizes that it can of itself be practical. A mixed theory of morals which is put together both from incentives of feelings and inclinations and from rational concepts must, on the other hand, make the mind vacillate between motives which cannot be brought under any principle and which can lead only accidentally to the good and often to the bad.

From what has been said it is clear that all moral concepts have their seat and origin entirely a priori in reason. This is just as much the case in the most ordinary reason as in reason which is speculative to the highest degree. It is obvious that they cannot be abstracted from any empirical and hence merely contingent cognitions. In the purity of their origin lies their worthiness to serve us as supreme practical principles, and to the extent that something empirical is added to them just this much is subtracted from their genuine influence and from the unqualified worth of actions. Furthermore, it is evident that it is not only of the greatest necessity in a theoretical point of view when it is a question of speculation but also of the utmost practical importance to derive the concepts and laws of morals from pure reason and to present them pure and

---

I might make it complete. The answer is only that the teachers themselves have not completely clarified their concepts, and when they wish to make up for this by hunting in every quarter for motives to the morally good so as to make their physic right strong, they spoil it. For the commonest observation shows that if we imagine an act of honesty performed with a steadfast soul and sundered from all view to any advantage in this or another world and even under the greatest temptations of need or allurement, it far surpasses and eclipses any similar action which was affected in the least by any foreign incentive; it elevates the soul and arouses the wish to be able to act in this way. Even moderately young children feel this impression, and one should never represent duties to them in any other way.

unmixed, and to determine the scope of this entire practical but pure rational knowledge (the entire faculty of pure practical reason) without making the principles depend upon [412] the particular nature of human reason as speculative philosophy may permit and even sometimes find necessary. But since moral laws should hold for every rational being as such, the principles must be derived from the universal concept of a rational being generally. In this manner all morals, which need anthropology for their application to men, must be completely developed first as pure philosophy, i.e., metaphysics, independently of anthropology (a thing which is easily done in such distinct fields of knowledge). For we know well that if we are not in possession of such a metaphysics, it is not merely futile to define accurately for the purposes of speculative judgment the moral element of duty in all actions which accord with duty, but impossible to base morals on legitimate principles for merely ordinary and practical use, especially in moral instruction; and it is only in this manner that pure moral dispositions can be produced and engrafted on men's minds for the purpose of the highest good in the world.

In this study we do not advance merely from the common moral judgment (which here is very worthy of respect) to the philosophical, as this has already been done, but we advance by natural stages from a popular philosophy (which goes no further than it can grope by means of examples) to metaphysics (which is not held back by anything empirical and which, as it must measure out the entire scope of rational knowledge of this kind, reaches even Ideas, where examples fail us). In order to make this advance, we must follow and clearly present the practical faculty of reason from its universal rules of determination to the point where the concept of duty arises from it.

Everything in nature works according to laws. Only a ra-

tional being has the capacity of acting according to the conception of laws, i.e., according to principles. This capacity is
will. Since reason is required for the derivation of actions
from laws, will is nothing else than practical reason. If reason
infallibly determines the will, the actions which such a being
recognizes as objectively necessary are also subjectively necessary. That is, the will is a faculty of choosing only that which
reason, independently of inclination, recognizes as practically
necessary, i.e., as good. But if reason of itself does not sufficiently determine the will, and if the will is subjugated to subjective conditions (certain incentives) which do not always
agree with objective conditions; in a word, if the will is [413]
not of itself in complete accord with reason (the actual case of
men), then the actions which are recognized as objectively
necessary are subjectively contingent, and the determination
of such a will according to objective laws is constraint. That
is, the relation of objective laws to a will which is not completely good is conceived as the determination of the will of a
rational being by principles of reason to which this will is not
by nature necessarily obedient.

The conception of an objective principle so far as it constrains a will, is a command (of reason), and the formula of
this command is called an *imperative*.

All imperatives are expressed by an "ought" and thereby
indicate the relation of an objective law of reason to a will
which is not in its subjective constitution necessarily determined by this law. This relation is that of constraint. Imperatives say that it would be good to do or to refrain from doing
something, but they say it to a will which does not always do
something simply because it is presented as a good thing to do.
Practical good is what determines the will by means of the
conception of reason and hence not by subjective causes but,
rather, objectively, i.e., on grounds which are valid for every

rational being as such. It is distinguished from the pleasant as that which has an influence on the will only by means of a sensation from merely subjective causes, which hold only for the senses of this or that person and not as a principle of reason which holds for everyone.[3]

A perfectly good will, therefore, would be equally [414] subject to objective laws (of the good), but it could not be conceived as constrained by them to act in accord with them, because, according to its own subjective constitution, it can be determined to act only through the conception of the good. Thus no imperatives hold for the divine will or, more generally, for a holy will. The "ought" is here out of place, for the volition of itself is necessarily in unison with the law. Therefore imperatives are only formulas expressing the relation of objective laws of volition in general to the subjective imperfection of the will of this or that rational being, e.g., the human will.

All imperatives command either hypothetically or categorically. The former present the practical necessity of a pos-

[3] The dependence of the faculty of desire on sensations is called [413] inclination, and inclination always indicates a need. The dependence of a contingently determinable will on principles of reason, however, is called interest. An interest is present only in a dependent will which is not of itself always in accord with reason; in the divine will we cannot conceive of an interest. But even the human will can take an interest in something without thereby acting from interest. The former means the practical interest in the action; the latter, the pathological interest in the object of the action. The former indicates only the dependence of the will on principles of reason in themselves, while the latter indicates dependence on the principles of reason for the purpose of inclination, since reason gives only the practical rule by which the needs of inclination are to be aided. In the former case the action interests me, and in the latter the object of the action (so far as it is pleasant for me) interests me. In the first section we have seen that, in the case of an action performed from duty, no regard must be given to the interest in the object, but merely in the action itself and its principle in reason (i.e., the law).

sible action as a means to achieving something else which one desires (or which one may possibly desire). The categorical imperative would be one which presented an action as of itself objectively necessary, without regard to any other end.

Since every practical law presents a possible action as good and thus as necessary for a subject practically determinable by reason, all imperatives are formulas of the determination of action which is necessary by the principle of a will which is in any way good. If the action is good only as a means to something else, the imperative is hypothetical; but if it is thought of as good in itself, and hence as necessary in a will which of itself conforms to reason as the principle of this will, the imperative is categorical.

The imperative thus says what action possible to me would be good, and it presents the practical rule in relation to a will which does not forthwith perform an action simply because it is good, in part because the subject does not always know that the action is good and in part (when he does know it) because his maxims can still be opposed to the objective principles of practical reason.

The hypothetical imperative, therefore, says only that the action is good to some purpose, possible or actual. In the former case it is a problematical,[4] in the latter an assertorical, [415]

---

[4] [The *First Introduction to the Critique of Judgment* says: "This is the place to correct an error into which I fell in the *Foundations of the Metaphysics of Morals*. After I had stated that the imperatives of prudence commanded only conditionally, and indeed only under the condition of merely possible, i.e., problematic, ends, I called that kind of practical precept 'problematic imperatives.' But there is certainly a contradiction in this expression. I should have called them 'technical imperatives,' i.e., imperatives of art. The pragmatic imperatives, or rules of prudence which command under the condition of an actual and even subjectively necessary end, belong also among the technical imperatives. (For what is prudence but the skill to use free men and even the natural dispositions and inclinations of oneself for one's own designs?) Only the fact that the end to which we submit ourselves and others, namely, our own happiness, does

practical principle. The categorical imperative, which declares the action to be of itself objectively necessary without making any reference to a purpose, i.e., without having any other end, holds as an apodictical (practical) principle.

We can think of that which is possible through the mere powers of some rational being as a possible purpose of any will. As a consequence, the principles of action, in so far as they are thought of as necessary to attain a possible purpose which can be achieved by them, are in reality infinitely numerous. All sciences have some practical part which consists of problems of some end which is possible for us and of imperatives as to how it can be reached. These can therefore generally be called imperatives of skill. Whether the end is reasonable and good is not in question at all, for the question is only of what must be done in order to attain it. The precepts to be followed by a physician in order to cure his patient and by a poisoner in order to bring about certain death are of equal value in so far as each does that which will perfectly accomplish his purpose. Since in early youth we do not know what ends may occur to us in the course of life, parents seek to let their children learn a great many things and provide for skill in the use of means to all sorts of arbitrary ends among which they cannot determine whether any one of them may later become an actual purpose of their pupil, though it is possible that he may some day have it as his actual purpose. And this anxiety is so great that they commonly neglect to form and correct their judgment on the worth of things which they may make their ends.

---

not belong to the merely arbitrary ends [which we may or may not have] justifies a special name for these imperatives because the problem does not require merely a mode of reaching the end as is the case with technical imperatives, but also requires a definition of what constitutes this end itself (happiness). The end must be presupposed as known in the case of technical imperatives" (Academy ed., XX, 200n.).]

There is one end, however, which we may presuppose as actual in all rational beings so far as imperatives apply to them, i.e., so far as they are dependent beings; there is one purpose not only which they *can* have but which we can presuppose that they all *do* have by a necessity of nature. This purpose is happiness. The hypothetical imperative which represents the practical necessity of action as means to the promotion of happiness is an assertorical imperative. We may not expound it as merely necessary to an uncertain and a merely possible purpose, but as necessary to a purpose which we can a priori and with assurance assume for everyone because it belongs [416] to his essence. Skill in the choice of means to one's own highest welfare can be called prudence[5] in the narrowest sense. Thus the imperative which refers to the choice of means to one's own happiness, i.e., the precept of prudence, is still only hypothetical; the action is not absolutely commanded but commanded only as a means to another end.

Finally, there is one imperative which directly commands a certain conduct without making its condition some purpose to be reached by it. This imperative is categorical. It concerns not the material of the action and its intended result but the form and the principle from which it results. What is essentially good in it consists in the intention, the result being what it may. This imperative may be called the imperative of morality.

Volition according to these three principles is plainly dis-

---

[5] The word "prudence" may be taken in two senses, and it may bear the name of prudence with reference to things of the world and private prudence. The former sense means the skill of a man in having an influence on others so as to use them for his own purposes. The latter is the ability to unite all these purposes to his own lasting advantage. The worth of the first is finally reduced to the latter, and of one who is prudent in the former sense but not in the latter we might better say that he is clever and cunning yet, on the whole, imprudent.

tinguished by dissimilarity in the constraint to which they subject the will. In order to clarify this dissimilarity, I believe that they are most suitably named if one says that they are either rules of skill, counsels of prudence, or commands (laws) of morality, respectively. For law alone implies the concept of an unconditional and objective and hence universally valid necessity, and commands are laws which must be obeyed, even against inclination. Counsels do indeed involve necessity, but a necessity that can hold only under a subjectively contingent condition, i.e., whether this or that man counts this or that as part of his happiness; but the categorical imperative, on the other hand, is restricted by no condition. As absolutely, though practically, necessary it can be called a command in the strict sense. We could also call the first imperative technical (belonging to art), the second pragmatic[6] (belonging to [417] welfare), and the third moral (belonging to free conduct as such, i.e., to morals).

The question now arises: how are all these imperatives possible? This question does not require an answer as to how the action which the imperative commands can be performed but merely as to how the constraint of the will, which the imperative expresses in the problem, can be conceived. How an imperative of skill is possible requires no particular discussion. Whoever wills the end, so far as reason has decisive influence on his action, wills also the indispensably necessary means to it that lie in his power. This proposition, in what concerns the will, is analytical; for, in willing an object as my effect, my causality as an acting cause, i.e., the use of the means, is al-

[6] It seems to me that the proper meaning of the word "pragmatic" could be most accurately defined in this way. For sanctions which properly flow not from the law of states as necessary statutes but from provision for the general welfare are called pragmatic. A history is pragmatically composed when it teaches prudence, i.e., instructs the world how it could provide for its interest better than, or at least as well as, has been done in the past.

ready thought, and the imperative derives the concept of necessary actions to this end from the concept of willing this end. Synthetical propositions undoubtedly are necessary in determining the means to a proposed end, but they do not concern the ground, the act of the will, but only the way to make the object real. Mathematics teaches, by synthetical propositions only, that in order to bisect a line according to an infallible principle I must make two intersecting arcs from each of its extremities; but if I know the proposed result can be obtained only by such an action, then it is an analytical proposition that, if I fully will the effect, I must also will the action necessary to produce it. For it is one and the same thing to conceive of something as an effect which is in a certain way possible through me and to conceive of myself as acting in this way.

If it were only easy to give a definite concept of happiness, the imperatives of prudence would completely correspond to those of skill and would be likewise analytical. For it could be said in this case as well as in the former that whoever wills the end wills also (necessarily according to reason) the only means to it which are in his power. But it is a [418] misfortune that the concept of happiness is so indefinite that, although each person wishes to attain it, he can never definitely and self-consistently state what it is he really wishes and wills. The reason for this is that all elements which belong to the concept of happiness are empirical, i.e., they must be taken from experience, while for the idea of happiness an absolute whole, a maximum, of well-being is needed in my present and in every future condition. Now it is impossible even for a most clear-sighted and most capable but finite being to form here a definite concept of that which he really wills. If he wills riches, how much anxiety, envy, and intrigue might he not thereby draw upon his shoulders! If he wills much knowledge and vision, perhaps it might become only an eye that much sharper to show him as more dreadful the evils which are now hidden from him and which are yet unavoidable, or to burden his desires—which already sufficiently engage him—with even more needs! If he wills a long life, who guarantees that it will not be long misery? If he wills at least health, how often has not the discomfort of the body restrained him from excesses into which perfect health would have led him? In short, he is not capable, on any principle and with complete certainty, of ascertaining what would make him truly happy; omniscience would be needed for his. He cannot, therefore, act according to definite principles so as to be happy, but only according to empirical counsels, e.g., those of diet, economy, courtesy, restraint, etc., which are shown by experience best to promote welfare on the average. Hence the imperatives of prudence cannot, in the strict sense, command, i.e., present actions objectively as practically necessary; thus they are to be taken as counsels (*consilia*) rather than as commands (*praecepta*) of reason, and the task of determining infallibly and universally what action will promote the happiness of a rational being is completely unsolvable. There can be no imperative which would, in the strict sense, command us to do what makes for happiness, because happiness is an ideal not of reason but of imagination,[7] depending only on empirical grounds which one would expect in vain to determine an [419] action through which the totality of consequences—which is in fact infinite—could be achieved. Assuming that the means

---

[7] [The distinction between happiness and pleasure, which Kant says the followers of Epicurus confused, is explained in a fragment dating back to perhaps 1775: "Happiness is not something sensed but something thought. Nor is it a thought which can be taken from experience but a thought which only makes its experience possible. Not as if one had to know happiness in all its elements, but [one must know] the a priori condition by which alone one can be capable of happiness" (*Lose Blätter*, Reicke ed., trans. Schilpp, in *Kant's Precritical Ethics*, p. 129).]

to happiness could be infallibly stated, this imperative of prudence would be an analytical proposition, for it differs from the imperative of skill only in that its end is given while in the latter case it is merely possible. Since both, however, only command the means to that which one presupposes, the imperative which commands the willing of the means to him who wills the end is in both cases analytical. There is, consequently, no difficulty in seeing the possibility of such an imperative.

To see how the imperative of morality is possible is, then, without doubt the only question needing an answer. It is not hypothetical, and thus the objectively conceived necessity cannot be supported by any presupposition, as was the case with the hypothetical imperatives. But it must not be overlooked that it cannot be shown by any example (i.e., it cannot be empirically shown) whether or not there is such an imperative; it is rather to be suspected that all imperatives which appear to be categorical may yet be hypothetical, but in a hidden way. For instance, when it is said, "Thou shalt not make a false promise," we assume that the necessity of this avoidance is not a mere counsel for the sake of escaping some other evil, so that it would read, "Thou shalt not make a false promise so that, if it comes to light, thou ruinest thy credit"; we assume rather that an action of this kind must be regarded as of itself bad and that the imperative of the prohibition is categorical. But we cannot show with certainty by any example that the will is here determined by the law alone without any other incentives, even though this appears to be the case. For it is always possible that secret fear of disgrace, and perhaps also obscure apprehension of other dangers, may have had an influence on the will. Who can prove by experience the nonexistence of a cause when experience shows us only that we do not perceive the cause? But in such a case the so-called moral imperative, which as such appears to be categorical and unconditional, would be actually only a pragmatic precept which makes us attentive to our own advantage and teaches us to consider it.

Thus we shall have to investigate purely a priori the possibility of a categorical imperative, for we do not have the advantage that experience would give us the reality of this [420] imperative, so that the [demonstration of its] possibility would be necessary only for its explanation and not for its establishment. In the meantime, this much may at least be seen: the categorical imperative alone can be taken as a practical *law*, while all the others may be called principles of the will but not laws. This is because what is necessary merely for the attainment of an arbitrary purpose can be regarded as itself contingent, and we get rid of the precept once we give up the purpose, whereas the unconditional command leaves the will no freedom to choose the opposite. Thus it alone implies the necessity which we require of a law.

Secondly, in the case of the categorical imperative or law of morality, the cause of difficulty in discerning its possibility is very weighty. This imperative is an a priori synthetical practical proposition,[8] and, since to discern the possibility of propositions of this sort is so difficult in theoretical knowledge, it may well be gathered that it will be no less difficult in the practical.

In attacking this problem, we will first inquire whether the mere concept of a categorical imperative does not also furnish

---

[8] I connect a priori, and hence necessarily, the action with the will without supposing as a condition that there is any inclination [to the action] (though I do so only objectively, i.e., under the idea of a reason which would have complete power over all subjective motives). This is, therefore, a practical proposition which does not analytically derive the willing of an action from some other volition already presupposed (for we do not have such a perfect will); it rather connects it directly with the concept of the will of a rational being as something which is not contained within it.

the formula containing the proposition which alone can be a categorical imperative. For even when we know the formula of the imperative, to learn how such an absolute law is possible will require difficult and special labors which we shall postpone to the last section.

If I think of a hypothetical imperative as such, I do not know what it will contain until the condition is stated [under which it is an imperative]. But if I think of a categorical imperative, I know immediately what it contains. For since the imperative contains besides the law only the necessity that the maxim[9] should accord with this law, while the law [421] contains no condition to which it is restricted, there is nothing remaining in it except the universality of law as such to which the maxim of the action should conform; and in effect this conformity alone is represented as necessary by the imperative.

There is, therefore, only one categorical imperative. It is: Act only according to that maxim by which you can at the same time will that it should become a universal law.

Now if all imperatives of duty can be derived from this one imperative as a principle, we can at least show what we understand by the concept of duty and what it means, even though it remain undecided whether that which is called duty is an empty concept or not.

The universality of law according to which effects are produced constitutes what is properly called nature in the most general sense (as to form), i.e., the existence of things so far

[9] A maxim is the subjective principle of acting and must be distinguished from the objective principle, i.e., the practical law. The former contains the practical rule which reason determines according to the conditions of the subject (often its ignorance or inclinations) and is thus the principle according to which the subject acts. The law, on the other hand, is the objective principle valid for every rational being, and the principle by which it ought to act, i.e., an imperative.

as it is determined by universal laws. [By analogy], then, the universal imperative of duty can be expressed as follows: Act as though the maxim of your action were by your will to become a universal law of nature.

We shall now enumerate some duties, adopting the usual division of them into duties to ourselves and to others and into perfect and imperfect duties.[10]

1. A man who is reduced to despair by a series of evils feels a weariness with life but is still in possession of his reason sufficiently to ask whether it would not be contrary [422] to his duty to himself to take his own life. Now he asks whether the maxim of his action could become a universal law of nature. His maxim, however, is: For love of myself, I make it my principle to shorten my life when by a longer duration it threatens more evil than satisfaction. But it is questionable whether this principle of self-love could become a universal law of nature. One immediately sees a contradiction in a system of nature whose law would be to destroy life by the feeling whose special office is to impel the improvement of life. In this case it would not exist as nature; hence that maxim cannot obtain as a law of nature, and thus it wholly contradicts the supreme principle of all duty.

2. Another man finds himself forced by need to borrow money. He well knows that he will not be able to repay it, but he also sees that nothing will be loaned him if he does not firmly promise to repay it at a certain time. He desires

---

[10] It must be noted here that I reserve the division of duties for a future *Metaphysics of Morals* and that the division here stands as only an arbitrary one (chosen in order to arrange my examples). For the rest, by a perfect duty I here understand a duty which permits no exception in the interest of inclination; thus I have not merely outer but also inner perfect duties. This runs contrary to the usage adopted in the schools, but I am not disposed to defend it here because it is all one to my purpose whether this is conceded or not.

to make such a promise, but he has enough conscience to ask himself whether it is not improper and opposed to duty to relieve his distress in such a way. Now, assuming he does decide to do so, the maxim of his action would be as follows: When I believe myself to be in need of money, I will borrow money and promise to repay it, although I know I shall never do so. Now this principle of self-love or of his own benefit may very well be compatible with his whole future welfare, but the question is whether it is right. He changes the pretension of self-love into a universal law and then puts the question: How would it be if my maxim became a universal law? He immediately sees that it could never hold as a universal law of nature and be consistent with itself; rather it must necessarily contradict itself. For the universality of a law which says that anyone who believes himself to be in need could promise what he pleased with the intention of not fulfilling it would make the promise itself and the end to be accomplished by it impossible; no one would believe what was promised to him but would only laugh at any such assertion as vain pretense.

3. A third finds in himself a talent which could, by means of some cultivation, make him in many respects a useful [423] man. But he finds himself in comfortable circumstances and prefers indulgence in pleasure to troubling himself with broadening and improving his fortunate natural gifts. Now, however, let him ask whether his maxim of neglecting his gifts, besides agreeing with his propensity to idle amusement, agrees also with what is called duty. He sees that a system of nature could indeed exist in accordance with such a law, even though man (like the inhabitants of the South Sea Islands) should let his talents rust and resolve to devote his life merely to idleness, indulgence, and propagation—in a word, to pleasure. But he cannot possibly will that this should become a universal law of nature or that it should be implanted in us by a natural

instinct. For, as a rational being, he necessarily wills that all his faculties should be developed, inasmuch as they are given to him for all sorts of possible purposes.

4. A fourth man, for whom things are going well, sees that others (whom he could help) have to struggle with great hardships, and he asks, "What concern of mine is it? Let each one be as happy as heaven wills, or as he can make himself; I will not take anything from him or even envy him; but to his welfare or to his assistance in time of need I have no desire to contribute." If such a way of thinking were a universal law of nature, certainly the human race could exist, and without doubt even better than in a state where everyone talks of sympathy and good will, or even exerts himself occasionally to practice them while, on the other hand, he cheats when he can and betrays or otherwise violates the rights of man. Now although it is possible that a universal law of nature according to that maxim could exist, it is nevertheless impossible to will that such a principle should hold everywhere as a law of nature. For a will which resolved this would conflict with itself, since instances can often arise in which he would need the love and sympathy of others, and in which he would have robbed himself, by such a law of nature springing from his own will, of all hope of the aid he desires.

The foregoing are a few of the many actual duties, or at least of duties we hold to be actual, whose derivation from the one stated principle is clear. We must be able to will that [424] a maxim of our action become a universal law; this is the canon of the moral estimation of our action generally. Some actions are of such a nature that their maxim cannot even be *thought* as a universal law of nature without contradiction, far from it being possible that one could will that it should be such. In others this internal impossibility is not found, though it is still impossible to *will* that their maxim should be raised to the universality of a law of nature, because such a will would contradict itself. We easily see that the former maxim conflicts with the stricter or narrower (imprescriptible) duty, the latter with broader (meritorious) duty. Thus all duties, so far as the kind of obligation (not the object of their action) is concerned, have been completely exhibited by these examples in their dependence on the one principle.

When we observe ourselves in any transgression of a duty, we find that we do not actually will that our maxim should become a universal law. That is impossible for us; rather, the contrary of this maxim should remain as a law generally, and we only take the liberty of making an exception to it for ourselves or for the sake of our inclination, and for this one occasion. Consequently, if we weighed everything from one and the same standpoint, namely, reason, we would come upon a contradiction in our own will, viz., that a certain principle is objectively necessary as a universal law and yet subjectively does not hold universally but rather admits exceptions. However, since we regard our action at one time from the point of view of a will wholly conformable to reason and then from that of a will affected by inclinations, there is actually no contradiction, but rather an opposition of inclination to the precept of reason (*antagonismus*). In this the universality of the principle (*universalitas*) is changed into mere generality (*generalitas*), whereby the practical principle of reason meets the maxim halfway. Although this cannot be justified in our own impartial judgment, it does show that we actually acknowledge the validity of the categorical imperative and allow ourselves (with all respect to it) only a few exceptions which seem to us to be unimportant and forced upon us.

We have thus at least established that if duty is a concept [425] which is to have significance and actual legislation for our actions, it can be expressed only in categorical imperatives and not at all in hypothetical ones. For every application of it we have also clearly exhibited the content of the categorical imperative which must contain the principle of all duty (if there is such). This is itself very much. But we are not yet advanced far enough to prove a priori that that kind of imperative really exists, that there is a practical law which of itself commands absolutely and without any incentives, and that obedience to this law is duty.

With a view to attaining this, it is extremely important to remember that we must not let ourselves think that the reality of this principle can be derived from the particular constitution of human nature. For duty is practical unconditional necessity of action; it must, therefore, hold for all rational beings (to which alone an imperative can apply), and only for that reason can it be a law for all human wills. Whatever is derived from the particular natural situation of man as such, or from certain feelings and propensities, or even from a particular tendency of the human reason which might not hold necessarily for the will of every rational being (if such a tendency is possible), can give a maxim valid for us but not a law; that is, it can give a subjective principle by which we might act only if we have the propensity and inclination, but not an objective principle by which we would be directed to act even if all our propensity, inclination, and natural tendency were opposed to it. This is so far the case that the sublimity and intrinsic worth of the command is the better shown in a duty the fewer subjective causes there are for it and the more there are against it; the latter do not weaken the constraint of the law or diminish its validity.

Here we see philosophy brought to what is, in fact, a precarious position, which should be made fast even though it is supported by nothing in either heaven or earth. Here philosophy must show its purity as the absolute sustainer of its laws, and not as the herald of those which an implanted sense or who knows what tutelary nature whispers to it. Those may be better than no laws at all, but they can never afford [426] fundamental principles, which reason alone dictates. These fundamental principles must originate entirely a priori and thereby obtain their commanding authority; they can expect nothing from the inclination of men but everything from the supremacy of the law and due respect for it. Otherwise they condemn man to self-contempt and inner abhorrence.

Thus everything empirical is not only wholly unworthy to be an ingredient in the principle of morality but is even highly prejudicial to the purity of moral practices themselves. For, in morals, the proper and inestimable worth of an absolutely good will consists precisely in the freedom of the principle of action from all influences from contingent grounds which only experience can furnish. We cannot too much or too often warn against the lax or even base manner of thought which seeks principles among empirical motives and laws, for human reason in its weariness is glad to rest on this pillow. In a dream of sweet illusions (in which it embraces not Juno but a cloud), it substitutes for morality a bastard patched up from limbs of very different parentage, which looks like anything one wishes to see in it, but not like virtue to anyone who has ever beheld her in her true form.[11]

The question then is: Is it a necessary law for all rational beings that they should always judge their actions by such maxims as they themselves could will to serve as universal

[11] To behold virtue in her proper form is nothing else than to exhibit morality stripped of all admixture of sensuous things and of every spurious adornment of reward or self-love. How much she then eclipses everything which appears charming to the senses can easily be seen by everyone with the least effort of his reason, if it be not spoiled for all abstraction.

laws? If it is such a law, it must be connected (wholly a priori) with the concept of the will of a rational being as such. But in order to discover this connection we must, however reluctantly, take a step into metaphysics, although into a region of it different from speculative philosophy, i.e., into metaphysics of morals. In a practical philosophy it is not a question of assuming grounds for what happens but of assuming laws of what ought to happen even though it may never happen— that is to say, objective, practical laws. Hence in practical philosophy we need not inquire into the reasons why [427] something pleases or displeases, how the pleasure of mere feeling differs from taste, and whether this is distinct from a general satisfaction of reason. Nor need we ask on what the feeling of pleasure or displeasure rests, how desires and inclinations arise, and how, finally, maxims arise from desires and inclination under the co-operation of reason. For all these matters belong to an empirical psychology, which would be the second part of physics if we consider it as philosophy of nature so far as it rests on empirical laws. But here it is a question of objectively practical laws and thus of the relation of a will to itself so far as it determines itself only by reason; for everything which has a relation to the empirical automatically falls away, because if reason of itself alone determines conduct it must necessarily do so a priori. The possibility of reason thus determining conduct must now be investigated.

The will is thought of as a faculty of determining itself to action in accordance with the conception of certain laws. Such a faculty can be found only in rational beings. That which serves the will as the objective ground of its self-determination is an end, and, if it is given by reason alone, it must hold alike for all rational beings. On the other hand, that which contains the ground of the possibility of the action, whose result is an end, is called the means. The subjective ground of desire is the incentive,[12] while the objective ground of volition is the motive. Thus arises the distinction between subjective ends, which rest on incentives, and objective ends, which depend on motives valid for every rational being. Practical principles are formal when they disregard all subjective ends; they are material when they have subjective ends, and thus certain incentives, as their basis. The ends which a rational being arbitrarily proposes to himself as consequences of his action are material ends and are without exception only relative, for only their relation to a particularly constituted faculty of desire in the subject gives them their worth. And this worth cannot, therefore, afford any universal principles for all rational beings or valid and necessary principles for every volition. That is, they [428] cannot give rise to any practical laws. All these relative ends, therefore, are grounds for hypothetical imperatives only.

But suppose that there were something the existence of which in itself had absolute worth, something which, as an end in itself, could be a ground of definite laws. In it and only in it could lie the ground of a possible categorical imperative, i.e., of a practical law.

Now, I say, man and, in general, every rational being exists as an end in himself and not merely as a means to be arbitrarily used by this or that will. In all his actions, whether they are directed to himself or to other rational beings, he must always be regarded at the same time as an end. All objects of inclinations have only a conditional worth, for if the inclinations and the needs founded on them did not exist, their object would be without worth. The inclinations themselves as the

---

[12] [*Triebfeder* in contrast to *Bewegungsgrund*. Abbott translates the former as "spring," but "urge" might better convey the meaning. I follow Greene and Hudson's excellent usage in their translation of the *Religion Within the Limits of Reason Alone*.]

sources of needs, however, are so lacking in absolute worth that the universal wish of every rational being must be indeed to free himself completely from them. Therefore, the worth of any objects to be obtained by our actions is at all times conditional. Beings whose existence does not depend on our will but on nature, if they are not rational beings, have only a relative worth as means and are therefore called "things"; on the other hand, rational beings are designated "persons" because their nature indicates that they are ends in themselves, i.e., things which may not be used merely as means. Such a being is thus an object of respect and, so far, restricts all [arbitrary] choice. Such beings are not merely subjective ends whose existence as a result of our action has a worth for us, but are objective ends, i.e., beings whose existence in itself is an end. Such an end is one for which no other end can be substituted, to which these beings should serve merely as means. For, without them, nothing of absolute worth could be found, and if all worth is conditional and thus contingent, no supreme practical principle for reason could be found anywhere.

Thus if there is to be a supreme practical principle and a categorical imperative for the human will, it must be one that forms an objective principle of the will from the conception of that which is necessarily an end for everyone because it is an end in itself. Hence this objective principle can serve [429] as a universal practical law. The ground of this principle is: rational nature exists as an end in itself. Man necessarily thinks of his own existence in this way; thus far it is a subjective principle of human actions. Also every other rational being thinks of his existence by means of the same rational ground which holds also for myself;[13] thus it is at the same

[13] Here I present this proposition as a postulate, but in the last section grounds for it will be found.

time an objective principle from which, as a supreme practical ground, it must be possible to derive all laws of the will. The practical imperative, therefore, is the following: Act so that you treat humanity, whether in your own person or in that of another, always as an end and never as a means only. Let us now see whether this can be achieved.

To return to our previous examples:

First, according to the concept of necessary duty to one's self, he who contemplates suicide will ask himself whether his action can be consistent with the idea of humanity as an end in itself. If, in order to escape from burdensome circumstances, he destroys himself, he uses a person merely as a means to maintain a tolerable condition up to the end of life. Man, however, is not a thing, and thus not something to be used merely as a means; he must always be regarded in all his actions as an end in himself. Therefore, I cannot dispose of man in my own person so as to mutilate, corrupt, or kill him. (It belongs to ethics proper to define more accurately this basic principle so as to avoid all misunderstanding, e.g., as to the amputation of limbs in order to preserve myself, or to exposing my life to danger in order to save it; I must, therefore, omit them here.)

Second, as concerns necessary or obligatory duties to others, he who intends a deceitful promise to others sees immediately that he intends to use another man merely as a means, without the latter containing the end in himself at the same time. For he whom I want to use for my own purposes by means of such a promise cannot possibly assent to my mode of acting against him and cannot contain the end of this action [430] in himself. This conflict against the principle of other men is even clearer if we cite examples of attacks on their freedom and property. For then it is clear that he who transgresses the rights of men intends to make use of the persons of others merely as a means, without considering that, as rational beings, they must always be esteemed at the same time as ends, i.e., only as beings who must be able to contain in themselves the end of the very same action.[14]

Third, with regard to contingent (meritorious) duty to one's self, it is not sufficient that the action not conflict with humanity in our person as an end in itself; it must also harmonize with it. Now in humanity there are capacities for greater perfection which belong to the end of nature with respect to humanity in our own person; to neglect these might perhaps be consistent with the preservation of humanity as an end in itself but not with the furtherance of that end.

Fourth, with regard to meritorious duty to others, the natural end which all men have is their own happiness. Humanity might indeed exist if no one contributed to the happiness of others, provided he did not intentionally detract from it; but this harmony with humanity as an end in itself is only negative rather than positive if everyone does not also endeavor, so far as he can, to further the ends of others. For the ends of any person, who is an end in himself, must as far as possible also be my end, if that conception of an end in itself is to have its full effect on me.

This principle of humanity and of every rational creature as an end in itself is the supreme limiting condition on freedom of the actions of each man. It is not borrowed from [431]

---

[14] Let it not be thought that the banal *quod tibi non vis fieri*, etc., could here serve as guide or principle, for it is only derived from the principle and is restricted by various limitations. It cannot be a universal law, because it contains the ground neither of duties to one's self nor of the benevolent duties to others (for many a man would gladly consent that others should not benefit him, provided only that he might be excused from showing benevolence to them). Nor does it contain the ground of obligatory duties to another, for the criminal would argue on this ground against the judge who sentences him. And so on.

experience, first, because of its universality, since it applies to all rational beings generally and experience does not suffice to determine anything about them; and, secondly, because in experience humanity is not thought of (subjectively) as the end of men, i.e., as an object which we of ourselves really make our end. Rather it is thought of as the objective end which should constitute the supreme limiting condition of all subjective ends, whatever they may be. Thus this principle must arise from pure reason. Objectively the ground of all practical legislation lies (according to the first principle) in the rule and in the form of universality, which makes it capable of being a law (at most a natural law); subjectively, it lies in the end. But the subject of all ends is every rational being as an end in itself (by the second principle); from this there follows the third practical principle of the will as the supreme condition of its harmony with universal practical reason, viz., the idea of the will of every rational being as making universal law.[15]

By this principle all maxims are rejected which are not consistent with the universal lawgiving of will. The will is thus not only subject to the law but subject in such a way that it must be regarded also as self-legislative and only for this reason as being subject to the law (of which it can regard itself as the author).

In the foregoing mode of conception, in which imperatives are conceived universally either as conformity to law by actions—a conformity which is similar to a natural order—or as the prerogative of rational beings as such, the imperatives exclude from their legislative authority all admixture of any interest as an incentive. They do so because they were

[15] [Following the suggestion of H. J. Paton, *The Categorical Imperative* (London: Hutchinson, 1946; Chicago: University of Chicago Press, 1949), p. 180.]

conceived as categorical. They were only assumed to be categorical, however, because we had to make such an assumption if we wished to explain the concept of duty. But that there were practical propositions which commanded categorically could not here be proved independently, just as little as it can be proved anywhere in this section. One thing, however, might have been done: to indicate in the imperative itself, by some determination which it contained, that in volition [432] from duty the renunciation of all interest is the specific mark of the categorical imperative, distinguishing it from the hypothetical. And this is now being done in the third formulation of the principle, i.e., in the idea of the will of every rational being as a will giving universal law. A will which stands under laws can be bound to this law by an interest. But if we think of a will giving universal laws, we find that a supreme legislating will cannot possibly depend on any interest, for such a dependent will would itself need still another law which would restrict the interest of its self-love to the condition that [the maxims of this will] should be valid as universal law.

Thus the principle of every human will as a will giving universal laws in all its maxims[16] is very well adapted to being a categorical imperative, provided it is otherwise correct. Because of the idea of universal lawgiving, it is based on no interest, and, thus of all possible imperatives, it alone can be unconditional. Or, better, converting the proposition: if there is a categorical imperative (a law for the will of every rational being), it can only command that everything be done from the maxim of its will as one which could have as its object only itself considered as giving universal laws. For only in this case are the practical principle and the imperative which the will

[16] I may be excused from citing examples to elucidate this principle, for those which have already illustrated the categorical imperative and its formula can here serve the same purpose.

obeys unconditional, because the will can have no interest as its foundation.

If we now look back upon all previous attempts which have ever been undertaken to discover the principle of morality, it is not to be wondered at that they all had to fail. Man was seen to be bound to laws by his duty, but it was not seen that he is subject only to his own, yet universal, legislation, and that he is only bound to act in accordance with his own will, which is, however, designed by nature to be a will giving universal laws. For if one thought of him as subject only to a law (whatever it may be), this necessarily implied some interest as a stimulus or compulsion to obedience because [433] the law did not arise from his will. Rather, his will was constrained by something else according to a law to act in a certain way. By this strictly necessary consequence, however, all the labor of finding a supreme ground for duty was irrevocably lost, and one never arrived at duty but only at the necessity of action from a certain interest. This might be his own interest or that of another, but in either case the imperative always had to be conditional and could not at all serve as a moral command. This principle I will call the principle of *autonomy* of the will in contrast to all other principles which I accordingly count under *heteronomy*.

The concept of each rational being as a being that must regard itself as giving universal law through all the maxims of its will, so that it may judge itself and its actions from this standpoint, leads to a very fruitful concept, namely, that of a *realm of ends*.

By "realm" I understand the systematic union of different rational beings through common laws. Because laws determine ends with regard to their universal validity, if we abstract from the personal difference of rational beings and thus from all content of their private ends, we can think of a whole of all ends in systematic connection, a whole of rational beings as ends in themselves as well as of the particular ends which each may set for himself. This is a realm of ends, which is possible on the aforesaid principles. For all rational beings stand under the law that each of them should treat himself and all others never merely as means but in every case also as an end in himself. Thus there arises a systematic union of rational beings through common objective laws. This is a realm which may be called a realm of ends (certainly only an ideal), because what these laws have in view is just the relation of these beings to each other as ends and means.

A rational being belongs to the realm of ends as a [434] member when he gives universal laws in it while also himself subject to these laws. He belongs to it as sovereign when he, as legislating, is subject to the will of no other. The rational being must regard himself always as legislative in a realm of ends possible through the freedom of the will, whether he belongs to it as member or as sovereign. He cannot maintain the latter position merely through the maxims of his will but only when he is a completely independent being without need and with power adequate to his will.

Morality, therefore, consists in the relation of every action to that legislation through which alone a realm of ends is possible. This legislation, however, must be found in every rational being. It must be able to arise from his will, whose principle then is to take no action according to any maxim which would be inconsistent with its being a universal law and thus to act only so that the will through its maxims could regard itself at the same time as universally lawgiving. If now the maxims do not by their nature already necessarily conform to this objective principle of rational beings as universally lawgiving, the necessity of acting according to that principle is called practical constraint, i.e., duty. Duty pertains not to the sovereign in the realm of ends, but rather to each member, and to each in the same degree.

The practical necessity of acting according to this principle, i.e., duty, does not rest at all on feelings, impulses, and inclinations; it rests merely on the relation of rational beings to one another, in which the will of a rational being must always be regarded as legislative, for otherwise it could not be thought of as an end in itself. Reason, therefore, relates every maxim of the will as giving universal laws to every other will and also to every action toward itself; it does so not for the sake of any other practical motive or future advantage but rather from the idea of the dignity of a rational being who obeys no law except that which he himself also gives.

In the realm of ends everything has either a *price* or a *dignity*. Whatever has a price can be replaced by something else as its equivalent; on the other hand, whatever is above all price, and therefore admits of no equivalent, has a dignity.

That which is related to general human inclinations and needs has a *market price*. That which, without presupposing any need, accords with a certain taste, i.e., with pleasure in the mere purposeless play of our faculties, has an *affective* [435] *price*. But that which constitutes the condition under which alone something can be an end in itself does not have mere relative worth, i.e., a price, but an intrinsic worth, i.e., *dignity*.

Now morality is the condition under which alone a rational being can be an end in itself, because only through it is it possible to be a legislative member in the realm of ends. Thus morality and humanity, so far as it is capable of morality, alone have dignity. Skill and diligence in work have a market value; wit, lively imagination, and humor have an affective price; but fidelity in promises and benevolence on principle (not from instinct) have intrinsic worth. Nature and likewise art contain nothing which could replace their lack, for their worth consists not in effects which flow from them, nor in advantage and utility which they procure; it consists only in intentions, i.e., maxims of the will which are ready to reveal themselves in this manner through actions even though success does not favor them. These actions need no recommendation from any subjective disposition or taste in order that they may be looked upon with immediate favor and satisfaction, nor do they have need for any immediate propensity or feeling directed to them. They exhibit the will which performs them as the object of an immediate respect, since nothing but reason is required in order to impose them on the will. The will is not to be cajoled into them, for this, in the case of duties, would be a contradiction. This esteem lets the worth of such a turn of mind be recognized as dignity and puts it infinitely beyond any price, with which it cannot in the least be brought into competition or comparison without, as it were, violating its holiness.

And what is it that justifies the morally good disposition or virtue in making such lofty claims? It is nothing less than the participation it affords the rational being in giving universal laws. He is thus fitted to be a member in a possible realm of ends to which his own nature already destined him. For, as an end in himself, he is destined to be legislative in the realm of ends, free from all laws of nature and obedient only to those which he himself gives. Accordingly, his maxims can belong to a universal legislation to which he is at the same time also subject. A thing has no worth other than that determined [436] for it by the law. The legislation which determines all worth must therefore have a dignity, i.e., unconditional and incomparable worth. For the esteem which a rational being must have for it, only the word "respect" is a suitable expression. Autonomy is thus the basis of the dignity of both human nature and every rational nature.

The three aforementioned ways of presenting the principle of morality are fundamentally only so many formulas of the very same law, and each of them unites the others in itself. There is, nevertheless, a difference in them, but the difference is more subjectively than objectively practical, for it is intended to bring an idea of reason closer to intuition (by means of a certain analogy) and thus nearer to feeling. All maxims have:

1. A form, which consists in universality; and in this respect the formula of the moral imperative requires that the maxims be chosen as though they should hold as universal laws of nature.
2. A material, i.e., an end; in this respect the formula says that the rational being, as by its nature an end and thus as an end in itself, must serve in every maxim as the condition restricting all merely relative and arbitrary ends.
3. A complete determination of all maxims by the formula that all maxims which stem from autonomous legislation ought to harmonize with a possible realm of ends as with a realm of nature.[17]

There is a progression here like that through the categories of the unity of the form of the will (its universality), the plurality of material (the objects, i.e., the ends), and the all-comprehensiveness or totality of the system of ends. But it is better in moral evaluation to follow the rigorous method and to make the universal formula of the categorical imperative

[17] Teleology considers nature as a realm of ends; morals regards a possible realm of ends as a realm of nature. In the former the realm of ends is a theoretical idea for the explanation of what actually is. In the latter it is a practical idea for bringing about that which is not actually real but which can become real through our conduct, and which is in accordance with this idea.

the basis: Act according to the maxim which can at the same time make itself a universal law. But if one wishes to [437] gain a hearing for the moral law, it is very useful to bring one and the same action under the three stated principles and thus, so far as possible, to bring it nearer to intuition.

We can now end where we started, with the concept of an unconditionally good will. That will is absolutely good which cannot be bad, and thus it is a will whose maxim, when made a universal law, can never conflict with itself. Thus this principle is also its supreme law: Always act according to that maxim whose universality as a law you can at the same time will. This is the only condition under which a will can never come into conflict with itself, and such an imperative is categorical. Because the validity of the will, as a universal law for possible actions, has an analogy with the universal connection of the existence of things under universal laws, which is the formal element of nature in general, the categorical imperative can also be expressed as follows: Act according to maxims which can at the same time have themselves as universal laws of nature as their object. Such, then, is the formula of an absolutely good will.

Rational nature is distinguished from others in that it proposes an end to itself. This end would be the material of every good will. Since, however, in the idea of an absolutely good will without any limiting condition of the attainment of this or that end, every end to be effected must be completely abstracted (as any particular end would make each will only relatively good), the end here is not conceived as one to be effected but as an independent end, and thus merely negatively. It is that which must never be acted against, and which must consequently never be valued as merely a means but in every volition also as an end. Now this end can never be other than the subject of all possible ends themselves, because this is at the same time the subject of a possible will which is absolutely good; for the latter cannot be made secondary to any other object without contradiction. The principle: Act with reference to every rational being (whether yourself or another) so that it is an end in itself in your maxim, is thus basically identical with the principle: Act by a maxim which involves its own universal validity for every rational being. [438]

That in the use of means to every end I should restrict my maxim to the condition of its universal validity as a law for every subject is tantamount to saying that the subject of ends, i.e., the rational being itself, must be made the basis of all maxims of actions and must thus be treated never as a mere means but as the supreme limiting condition in the use of all means, i.e., as an end at the same time.

It follows incontestably that every rational being must be able to regard himself as an end in himself with reference to all laws to which he may be subject, whatever they may be, and thus as giving universal laws. For it is just the fitness of his maxims to a universal legislation that indicates that he is an end in himself. It also follows that his dignity (his prerogative) over all merely natural beings entails that he must take his maxims from the point of view which regards himself, and hence also every other rational being, as legislative. (The rational beings are, on this account, called persons.) In this way, a world of rational beings (*mundus intelligibilis*) is possible as a realm of ends, because of the legislation belonging to all persons as members. Consequently, every rational being must act as if he, by his maxims, were at all times a legislative member in the universal realm of ends. The formal principle of these maxims is: So act as if your maxims should serve at the same time as the universal law (of all rational beings). A realm of ends is thus possible only by analogy with a realm of nature. The former, however, is possible only by maxims, i.e.,

self-imposed rules, while the latter is possible by laws of efficient causes of things externally necessitated. Regardless of
this difference, by analogy we call the natural whole a realm
of nature so far as it is related to rational beings as its end;
we do so even though the natural whole is looked at as a
machine. Such a realm of ends would actually be realized
through maxims whose rule is prescribed to all rational beings
by the categorical imperative, if they were universally obeyed.
But a rational being, though he scrupulously follow this
maxim, cannot for that reason expect every other rational
being to be true to it; nor can he expect the realm of nature
and its orderly design to harmonize with him as a fitting member of a realm of ends which is possible through himself. That
is, he cannot count on its favoring his expectation of happiness.
[439] Still the law: Act according to the maxims of a universally legislative member of a merely potential realm of ends,
remains in full force, because it commands categorically. And
just in this lies the paradox that merely the dignity of humanity as rational nature without any end or advantage to be
gained by it, and thus respect for a mere idea, should serve as
the inflexible precept of the will. There is the further paradox
that the sublimity of the maxims and the worthiness of every
rational subject to be a legislative member in the realm of ends
consist precisely in independence of the maxims from all such
incentives. Otherwise he would have to be viewed as subject
only to the natural law of his needs. Although the realm of
nature as well as that of ends would be thought of as united
under a sovereign so that the latter would no longer remain a
mere idea but would receive true reality, the realm of ends
would undoubtedly gain a strong urge in its favor, but its intrinsic worth would not be augmented. Regardless of this,
even the one and only absolute legislator would still have
to be conceived as judging the worth of rational beings only

by the disinterested conduct which they prescribe to themselves merely from the idea [of dignity]. The essence of things is not changed by their external relations, and without reference to these relations a man must be judged only by what constitutes his absolute worth; and this is true whoever his judge is, even if it be the Supreme Being. Morality is thus the relation of actions to the autonomy of the will, i.e., to possible universal lawgiving by maxims of the will. The action which can be compatible with the autonomy of the will is permitted; that which does not agree with it is prohibited. The will whose maxims necessarily are in harmony with the laws of autonomy is a holy will or an absolutely good will. The dependence of a will not absolutely good on the principle of autonomy (moral constraint) is *obligation*. Hence obligation cannot be applied to a holy will. The objective necessity of an action from obligation is called *duty*.

From what has just been said, it can easily be explained how it happens that, although in the concept of duty we think of subjection to law, we do nevertheless ascribe a certain sublimity and dignity to the person who fulfills all his duties. [440] For though there is no sublimity in him in so far as he is subject to the moral law, yet he is sublime in so far as he is legislative with reference to the law and subject to it only for this reason. We have also shown above how neither fear of nor inclination to the law is the incentive which can give a moral worth to action; only respect for it can do so. Our own will, so far as it would act only under the condition of a universal legislation rendered possible by its maxims—this will, ideally possible for us, is the proper object of respect, and the dignity of humanity consists just in its capacity of giving universal laws, although with the condition that it is itself subject to this same legislation.

The autonomy of the will as the supreme principle of morality

Autonomy of the will is that property of it by which it is a law to itself independently of any property of objects of volition. Hence the principle of autonomy is: Never choose except in such a way that the maxims of the choice are comprehended in the same volition as a universal law. That this practical rule is an imperative, that is, that the will of every rational being is necessarily bound to it as a condition, cannot be proved by a mere analysis of the concepts occurring in it, because it is a synthetical proposition. To prove it, we would have to go beyond the knowledge of objects to a critical examination of the subject, i.e., of the pure practical reason, for this synthetical proposition which commands apodictically must be susceptible of being known completely a priori. This matter, however, does not belong in the present section. But that the principle of autonomy, which is now in question, is the sole principle of morals can be readily shown by mere analysis of concepts of morality; for by this analysis we find that its principle must be a categorical imperative and that the imperative commands neither more nor less than this very autonomy.

The heteronomy of the will as the source of all spurious principles of morality

If the will seeks the law which is to determine it anywhere [441] else than in the fitness of its maxims to its own universal legislation, and if it thus goes outside itself and seeks this law in the property of any of its objects, heteronomy always results. For then the will does not give itself the law, but the object through its relation to the will gives the law to it. This relation, whether it rests on inclination or on conceptions of reason, only admits of hypothetical imperatives: I should do something for the reason that I will something else. The moral, and therewith categorical, imperative, on the other hand, says I should act this or that way even though I will nothing else. For example, the former says I should not lie if I wish to keep my reputation. The latter says I should not lie even though it would not cause me the least injury. The latter, therefore, must disregard every object to such an extent that it has absolutely no influence on the will, so that practical reason (will) may not merely minister to an interest not its own but rather may show its commanding authority as the supreme legislation. Thus, for instance, I should seek to further the happiness of others, not as though its realization was any concern of mine (whether because of direct inclination or of some satisfaction related to it indirectly through reason); I should do so merely because the maxim which excludes it from my duty cannot be comprehended as a universal law in one and the same volition.

Classification of all possible principles of morality following from the assumed principle of heteronomy

Here as everywhere in the pure use of reason, so long as a critical examination of it is lacking, human reason at first tries all possible wrong ways before it succeeds in finding the one true way.

All principles which can be taken in this point of view are either empirical or rational. The former, drawn from the principle of happiness, are based on physical or moral [442] feeling; the latter, drawn from the principle of perfection, are based either on the rational concept of perfection as a possible result or on the concept of an independent perfection (the will of God) as the determining cause of our will.

Empirical principles are not at all suited to serve as the basis of moral laws. For if the basis of the universality by which they should be valid for all rational beings without distinction (the unconditional practical necessity which is thereby imposed upon them) is derived from a particular tendency of human nature or the accidental circumstance in which it is found, that universality is lost. But the principle of one's own happiness is the most objectionable of all. This is not merely because it is false and because experience contradicts the supposition that well-being is always proportional to good conduct, nor yet because this principle contributes nothing to the establishment of morality, inasmuch as it is a very different thing to make a man happy from making him good, and to make him prudent and farsighted for his own advantage is far from making him virtuous. Rather, it is because this principle supports morality with incentives which undermine it and destroy all its sublimity, for it puts the motives to virtue and those to vice in the same class, teaching us only to make a better calculation while obliterating the specific difference between them. On the other hand, there is the alleged special sense,[18] the moral feeling. The appeal to it is superficial, since those who cannot think expect help from feeling, even with respect to that which concerns universal laws; they do so even though feelings naturally differ so infinitely in degree that they are incapable of furnishing a uniform standard of the good and bad, and also in spite of the fact that one cannot

[18] I count the principle of moral feeling under that of happiness, because every empirical interest promises to contribute to our well-being by the agreeableness that a thing affords, either directly and without a view to future advantage or with a view to it. We must likewise, with Hutcheson, count the principle of sympathy with the happiness of others under the moral sense which he assumed.

validly judge for others by means of his own feeling. Nevertheless, the moral feeling is nearer to morality and its dignity, inasmuch as it pays virtue the honor of ascribing the satisfaction and esteem for her directly to morality, and does not, as it were, say to her face that it is not her beauty but only [443] our advantage which attaches us to her.

Among the rational principles of morality, there is the ontological concept of perfection. It is empty, indefinite, and consequently useless for finding in the immeasurable field of possible reality the greatest possible sum which is suitable to us; and, in specifically distinguishing the reality which is here in question from all other reality, it inevitably tends to move in a circle and cannot avoid tacitly presupposing the morality which it ought to explain. Nevertheless, it is better than the theological concept, which derives morality from a most perfect divine will. It is better not merely because we cannot intuit its perfection, having rather to derive it only from our own concepts of which morality itself is foremost, but also because if we do not so derive it (and to do so would involve a most flagrant circle in explanation), the only remaining concept of the divine will is made up of the attributes of desire for glory and dominion combined with the awful conceptions of might and vengeance, and any system of ethics based on them would be directly opposed to morality.

But if I had to choose between the concept of the moral sense and that of perfection in general (neither of which at any rate weakens morality, although they are not capable of serving as its foundations), I would decide for the latter, because it preserves the indefinite idea (of a will good in itself) free from corruption until it can be more narrowly defined. It at least withdraws the decision of the question from sensibility and brings it to the court of pure reason, although it does not even here decide the question.

For the rest, I think that I may be excused from a lengthy

refutation of all these doctrines. It is so easy, and presumably so well understood even by those whose office requires them to decide for one of these theories (since the hearers would not tolerate suspension of judgment), that such a refutation would be only superfluous work. What interests us more, however, is to know that all these principles set up nothing other than the heteronomy of the will as the first ground of morality and thus necessarily miss their aim.

In every case in which an object of the will must be [444] assumed as prescribing the rule which is to determine the will, the rule is nothing else but heteronomy. The imperative in this case is conditional, stating that if or because one wills this object, one should act thus or so. Therefore the imperative can never command morally, that is, categorically. The object may determine the will by means of inclination, as in the principle of one's own happiness, or by means of reason directed to objects of our possible volition in general, as in the principle of perfection; but the will in these cases never determines itself directly by the conception of the action itself but only by the incentive which the foreseen result of the action incites in the will—that is, "I ought to do something because I will something else." And here still another law must be assumed in my person as the basis of this imperative; it would be a law by which I would necessarily will that other thing; but this law would again require an imperative to restrict this maxim. Since the conception of an object commensurate to our power incites in the will an impulse according to the natural characteristic of our person, this impulse belongs to the nature of the subject (either to the sensibility, i.e., inclination and taste, or to understanding and reason, which faculties, according to the particular constitution of their nature, take pleasure in exercising themselves on an object). It follows that it would be really nature that would give the law. As a law of nature, known and proved by experience, it would be contingent and therefore unfit to be an apodictical practical rule such as the moral rule must be. Such a law always represents heteronomy of the will; the will does not give itself the law, but an external impulse gives it to the will according to the nature of the subject which is adapted to receive it.

The absolutely good will, the principle of which must be a categorical imperative, is thus undetermined with reference to any objects. It contains only the form of volition in general, and this form is autonomy. That is, the capability of the maxims of every good will to make themselves universal laws is itself the sole law which the will of every rational being imposes on itself, and it does not need to support this on any incentive or interest.

How such a synthetical practical a priori proposition is possible and why it is necessary is a problem whose solution does not lie within the boundaries of the metaphysics of morals. Moreover, we have not here affirmed its truth, and [445] even less professed to command a proof of it. We showed only through the development of the universally received concept of morals that autonomy of the will is unavoidably connected with it, or rather that it is its foundation. Whoever, therefore, holds morality to be something real and not a chimerical idea without truth must also concede its principle which has been adduced here. Consequently, this section was merely analytical, like the first. To prove that morality is not a mere phantom of the mind—and if the categorical imperative, and with it the autonomy of the will, is true and absolutely necessary as an a priori principle, it follows that it is no phantom—requires that a synthetical use of pure practical reason is possible. But we must not venture on this use without first making a critical examination of this faculty of reason. In the last section we shall give the principal features of such an examination that will be sufficient for our purpose.

Third section / Transition from

the metaphysics of morals

to the critical examination of

pure practical reason

*The concept of freedom is the key to the explanation
of the autonomy of the will*

As will is a kind of causality of living beings so far as [446]
they are rational, freedom would be that property of this causality by which it can be effective independently of foreign
causes determining it, just as natural necessity is the property
of the causality of all irrational beings by which they are determined in their activity by the influence of foreign causes.

The preceding definition of freedom is negative and therefore affords no insight into its essence. But a positive concept
of freedom flows from it which is so much the richer and more
fruitful. Since the concept of a causality entails that of laws
according to which something, i.e., the effect, must be established through something else which we call cause, it follows

that freedom is by no means lawless even though it is not a property of the will according to laws of nature. Rather, it must be a causality according to immutable laws, but of a peculiar kind. Otherwise a free will would be an absurdity. Natural necessity is, as we have seen, a heteronomy of efficient causes, for every effect is possible only according to the law that something else determines the efficient cause to its causality. What else, then, can the freedom of the will be but [447] autonomy, i.e., the property of the will to be a law to itself? The proposition that the will is a law to itself in all its actions, however, only expresses the principle that we should act according to no other maxim than that which can also have itself as a universal law for its object. And this is just the formula of the categorical imperative and the principle of morality. Therefore a free will and a will under moral laws are identical.

Thus if freedom of the will is presupposed, morality together with its principle follows from it by the mere analysis of its concept. But the principle is nevertheless a synthetical proposition: an absolutely good will is one whose maxim can always include itself as a universal law. It is synthetical because by analysis of the concept of an absolutely good will that property of the maxim cannot be found. Such synthetical propositions, however, are possible only by the fact that both cognitions are connected through their union with a third in which both of them are to be found. The positive concept of freedom furnishes this third cognition, which cannot be, as in the case of physical causes, the nature of the sensuous world, in the concept of which we find conjoined the concepts of something as cause in relation to something else as effect. We cannot yet show directly what this third cognition is to which freedom directs us and of which we have an a priori idea, nor can we explain the deduction of the concept of freedom from pure practical reason and therewith the possibility of a categorical imperative. For this some further preparation is needed.

Freedom must be presupposed as the property of the will of all rational beings

It is not enough to ascribe freedom to our will, on any grounds whatever, if we do not also have sufficient grounds for attributing it to all rational beings. For since morality serves as a law for us only as rational beings, morality must hold valid for all rational beings, and since it must be derived exclusively from the property of freedom, freedom as the property of the will of all rational beings must be demonstrated. And it does not suffice to prove it from certain alleged experiences of human nature (which is indeed impossible, as it can be proved [448] only a priori), but we must prove it as belonging generally to the activity of rational beings endowed with a will. Now I say that every being which cannot act otherwise than under the idea of freedom is thereby really free in a practical respect. That is to say, all laws which are inseparably bound up with freedom hold for it just as if its will were proved free in itself by theoretical philosophy.[1] Now I affirm that we must necessarily grant that every rational being who has a will also has the idea of freedom and that it acts only under this idea. For in such a being we think of a reason which is practical, i.e., a reason which has causality with respect to its objects. Now, we cannot conceive of a reason which consciously responds to a bidding from the outside with respect to its judgments, for

[1] I follow this method, assuming that it is sufficient for our purpose that rational beings take merely the idea of [*in der Idee*] freedom as basic to their actions, in order to avoid having also to prove freedom in its theoretical aspect. For if the latter is left unproved, the laws which would obligate a being who was really free would hold for a being who cannot act except under the idea of his own freedom. Thus we can escape here from the onus which presses on the theory.

then the subject would attribute the determination of its power of judgment not to reason but to an impulse. Reason must regard itself as the author of its principles, independently of foreign influences; consequently, as practical reason or as the will of a rational being, it must regard itself as free. That is to say, the will of a rational being can be a will of its own only under the idea of freedom, and therefore in a practical point of view such a will must be ascribed to all rational beings.

Of the interest attaching to the ideas of morality

We have finally reduced the definite concept of morality to the idea of freedom, but we could not prove freedom to be real in ourselves and in human nature. We saw only that [449] we must presuppose it if we would think of a being as rational and conscious of his causality with respect to actions, that is, as endowed with a will; and so we find that on the very same grounds we must ascribe to each being endowed with reason and will the property of determining himself to action under the idea of freedom.

From presupposing this idea [of freedom] there followed also consciousness of a law of action: that the subjective principles of actions, i.e., maxims, in every instance must be so chosen that they can hold also as objective, i.e., universal, principles, and thus can serve as principles for the universal laws we give. But why should I subject myself as a rational being, and thereby all other beings endowed with reason, to this law? I will admit that no interest impels me to do so, for that would then give no categorical imperative. But I must nevertheless take an interest in it and see how it comes about, for this "ought" is properly a "would" that is valid for every rational being provided reason is practical for him without hindrance [i.e., exclusively determines his action]. For beings who like ourselves are affected by the senses as incentives different from reason and who do not always do that which reason for itself alone would have done, that necessity of action is expressed only as an "ought." The subjective necessity is thus distinguished from the objective.

It therefore seems that the moral law, i.e., the principle of the autonomy of the will, is, properly speaking, only presupposed in the idea of freedom, as if we could not prove its reality and objective necessity by itself. Even if that were so, we would still have gained something because we would at least have defined the genuine principle more accurately than had been done before. But with regard to its validity and to the practical necessity of subjection to it, we would not have advanced a single step, for we could give no satisfactory answer to anyone who asked us why the universal validity of our maxims as of a law had to be the restricting condition of our action. We could not tell on what is based the worth we ascribe to actions of this kind—a worth so great that there can be no higher interest, nor could we tell how it happens that man believes it is only through this that he feels his own personal worth, in contrast to which the worth of a [450] pleasant or unpleasant condition is to be regarded as nothing.

We do find sometimes that we can take an interest in a personal quality which involves no [personal] interest in any [external] condition, provided only that [possession of] this quality makes us capable of participating in the [desired] condition in case reason were to effect the allotment of it. That is, mere worthiness to be happy even without the motive of participating in it can interest us of itself. But this judgment is in fact only the effect of the already assumed importance of moral laws (if by the idea of freedom we detach ourselves from every empirical interest). But that we ought to detach ourselves, i.e., regard ourselves as free in acting and yet as subject to certain laws, in order to find a worth merely in our person which would compensate for the loss of everything which makes our situation desirable—how this is possible and hence on what grounds the moral law obligates us we still cannot see in this way.

We must openly confess that there is a kind of circle here from which it seems that there is no escape. We assume that we are free in the order of efficient causes so that we can conceive of ourselves as subject to moral laws in the order of ends. And then we think of ourselves as subject to these laws because we have ascribed freedom of the will to ourselves. This is circular because freedom and self-legislation of the will are both autonomy and thus are reciprocal concepts, and for that reason one of them cannot be used to explain the other and to furnish a ground for it. At most they can be used for the logical purpose of bringing apparently different conceptions of the same object under a single concept (as we reduce different fractions of the same value to the lowest common terms).

One recourse, however, remains open to us, namely, to inquire whether we do not assume a different standpoint when we think of ourselves as causes a priori efficient through freedom from that which we occupy when we conceive of ourselves in the light of our actions as effects which we see before our eyes.

The following remark requires no subtle reflection, and we may suppose that even the commonest understanding can make it, though it does so, after its fashion, by an obscure discernment of judgment which it calls feeling: all conceptions, [451] like those of the senses, which come to us without our choice enable us to know the objects only as they affect us, while what they are in themselves remains unknown to us;

therefore, as regards this kind of conception, even with the closest attention and clearness which understanding may ever bring to them we can attain only to knowledge of appearances and never to knowledge of things in themselves. As soon as this distinction is made (perhaps merely because of a difference noticed between conceptions which are given to us from somewhere else and to which we are passive and those which we produce only from ourselves and in which we show our own activity), it follows of itself that we must admit and assume behind the appearances something else which is not appearance, namely, things in themselves; we do so although we must admit that we cannot approach them more closely and can never know what they are in themselves, since they can never be known by us except as they affect us. This must furnish a distinction, though a crude one, between a world of sense and a world of understanding. The former, by differences in the sensuous faculties, can be very different among various observers, while the latter, which is its foundation, remains always the same. A man may not presume to know even himself as he really is by knowing himself through inner sensation. For since he does not, as it were, produce himself or derive his concept of himself a priori but only empirically, it is natural that he obtains his knowledge of himself through inner sense and consequently only through the appearance of his nature and the way in which his consciousness is affected. But beyond the characteristic of his own subject which is compounded of these mere appearances, he necessarily assumes something else as its basis, namely, his ego as it is in itself. Thus in respect to mere perception and receptivity to sensations he must count himself as belonging to the world of sense; but in respect to that which may be pure activity in himself (i.e., in respect to that which reaches consciousness directly and not by affecting the senses) he must reckon himself as belonging to the intellectual world. But he has no further knowledge of that world.

To such a conclusion, the thinking man must come with respect to all things which may present themselves to [452] him. Presumably it is to be met with in the commonest understanding which, as is well known, is very much inclined to expect behind the objects of the senses something else invisible and acting of itself. But such an understanding soon spoils it by trying to make the invisible again sensuous, i.e., to make it an object of intuition. Thus common understanding becomes not in the least wiser.

Now man really finds in himself a faculty by which he distinguishes himself from all other things, even from himself so far as he is affected by objects. This faculty is reason. As a pure spontaneous activity it is elevated even above understanding. For though the latter is also a spontaneous activity and does not, like sense, merely contain conceptions which arise only when one is affected by things, being passive, it nevertheless cannot produce by its activity any other concepts than those which serve to bring the sensuous conceptions under rules, and thereby to unite them in one consciousness. Without this use of sensibility it would not think at all, while, on the other hand, reason shows such a pure spontaneity in the case of ideas that it[2] far transcends everything that sensibility can give to consciousness and shows its chief occupation in distinguishing the world of sense from the world of understanding, thereby prescribing limits to the understanding itself.

For this reason a rational being must regard himself as intelligence (and not from the side of his lower powers), as be-

---

[2] [Kant wrote *er . . . ihm*, which gives no tenable meaning. Adickes suggested *sie . . . ihr* = reason . . . to reason. But as sensibility does not give material to reason, at least directly, Vorländer and the Cassirer ed. read *sie . . . ihm*, and they are followed here.]

longing to the world of understanding and not to that of the senses. Thus he has two standpoints from which he can consider himself and recognize the laws of the employment of his powers and consequently of all his actions: first, as belonging to the world of sense under laws of nature (heteronomy), and, second, as belonging to the intelligible world under laws which, independent of nature, are not empirical but founded only on reason.

As a rational being and thus as belonging to the intelligible world, man cannot think of the causality of his own will except under the idea of freedom, for independence from the determining causes of the world of sense (an independence which reason must always ascribe to itself) is freedom. The concept of autonomy is inseparably connected with the idea of freedom, and with the former there is inseparably bound the universal principle of morality, which ideally is the ground of all actions of rational beings, just as natural law is the [453] ground of all appearances.

Now we have removed the suspicion which we raised that there might be a hidden circle in our reasoning from freedom to autonomy and from the latter to the moral law. This suspicion was that we laid down the idea of freedom for the sake of the moral law in order later to derive the latter from freedom, and that we were thus unable to give any ground for the law, presenting it only as a *petitio principii* that well-disposed minds would gladly allow us but which we could never advance as a demonstrable proposition. But we now see that, if we think of ourselves as free, we transport ourselves into the intelligible world as members of it and know the autonomy of the will together with its consequence, morality; while, if we think of ourselves as obligated, we consider ourselves as belonging both to the world of sense and at the same time to the intelligible world.

How is a categorical imperative possible?

The rational being counts himself, qua intelligence, as belonging to the intelligible world, and only as an efficient cause belonging to it does he call his causality a will. On the other side, however, he is conscious of himself as a part of the world of sense in which his actions are found as mere appearances of that causality. But we do discern how they are possible on the basis of that causality which we do not know; rather, those actions must be regarded as determined by other appearances, namely, desires and inclinations, belonging to the world of sense. As a mere member of the intelligible world, all my actions would completely accord with the principle of the autonomy of the pure will, and as a part only of the world of sense would they have to be assumed to conform wholly to the natural law of desires and inclinations and thus to the heteronomy of nature. (The former actions would rest on the supreme principle of morality, and the latter on that of happiness.) But since the intelligible world contains the ground of the world of sense and hence of its laws, the intelligible world is (and must be conceived as) directly legislative for my will, which belongs wholly to the intelligible world. Therefore I recognize myself qua intelligence as subject to the law of the world of understanding and to the autonomy [454] of the will. That is, I recognize myself as subject to the law of reason which contains in the idea of freedom the law of the intelligible world, while at the same time I must acknowledge that I am a being which belongs to the world of sense. Therefore I must regard the laws of the intelligible world as imperatives for me, and actions in accord with this principle as duties.

Thus categorical imperatives are possible because the idea

of freedom makes me a member of an intelligible world. Consequently, if I were a member of only that world, all my actions *would* always be in accordance with the autonomy of the will. But since I intuit myself at the same time as a member of the world of sense, my actions *ought* to conform to it, and this categorical ought presents a synthetic a priori proposition, since besides my will affected by my sensuous desires there is added the idea of exactly the same will as pure, practical of itself, and belonging to the intelligible world, which according to reason contains the supreme condition of the former [sensuously affected] will. It is similar to the manner in which concepts of the understanding, which of themselves mean nothing but lawful form in general, are added to the intuitions of the sensuous world, thus rendering possible a priori synthetic propositions on which all knowledge of a system of nature rests.

The practical use of common human reason confirms the correctness of this deduction. When we present examples of honesty of purpose, of steadfastness in following good maxims, and of sympathy and general benevolence even with great sacrifice of advantages and comfort, there is no man, not even the most malicious villain (provided he is otherwise accustomed to using his reason), who does not wish that he also might have these qualities. But because of his inclinations and impulses he cannot bring this about, yet at the same time he wishes to be free from such inclinations which are burdensome even to himself. He thus proves that, with a will free from all impulses of sensibility, he in thought transfers himself into an order of things altogether different from that of his desires in the field of sensibility. He cannot expect to obtain by that wish any gratification of desires or any condition which would satisfy his real or even imagined inclinations, for the idea itself, which elicits this wish from him, would lose its pre-eminence if he had any such expectation. He can expect only a greater inner worth of his person. He imagines himself to be this better person when he transfers [455] himself to the standpoint of a member of the intelligible world to which he is involuntarily impelled by the idea of freedom, i.e., independence from the determining causes of the world of sense; and from this standpoint he is conscious of a good will, which on his own confession constitutes the law for his bad will as a member of the world of sense. He acknowledges the authority of this law even while transgressing it. The moral ought is therefore his own volition as a member of the intelligible world, and it is conceived by him as an ought only in so far as he regards himself at the same time as a member of the world of sense.

On the extreme limit of all practical philosophy

In respect to their will, all men think of themselves as free. Hence arise all judgments of actions as being such as ought to have been done, although they were not done. But this freedom is not an empirical concept and cannot be such, for it still remains even though experience shows the contrary of the demands which are necessarily conceived as consequences of the supposition of freedom. On the other hand, it is equally necessary that everything which happens should be inexorably determined by natural laws, and this natural necessity is likewise no empirical concept, because it implies the concept of necessity and thus of a priori knowledge. But this concept of a system of nature is confirmed by experience, and it is inevitably presupposed if experience, which is knowledge of the objects of the senses interconnected by universal laws, is to be possible. Therefore freedom is only an idea of reason whose objective reality in itself is doubtful, while nature is a concept of the understanding which shows and necessarily must show its reality by examples in experience.

There now arises a dialectic of reason, since the freedom ascribed to the will seems to stand in contradiction to natural necessity. At this parting of the ways reason in its speculative purpose finds the way of natural necessity more well-beaten and usable than that of freedom; but in its practical purpose the footpath of freedom is the only one on which it is possible to make use of reason in our conduct. Hence it is as [456] impossible for the subtlest philosophy as for the commonest reasoning to argue freedom away. Philosophy must therefore assume that no true contradiction will be found between freedom and natural necessity in the same human actions, for it cannot give up the concept of nature any more than that of freedom.

Hence even if we should never be able to conceive how freedom is possible, at least this apparent contradiction must be convincingly eradicated. For if even the thought of freedom contradicts itself or nature, which is equally necessary, it would have to be surrendered in competition with natural necessity.

But it would be impossible to escape this contradiction if the subject, who seems to himself free, thought of himself in the same sense or in the same relationship when he calls himself free as when he assumes that in the same action he is subject to natural law. Therefore it is an inescapable task of speculative philosophy to show at least that its illusion about the contradiction rests in the fact that we [do not]³ think of man in a different sense and relationship when we call him free from that in which we consider him as a part of nature and subject to its laws. It must show not only that they can

³ [Following the suggestion of R. F. A. Hoernlé, *Mind*, XLV (N. S. 1936), 127–128.]

very well coexist but also that they must be thought of as necessarily united in one and the same subject; for otherwise no ground could be given why we should burden reason with an idea which, though it may without contradiction be united with another that is sufficiently established, nevertheless involves us in a perplexity which sorely embarrasses reason in its speculative use. This duty is imposed only on speculative philosophy, so that it may clear the way for practical philosophy. Thus the philosopher has no choice as to whether he will remove the apparent contradiction or leave it untouched, for in the latter case the theory of it would be *bonum vacans*, into the possession of which the fatalist can rightly enter and drive all morality from its alleged property as occupying it without title.

Yet we cannot say here that we have reached the beginnings of practical philosophy. For the settlement of the controversy does not belong to practical philosophy, as the latter demands from speculative reason only that it put an end to the discord in which it entangles itself in theoretical questions, so that practical reason may have rest and security from [457] outer attacks which could dispute with it the ground on which it desires to erect its edifice.

The title to freedom of the will claimed by common reason is based on the consciousness and the conceded presupposition of the independence of reason from merely subjectively determining causes which together constitute what belongs only to sensation, being comprehended under the general name of sensibility. Man, who in this way regards himself as intelligence, puts himself in a different order of things and in a relationship to determining grounds of an altogether different kind when he thinks of himself as intelligence with a will and thus as endowed with causality, compared with that other order of things and that other set of determining grounds which become relevant when he perceives himself as a phenomenon in the world of sense (as he really also is) and submits his causality to external determination according to natural laws. Now he soon realizes that both can subsist together—indeed, that they must. For there is not the least contradiction between a thing in appearance (as belonging to the world of sense) being subject to certain laws of which it is independent as a thing or a being in itself. That it must think of itself in this twofold manner rests, with regard to the first, on the consciousness of itself as an object affected through the senses, and, with regard to what is required by the second, on the consciousness of itself as intelligence, i.e., as independent of sensuous impressions in the use of reason and thus as belonging to the intelligible world.

This is why man claims to possess a will which does not let him become accountable for what belongs merely to his desires and inclinations, but thinks of actions which can be performed only by disregarding all desires and sensuous attractions, as possible and indeed necessary for him. The causality of these actions lies in him as an intelligence and in effects and actions in accordance with principles of an intelligible world, of which he knows only that reason alone and indeed pure reason independent of sensibility gives the law in it. Moreover, since it is only as intelligence that he is his proper self (being as man only appearance of himself), he knows that those laws apply to him directly and categorically, so that that to which inclinations and impulses and hence the entire nature of the world of sense incite him cannot in the least impair the laws of his volition as an intelligence. He does not even hold himself [458] responsible for these inclinations and impulses or attribute them to his proper self, i.e., his will, though he does ascribe to his will the indulgence which he may grant to them when he permits them an influence on his maxims to the detriment of the rational laws of his will.

When practical reason thinks itself into an intelligible world, it does in no way transcend its limits. It would do so, however, if it tried to intuit or feel itself into it. The intelligible world is only a negative thought with respect to the world of sense, which does not give reason any laws for determining the will. It is positive only in the single point that freedom as negative determination is at the same time connected with a positive faculty and even a causality of reason. This causality we call a will to act so that the principle of actions will accord with the essential characteristic of a rational cause, i.e., with the condition of the universal validity of a maxim as a law. But if it were to borrow an object of the will, i.e., a motive, from the intelligible world, it would overstep its boundaries and pretend to be acquainted with something of which it knows nothing. The concept of a world of understanding is therefore only a standpoint which reason sees itself forced to take outside of appearances, in order to think of itself as practical. If the influences of sensibility were determining for man, this would not be possible; but it is necessary unless he is to be denied the consciousness of himself as an intelligence, and thus as a rational and rationally active cause, i.e., a cause acting in freedom. This thought certainly implies the idea of an order and legislation different from that of natural mechanism which applies to the world of sense; and it makes necessary the concept of an intelligible world, the whole of rational beings as things in themselves. But it does not give us the least occasion to think of it otherwise than according to its formal condition only, i.e., the universality of the maxim of the will as law and thus the autonomy of the will, which alone is consistent with freedom. All laws, on the other hand, which are directed to an object make for heteronomy, which belongs only to natural laws and which can apply only to the world of sense.

But reason would overstep all its bounds if it undertook to explain how pure reason can be practical, which is the same problem as explaining how freedom is possible. [459]

For we can explain nothing but what we can reduce to laws whose object can be given in some possible experience. But freedom is a mere idea, the objective reality of which can in no way be shown according to natural laws or in any possible experience. Since no example in accordance with any analogy can support it, it can never be comprehended or even imagined. It holds only as the necessary presupposition of reason in a being that believes itself conscious of a will, i.e., of a faculty different from the mere faculty of desire, or a faculty of determining itself to act as intelligence and thus according to laws of reason independently of natural instincts. But where determination according to natural laws comes to an end, there too all explanation ceases and nothing remains but defense, i.e., refutation of the objections of those who pretend to have seen more deeply into the essence of things and therefore boldly declare freedom to be impossible. We can only show them that the supposed contradiction they have discovered lies nowhere else than in their necessarily regarding man as appearance in order to make natural law valid with respect to human actions. And now when we require them to think of him qua intelligence as a thing in itself, they still persist in considering him as appearance. Obviously, then, the separation of his causality (his will) from all natural laws of the world of sense in one and the same object is a contradiction, but this disappears when they reconsider and confess, as is reasonable, that behind the appearances things in themselves must stand as their hidden ground and that we cannot expect the laws of the activity of these grounds to be the same as those under which their appearances stand.

The subjective impossibility of explaining the freedom of the will is the same as the impossibility of discovering and explaining an interest[4] which man can take in moral laws. [460] Nevertheless, he does actually take an interest in them, and the foundation in us of this interest we call the moral feeling. This moral feeling has been erroneously construed by some as the standard for our moral judgment, whereas it must rather be regarded as the subjective effect which the law has upon the will to which reason alone gives objective grounds.

In order to will that which reason alone prescribes to the sensuously affected rational being as that which he ought to will, certainly there is required a power of reason to instill a feeling of pleasure or satisfaction in the fulfillment of duty, and hence there must be a causality of reason to determine the sensibility in accordance with its own principles. But it is wholly impossible to discern, i.e., to make a priori conceivable, how a mere thought containing nothing sensuous is to produce a sensation of pleasure or displeasure. For that is a particular kind of causality of which, as of all causality, we can-

---

[4] Interest is that by which reason becomes practical, i.e., a cause determining the will. We therefore say only of a rational being that he takes an interest in something; irrational creatures feel only sensuous impulses. A direct interest in the action is taken by reason only if the universal validity of its maxim is a sufficient determining ground of the will. Only such an interest is pure. But if reason can determine the will only by means of another object of desire or under the presupposition of a particular feeling of the subject, reason takes merely an indirect interest in the action, and since reason by itself alone without experience can discover neither objects of the will nor a particular feeling which lies at its root, that indirect interest would be only empirical and not a pure interest of reason. The logical interest of reason in advancing its insights is never direct but rather presupposes purposes for which they are to be used.

not determine anything a priori but must consult experience only. But since experience can exemplify the relation of cause to effect only as subsisting between two objects of experience, while here pure reason by mere Ideas (which furnish no object for experience) is to be the cause of an effect which does lie in experience, an explanation of how and why the universality of the maxim as law (and hence morality) interests us is completely impossible for us men. Only this much is certain: that it is valid for us not because it interests us (for that is heteronomy and dependence of practical reason on sensibility, i.e., on a basic feeling, and thus it could never be morally [461] legislative), but that it interests us because it is valid for us as men, inasmuch as it has arisen from our will as intelligence and hence from our proper self; but what belongs to mere appearance is necessarily subordinated by reason to the nature of the thing in itself.

Thus the question, "How is a categorical imperative possible?" can be answered to this extent: We can cite the only presupposition under which it is alone possible. This is the Idea of freedom, and we can discern the necessity of this presupposition which is sufficient to the practical use of reason, i.e., to the conviction of the validity of this imperative and hence also of the moral law. But how this presupposition itself is possible can never be discerned by any human reason. However, on the presupposition of freedom of the will of an intelligence, its autonomy as the formal condition under which alone it can be determined is a necessary consequence. To presuppose the freedom of the will is not only quite possible, as speculative philosophy itself can prove, for it does not involve itself in a contradiction with the principle of natural necessity in the interconnection of appearances in the world of sense. But it is also unconditionally necessary that a rational being conscious of his causality through reason and thus conscious of a will different from desires should practically presuppose it, i.e., presuppose it in the idea as the fundamental condition of all his voluntary actions. Yet how pure reason, without any other incentives, wherever they may be derived, can by itself be practical, i.e., how the mere principle of the universal validity of all its maxims as laws (which would certainly be the form of a pure practical reason), without any material (object) of the will in which we might in advance take some interest, can itself furnish an incentive and produce an interest which would be called purely moral; or, in other words, how pure reason can be practical—to explain this, all human reason is wholly incompetent, and all the pains and work of seeking an explanation of it are wasted.

It is just the same as if I sought to find out how freedom itself as causality of a will is possible; for, in so doing, I would leave the philosophical basis of explanation behind, and [462] I have no other. Certainly I could revel in the intelligible world, the world of intelligences, which still remains to me; but although I have a well-founded idea of it, still I do not have the least knowledge of it, nor can I ever attain to it by all the exertions of my natural capacity of reason. This intelligible world signifies only a something which remains when I have excluded from the determining grounds of my will everything belonging to the world of sense in order to withhold the principle of motives from the field of sensibility. I do so by limiting it and showing that it does not contain absolutely everything in itself but that outside it there is still more; but this more I do not further know. After banishing all material, i.e., knowledge of objects, from pure reason which formulates this ideal, there remain to me only the form, the practical law of universal validity of maxims, and, in conformity with this, reason in relation to a pure intelligible world as a possible effective cause, i.e., as determining the will. An incentive must here be wholly absent unless this idea of an intelligible world itself be the incentive or that in which reason primarily takes an interest. But to make this conceivable is precisely the problem we cannot solve.

Here is, then, the supreme limit of all moral inquiry. To define it is very important, both in order that reason may not seek around, on the one hand, in the world of sense, in a way harmful to morals, for the supreme motive and for a comprehensible but empirical interest; and so that it will not, on the other hand, impotently flap its wings in the space (for it, an empty space) of transcendent concepts which we call the intelligible world, without being able to move from its starting point, or lose itself amid phantoms. Furthermore, the idea of a pure intelligible world as a whole of all intelligences to which we ourselves belong as rational beings (though on the other side we are at the same time members of the world of sense) is always a useful and permissible idea for the purpose of a rational faith. This is so even though all knowledge terminates at its boundary, for through the glorious ideal of a universal realm of ends-in-themselves (rational beings) a lively interest in the moral law can be awakened in us. To that realm we can belong as members only when we carefully [463] conduct ourselves according to maxims of freedom as if they were laws of nature.

Concluding remark

The speculative use of reason with respect to nature leads to the absolute necessity of some supreme cause of the world. The practical use of reason with respect to freedom leads also to an absolute necessity, but to the necessity only of laws of actions of a rational being as such. Now it is an essential principle of all use of reason to push its knowledge to a consciousness of its necessity, for otherwise it would not be rational knowledge. But it is also an equally essential restriction of this very same reason that it cannot discern the necessity of what is or what occurs or what ought to be done, unless a condition under which it is or occurs or ought to be done is presupposed. In this way, however, the satisfaction of reason is only further and further postponed by the constant inquiry after the condition. Therefore, reason restlessly seeks the unconditionally necessary and sees itself compelled to assume it, though it has no means by which to make it comprehensible and is happy enough if it can only discover the concept which is consistent with this presupposition. It is therefore no objection to our deduction of the supreme principle of morality, but a reproach which we must make to human reason generally, that it cannot render comprehensible the absolute necessity of an unconditional practical law (such as the categorical imperative must be). Reason cannot be blamed for being unwilling to explain it by a condition, i.e., by making some interest its basis, for the law would then cease to be moral, i.e., a supreme law of freedom. And so we do not indeed comprehend the practical unconditional necessity of the moral imperative; yet we do comprehend its incomprehensibility, which is all that can be fairly demanded of a philosophy which in its principles strives to reach the limit of human reason.

Critical

essays

Julius Ebbinghaus / Interpretation

and misinterpretation of the

categorical imperative

The concept connected by Kant with the phrase "categorical imperative" seems easy to explain. It means a law valid for the will of every rational being and therefore valid unconditionally. This is in no need of interpretation: it can hardly be misinterpreted. Kant has stated it in the clearest and most intelligible terms. Understanding becomes much more difficult if we are concerned, not merely with the verbal definition, but

Reprinted from THE PHILOSOPHICAL QUARTERLY, *Vol. IV, No. 15 (April 1954), pp. 97–108, by permission of the author and editors. This article was originally published, under the title* DEUTUNG UND MISSDEUTUNG DES KATEGORISCHEN IMPERATIVS, *in* STUDIUM GENERALE, *I Jahrgang (1948), Heft 7. This translation, by Professor H. J. Paton, was printed in* THE PHILOSOPHICAL QUARTERLY *by permission of Professor Ebbinghaus and the Springer-Verlag of Berlin, Goettingen, and Heidelberg, the publishers of* STUDIUM GENERALE.

with the content of the categorical command and with the inferences to be drawn from it. Even specialists have fallen into confusion about these questions and have, as it were, begun to see ghosts in quarters where reason prevails; but, quite apart from this, the doctrine of a categorical imperative inherent in the will of man himself appears at present to meet with most unexpected and most unwanted repercussions in the common opinion, not merely of Germany, but almost of the whole world. To lovers of humanity it may seem a lofty and worthy aim that doctrines elaborated by science and claiming to determine the conduct of every man should gradually spread wider and wider until at last every cottage is illuminated by the light this labour generates. But it also seems as if precisely this welcome process, which has gained greatly in intensity since the eighteenth century, has merely added one more to those evils of civilization by which mankind is afflicted. When we argue with experts in our own subject, we can pretty well manage at least to be correctly understood and not to be saddled with conclusions in direct contradiction to our own thought; but we are, so to speak, robbed of all protection when matters of controversy among the learned are thrust, through the efforts of more or less unfriendly publicists, upon the wide masses of the educated or half-educated, are there passed from hand to hand, and are finally hurled into a sea of surging passion. This happens most of all when we are concerned with the propositions of a science which—like philosophy—is still having to *fight* for its existence so that attacks upon any doctrinal structure attempted in its name will never fail to find authorities prepared to back them. No matter how ludicrous men may consider the claim of philosophy as a guide to life, they are always ready, when they have reduced their affairs to utter disorder, to listen to those who find its cause in some philosophy they dislike.

No one need be surprised if in the present miseries of the world voices are raised expressing all too clearly the view that the susceptibility to National Socialism displayed by wide ranges of the German people springs properly from that readiness for unconditioned obedience, that spirit of unconditioned sacrifice, which is undoubtedly demanded by Kant in his law of duty; or at least—not going quite so far—the view that Kant's law voices precisely that Prussian or German inclination for discipline and subjection, that readiness for harshness and rigour, that insensitiveness to all the gentler movements of the spirit, which celebrated their frightful triumphs in the years of Terror. "All that is worthy of respect in me is my capacity to obey—and the same must hold for you as it does for me." In these words Friedrich Nietzsche already gave utterance to an interpretation of Kant's ethics in which the above view is anticipated. The morality of the categorical imperative as the morality of the correct Prussian official, who regards his superiors as gods or demi-gods and disdains the pleasures of life as sour grapes—this is one of the travesties into which the greatest achievement in the field of ethics since Plato has been distorted by a sociological treatment that has lost its bearings.

I

If we turn its own methods upon this treatment itself, we discover behind it a tendency to interpret statements, not by the real necessities which led to them, but by some sort of assumed subjective motive. The law formulated by Kant in his categorical imperative is not one by which any principle whatever to which a man may find himself drawn under conditions of experience—such as obedience to potentates or abstention from the pleasures of life—can be imposed on him categorically. Kant's law is rather a way of expressing the conditions under which alone a principle can have the character of a categorical demand. The categorical imperative is thus conceived as the fundamental principle determining which possible principles can be objectively valid for the decisions of our will as such. When we say it is our duty to do something or to refrain from doing it, we manifestly have in mind such a categorical demand or such an objectively valid principle. Hence we can also say that on Kant's view the categorical imperative contains nothing but the concept of being under a possible moral obligation as such. If he was wrong in maintaining that such a command is binding upon our will, it is not to be inferred that duty must be determined by some other law; what it would mean is that there are no universally valid demands on human behaviour, so far as this depends on our will, and consequently that nothing whatever can be our duty and that we are entirely free to do whatever we may happen to want. We might indeed by acting in this way get entangled in all sorts of disagreeable consequences, or we might be astute enough to find means of escaping these disagreeable consequences; but what Kant maintains is this: The sum total of these means could never have the character of a system of precepts for the will such that men would be under an objective obligation to obey them; nor could a necessary harmony of these means be discovered (independently of a categorical imperative) such that it would be free from all possible conflict of the will with itself and with the will of others.

We can sum all this up in the proposition that the categorical imperative determines the concept of duty *solely as regards its form*. It states only what duty as such is and consequently what all duties have in common; but it contains nothing to show how the particular duties determined by it are materially different from one another. Yet we ought not to imagine that this purely formal character of the categorical im-

perative as the law of duty is identical with the property envisaged by those who describe as "formal" both the principle
of Kant's ethical theory and consequently this theory itself in
distinction from other systems of morality. Here we find the
first misinterpretation of the categorical imperative—the view
that this necessarily confines moral philosophy to stating what
the concept of duty is simply as regards its form and makes impossible the articulation of particular duties that are materially
different. Every doctrine of duties, if it is based on any principle at all, must begin by stating in what duty consists—that
is, by stating what is the concept of duty simply as regards its
form. If we say, for example, that duty consists in performing
the actions required to realise the happiness of the greatest
number, we have determined the concept of duty simply as
regards its form—that is, without specifying the content of the
actions that are thus required. If Kant's principle has a still
further special characteristic of formality, this is to be found
in the *way* he determines the concept of duty simply as regards
its form. This special characteristic may be described—negatively—as the assertion that if we are to discover the concept
of duty, we must abstract, not merely from all the matter of
duty, as is obvious, but also—as is not so obvious—from all
the matter of the will; that is, from all purposes or ends.

Naturally, if anyone intends to realise something that he
has made the end of his action, it is necessary that he should
adopt the means adequate to realise it. But such necessity is a
conditioned one (hypothetical, not categorical); and it contains
no immediate law for his will since he must already will something definite before he can become subject to this necessity.
"Yes"—it may be replied—"we must naturally begin with
some final end; this is already stated by Aristotle. And just as
naturally such an end must possess some kind of necessity for
the human will." "We are not to infer," says John Stuart Mill,

"that its acceptance or rejection must depend on blind impulse or arbitrary choice" (*Utilitarianism*, Chapter I). But if, with Aristotle and Mill, we take happiness as the final end on which we may hope to find all men agreed, can we then say that there is for man an unconditioned command to make his own happiness his end? Even if he may in fact always make this his end, no one can say that this inevitability to be found in experience is the necessity characterizing a *demand*, in virtue of which man has the duty of adopting this end. And is it not at least conceivable that it may be both possible and necessary for the will of man to subordinate the end of his own happiness to a higher condition of his actions?

Suppose one answers: "Yes, admittedly there must be an end necessary in and for itself—that is, necessary for the will of every rational being independently of all subjective conditions—an end which alone can supply the ground for an unconditioned demand that it be adopted." The question then arises: In what way is it possible for us to have such an end? If we assume that man by nature can have no ends conflicting with the end that is necessary in itself, then clearly he can be subject to no command at all about the decisions of his will: his will must always of itself have this highest good as its object. In that case there can be no question of duty. If we admit, on the other hand, that he can decide to act contrary to this end which is necessary in and for itself, there must be, even beyond this highest end, a motive which can move him to do what he does not already do of himself—namely, to make this end his own. He would then need to have, above this highest end, a still prior end by which he would be required to take as his end what was good in and for itself. But such a prior end contains a contradiction; for all possible ends must naturally be subordinated to the end which is by definition the highest. Hence along this line we could produce neither a categorical nor a hypothetical imperative for adopting the end on which the whole necessity of human action is supposed to be dependent. We should be left merely with a choice between a will that was infallibly good and a will that could not even be asked to be good at all.

It is purely analytic considerations like these that ought to be adduced if we want to understand the real motive which led Kant to what constitutes the strictly formal character of his ethics. This character is to be found in the fact that in place of some previously given end—that is, in place of some matter of the will—Kant asserts that the mere form of maxims (that is, of the subjective principles of our arbitrary choice), so far as this fits them for the making of universal law, is what determines duty as regards its form. After what has been said, there should be no need to explain further why in this statement the word "form" occurs twice. The form which fits maxims for the making of universal law—whatever may be their matter, that is, their end—is here identified with that demand by which alone an imperative can have the character of being categorical, or—in other words—by which duty is determined as regards its form. If in the language of abbreviation we call this imperative "formal," this does not mean that *it* has no content. It has precisely the content we have just adduced; and we cannot infer conversely that because the categorical imperative has in fact a content, therefore Kant must be in error when he maintains that only the form which fits maxims for the making of laws can supply a universally valid ground for determining our will. Yet this is precisely the inference which one of the more recent writers on ethics has in fact drawn.

Apart from objections of this kind, which rest merely on a play of words, the fact that Kant has calmly built up a whole system of commands and prohibitions on the basis of his moral law has been looked on with the utmost suspicion and indeed with open scorn. "When he begins," says John Stuart Mill again of Kant, "to deduce from this precept any of the actual duties of morality, he fails, almost grotesquely, to show that there would be any contradiction, any logical impossibility, in the adoption by all rational beings of the most outrageously immoral rules of conduct" (*op. cit.*). This charge has its history. It is already present in Hegel's assertion that when Kant deduces particular duties, he goes continually round in circles, since in order to show a contradiction between a maxim and the possibility of willing it as a universal law he has always to presuppose as necessary the very volition whose necessity it is his business to prove. By this method it would be open to us to put forward any kind of arbitrary conduct as a demand of duty. This seems to confirm one view of the history of moral evaluation. "It can almost be said," writes one recent moralist (E. Becher, *Die Grundfrage der Ethik* [Köln: M. Dumont-Schauberg'sche Buchhandlung, 1908], pp. 88 ff.), "that there is no atrocity and no crime which has not been enjoined at some time and some place by conscience and duty or which is not still enjoined today. Murder, scorching and laying waste, the slaughter of the defenceless, of women and children without regard to guilt or innocence, robbery and betrayal, debauchery and orgies count as in accord with duty or at least as not against conscience; and so too actions that appear to us as morally quite indifferent are enjoined by this strict command." Yet we cannot say in Kant's sense that the atrocities cited have been commanded "at some time and some place" by conscience and duty, or are still commanded, unless we have first shown that such conduct is contained in the demand of his moral law. Obviously in the opinion of the author the formalism of Kant's ethics consists in this—that his concept of duty can be applied to any arbitrary behaviour, so far as man believes himself constrained to it *by any will* beyond which, for some subjective reason, he recognises no higher.

It is only one step from this to the sensational reasoning we find in a recently resurrected book of Dewey's—*German Philosophy and Politics* (2nd edition [New York: G. P. Putnam's Sons], 1944), p. 87. "The gospel of a duty devoid of content (!) naturally lent itself to the consecration and idealisation of such specific duties as the existing national order might prescribe." Even if any one should be found who believes himself entitled by the formalization of Kant's moral law to declare the prescriptions of an existing national order to be prescriptions imposed upon the subjects of that order by the moral law itself, it is still barely comprehensible how Dewey could take such an interpretation of the "gospel of duty" as a proceeding to which this gospel "naturally lent itself." If, as Dewey imagines, the thought of duty in Kant is "devoid of content"—and so cannot contain any possibility of recognising any definite rule as either lawful or unlawful for human action—it is *quite impossible* to suppose that any definite prescription of the existing national order is "consecrated" by the moral law; for in that case we should have to be able to show either that this prescription itself or that the competence of the national will to lay down such a prescription arbitrarily was required by the moral law. But if, in the opinion of the pseudo-Kantian who fills up the moral law with national prescriptions, the national order has to be sovereign in *arbitrary* ordinances, how can this rank as a categorical imperative (a law of duty)? If national prescriptions are such as are subject to absolutely no law in their volition, we can at least say this much with certainty—that we can be subject to them only *in contradiction* with the moral law of Kant. Otherwise his moral law itself would have to be able to agree with subjection to an arbitrary will that in and for itself was lawless.

Yet this is precisely what Dewey in fact thinks. He goes so far as to say: "Idealism and personality separated from empirical analysis and experimental utilization of concrete social situations are worse than vague mouthings. They stand for realities, but these realities are the plans and desires of those who wish to gain control, under the alleged cloak of high ends, of the activities of other human beings" (pp. 29–30). If this is to be applied to Kant's Ideas of duty and personality, we are faced with the contention that these Ideas can serve to disguise any form of arbitrary despotism. On Dewey's view it would manifestly be possible for any tyrant to supply the content alleged to be lacking in these Ideas of Kant by telling those in his power that the unconditional obedience required by the command of duty was obedience to himself, and that their personality was manifested in a purity of will which in the interests of this obedience would shrink from no sacrifice of life or happiness. Such an abuse of *words* may be possible—but certainly not to any one who connects with the words "duty" and "person" the meanings attached to them by Kant. If the will of the tyrant himself is to have the character of a categorical imperative, this means that his subjects must be subject to him in *every possible exercise of their will*. But how can they be subjected to him *as regards their will* except on the ground that their own will determines them to this subjection. No one will wish to maintain that in virtue of some necessity independent of the exercise of his own will (and so by a law of nature) a man's will can, as it were, be transferred to the willing of another man. But the *maxim* by means of which a man makes this transference, if he subjects himself in every possible exercise of his own will to the arbitrary will of another, cannot possibly have the character of a law for *his* will, and therefore cannot possibly be a categorical imperative; for such a law would make him have no will of his own at all—and consequently he would also cease to be a person.

This is the answer, in the spirit and letter of Kant's moral doctrine, that should have been given to the despot when he sought to prescribe to persons his own arbitrary lawless will as the law of their duty. For the formalism of this doctrine does not, as Dewey and a host of empiricists before him imagine, contain a warrant for man *to select at random absolutely any will as his supreme lawgiver.* On the contrary: with the greatest possible determinateness of content this doctrine forbids man to subject himself to any will other than his own will so far as its maxims are capable of being laws. It forbids this because the maxim of such subjection, if taken as a law, is in necessary and irremovable conflict with his own will. Such a law cannot in the strict sense of the word be willed by him; for it is self-contradictory that a will should be able to will its own annulment with the necessity of law in every possible exercise of its own volition.

II

We have at least established this—that the obedience required by the categorical imperative is the direct opposite of an obedience by which a man could subject himself at random to any arbitrary power. If anybody is looking for definite precepts contained in the categorical imperative, he can put this down as the first—that such subjection is forbidden. The ban admittedly is only another way of saying that the categorical imperative is in fact nothing but the law of the will's autonomy (its making of its own laws). But with this view of it are we not plunged into a difficulty of the opposite kind? Instead of inferring that our will must be unconditionally fettered to the will of another are we not bound to infer that our own arbitrary will must be unconditionally unfettered? Must not a will subjected solely to its own legislation be able to pass any law it likes? Must it not be able in virtue of its autonomy "to will as a law" any arbitrary maxim it sees fit to use in regulating its choice of ends? At any rate Kant—as we have already heard —fails "almost grotesquely" in the eyes of his critics when he tries to persuade us that we must will any particular maxim as a law or that we cannot will it as a law. This failure is obviously called "grotesque" because, in the examples he gives of such necessities and impossibilities, it looks as if he casually introduces, in order to reach a decision, *that very consideration of the agent's personal advantage* which the categorical imperative professes to set aside as a principle of moral evaluation. Suppose, for example, he wants to show that nobody can will as a law the maxim of not bothering about the distress of others: "For," he says, "a will which decided in this way would be in conflict with itself, since many a situation might arise in which the man needed love and sympathy from others, and in which by such a law of nature sprung from his own will, he would rob himself of *all hope of the help he wants for himself.*" A clear case, it might seem. "This type of reason," says G. Simmel (*Kant* [Leipzig: Duncker & Humblot], 1904, pp. 97–98), "will satisfy no one today, and indeed I must admit that in Kant it is to me quite incomprehensible. Why should an appeal to personal interest, which he nowhere else recognises as a moral criterion, be all of a sudden taken here as decisive?" This is a repetition of John Stuart Mill's criticism— except that the forecast is reversed. Kant cannot possibly be free to appeal to personal interest (in happiness), says Simmel. He must inevitably appeal to happiness, says Mill, when he wants to come down to concrete events; and Mill's follower, Fr. Jodl (*Geschichte der Ethik* [*in der neueren Philosophie*, Band] II [Stuttgart: J. G. Cotta], 1889, p. 18), repeats: "In alleging reasons that make the universalisation of immoral maxims impossible, the decisive word in Kant's own exposition is kept for "empirically material" principles—not, however, the principle of general happiness, but rather of the most commonplace egoism."

Do such principles really have the last word? The opinion that they do rests manifestly on Kant's argument that we cannot will hardheartedness as a law because we should then rob ourselves of all hope of (possible) help even when we stood in need of it. Naturally, this can be a reason only for an agent to whom personal happiness is an end. But certainly it cannot be said that personal happiness *to the exclusion of the happiness of others* must be his end, and therefore that his interest in happiness must be a *selfish* interest if it is to prevent him from making his own possible need irremediable by a decision of his own will. What can be said is this. Whether he subordinates his whole interest to his own happiness as a supreme principle or considers also the happiness of others, he cannot possibly will, *so far as his happiness is an end for him*, to be abandoned in his need by all who could save him, and consequently he cannot will his own unhappiness. This is a purely analytic proposition: its truth is in no way affected by questions about the principle on which he acts. Hence Jodl's contention—that here "the most commonplace egoism" has the decisive word—is false.

Nevertheless—it may be insisted—the whole business still leaves a disagreeable aftertaste. The reason why we cannot will hardheartedness as a law is simply that we must be afraid of damaging ourselves if we do so. "Here it is stated as plainly as can be," says Schopenhauer in his prize essay *Über die Grundlage der Moral*, § 7, "that moral obligation rests entirely on a presupposed reciprocity. Hence it is completely egoistic and is to be understood as a form of egoism that prudently commits itself to a compromise on the condition of reciprocity." If we abandon this condition and imagine a man who assumes (rightly or wrongly) that he will never get into a position where he is in need of help, such a man can perfectly well agree that everybody should act on the maxim of hard-heartedness. Admittedly, if a man is prepared to act on the maxim of kindness only so far as he can in this way purchase the kindness of others, and if he would immediately withdraw his assent to this maxim as soon as he believed himself immune from need—such a man would be an egoist. But if he wills kindness only under such reservations, can he be said to will it *as a law?* Obviously he will never once show kindness himself except insofar as readiness on the part of others to help him will be its outcome. This is precisely the "reciprocity" that Schopenhauer has in mind; but he fails to notice that if a man shows kindness only on condition that others are kind to him, his maxim of kindness is such that, if it were made into a law, it would remove the possibility of kindness altogether. For if every one makes his kindness depend on another's being kind to him, it is obvious that there is no possibility of anyone being kind at all.

Equally astray is the contention that if we feel ourselves immune from need, we can perfectly well will *the maxim of indifference* as a law. This maxim *as a law* would run as follows: Every one who feels himself immune from need may be deaf to the need of others. It is manifest that however immune from need we may imagine ourselves to be, we *cannot* will this law. The reason is that the universalised maxim of the hard-hearted, let him turn and twist as he will—and indeed every case in which no help is given to him—does not hold subject to the condition on which he agreed to do it, namely, that *he* should be immune from need. *Everybody* is authorized by the maxim to refuse help so far as he himself is immune from need —without regard to the position of the man to whom help is refused. Consequently a will which wills the maxim of hardheartedness as a law necessarily contains in itself a will to be abandoned in the not absolutely impossible case of the agent's own need, and therefore it is a will in conflict with itself.

Naturally this is based on "reciprocity"—not, however, as Schopenhauer thinks, on the arbitrarily arranged reciprocity of a deal in cattle, but on a situation entirely withdrawn from human choice, namely, that "help" is a human relation with two terms: there is always one partner who gives help and another who receives it. Consequently nothing can alter the fact that if we lay down conditions for giving help, we also lay down conditions for receiving help. Hence if I wish the condition under which I can agree to the impossibility of receiving help to remain in force when my maxim about giving help is made universal, I must incorporate this condition in the maxim itself. The maxim will then take this form; I will never help any one who is immune from need. That such a maxim can be willed as a law without the slightest difficulty is certainly not a proposition that Kant would have been anxious to deny.

The series of fallacies into which Kant's critics fall again and again could never have been constructed but for a failure to observe that in a decisive passage in the *Groundwork of the Metaphysic of Morals* Kant has given the categorical imperative this form: Act only on that maxim *through* which you can at the same time will that it should become a universal law. The word "through" has not only been disregarded: there has been such a failure to understand it that the patchwork theorists (to use a phrase coined by Professor Paton) have proposed to see in it a textual corruption and to cut it out. This would mean cutting out the very word that first gives the formula its greatest precision. You must be able to will the character of law "through" the maxim; that is to say, the reason for the possibility of willing the maxim as a law must be found in the maxim itself—not in any external circumstances of the agent which are in no way determined by the maxim. If any one agrees to make the maxim of hardheartedness universally valid merely because he believes himself to need no help, he makes the possibility of his agreement depend on circumstances which on their side are not determinable by his maxim. For in the principle "Help yourself" there is no warrant for the ground on which he assents to the universality of the maxim —namely, that he should be free from the need of others' help. Thus he cannot will *through* his maxim that it should become a law; and consequently he cannot conform to the conditions laid down by Kant.

After all this what remains of the charge of egoism? All that remains is this: Kant rests his argument on the supposition that a man cannot in harmony with his own will choose to be abandoned in misfortune by those who could give him help. We have already said that this has nothing to do with egoism. If I have fallen into the water without being able to swim, and champion swimmers are all around me in lifeboats some twenty yards away, is my wish that they should pull me out to be explained only on the ground that I am an egoist— that is, a man who bothers about the need of others only when he can count on getting some advantage out of it for himself? And how is this to be distinguished in principle from any other arbitrary case where a man is in need of help and other people have the power to help him?

But—it will be said—Kant does insist that for the sake of a higher interest we must be prepared to make unlimited sacrifices of our own happiness. He undoubtedly does require this; but what he has certainly never claimed is that we must therefore be prepared to sacrifice our own happiness *as a possible end altogether*. This is precisely the claim he would have had to make if it were to be inferred from his principles that a man must be able to will his own abandonment in need. In that case the categorical imperative would have to forbid a man to make his own happiness an end. How could we possibly find a reason for any such prohibition? One's own happiness as an end is admittedly not the *ground* on which a will can be in law-abiding harmony with itself and with the will of all others; but it does not follow that *by having this end* the will is split in such a way that there could never be any conditions under which the maxim of making one's happiness an end might be willed as a law. If we wanted to take the contrary view, we should have to be able to say that man can make his own happiness an end only by reference to the unhappiness of others or even of himself—only if he is made unhappy by the happiness of others or perhaps by his own happiness at some past or future time. Under special conditions something like this may perhaps actually happen. But no one can say that this is among the universal and necessary conditions of human happiness as such. And consequently we cannot say that the categorical imperative forbids us to make our own happiness an end. We are therefore in error if we take Kant's statement—that a man cannot will his own unhappiness—to be false on the ground that on Kant's own principles a man ought never to make happiness his end and consequently that on these same principles he must be able to will his own happiness.

Not only does Kant's statement not contradict the categorical imperative: it is in itself completely justified. Man cannot renounce happiness altogether as a possible end: to have or not have this end in no way depends on his own choice. Nature forces this end upon him as soon as he begins to have ends at all. We cannot even conceive beyond this end any further motive which might induce him to make this end his own. This is why Aristotle declared happiness to be the final end of man; and he was perfectly right as long as we look for ends only within the bounds of experience. This amounts to saying that the categorical imperative does not prescribe this end to man—at least not directly. But no more does the categorical imperative prevent me—as has just been shown—from treating this end as one which is naturally common to all human beings. The categorical imperative *abstracts from all ends* because, in deriving from it an absolute demand as such, I cannot rest my case on any end that I presuppose; but this does not mean that the categorical imperative demands a will *that has no ends at all* and so wills nothing. It abstracts from all ends—that is, in the present case, it does not say with the utilitarians: "You must help others in need because by this you will promote your own happiness." Rather it says: "You must help them, whether this promotes your own happiness or not, since to will the maxim of indifference as a law is in contradiction with your inevitable and permissible end, namely, to receive help from them." When therefore the empiricist E. Becher asserts that if there is no question of consequences, I can will any arbitrary maxim whatever as a law, he must be told that he is a victim of the loose expression "there is (for Kant) no question of consequences." If we make this expression precise, it runs as follows: In deciding the unlawfulness of the maxim "Never help any one in need," there is no question of consequences so far as these concern the *possibility of attaining my own happiness as an end* if this maxim is followed by myself and others. But in coming to this decision there is indeed a question of consequences so far as these concern the possibility *of taking my own happiness*, and consequently my own rescue in distress, *as an end*, if I will the maxim of hardheartedness as a law. Inability to distinguish these two points of view is the secret—to use the language of John Stuart Mill—of the almost grotesque failure of those who have attempted to criticise Kant's deductions of particular moral duties. The reason why I cannot will the maxim of indifference as a law is not that by so doing I should stand in the

way of my own happiness. Whether my chance of happiness
will be improved or impaired by freeing every one, and consequently myself, from all obligation to help others depends
on circumstances about which there can never be any *a priori*
decision. But I can indeed decide *a priori*, as in the case of
every analytic truth, that if my will includes a will to be left
without help in need, I cannot possibly take happiness as my
end and consequently must be able to will my own unhappiness.

With the help of this analysis we must try to penetrate a
little more deeply into the seemingly paradoxical mechanism
which makes it possible for a will to fall into contradiction
with itself by willing that a maxim it can have should be a law.
The decisive consideration here is obviously that the will is
viewed in a situation where the object of its volition can itself
be a volition. I do will my own happiness—there is no further
problem in that. I *can*, secondly, will the happiness of others.
But, in the third place, in willing my own happiness, I also will
on the principle that others should will my happiness. Now if
on my side I do *not* will the happiness of others, I cannot (without willing contrary to my own volition) will that my maxim
should be acted on by others, and consequently I cannot will
that it should be a law. Hence if the categorical imperative is
valid, there follows from it *as a definite command* of duty that
I must include within my end of happiness the happiness of
others.

With this we conclude our discussion of one *example* by
which Kant has illustrated the possibility of deriving particular
precepts from the categorical imperative. I cannot hope that
this discussion will be enough to show in a new light the world-
wide practice of talking as if philosophy were not in a position
to tell men quite precisely what they ought to do and ought not
to do. But perhaps it will be enough to raise doubts about the

reliability of those who want to dismiss Kant's moral philosophy and its categorical imperative as a *causa judicata*.

If this is the situation, would it not be better to refrain from dragging questions of philosophy into regions where they may enter even a stray breath of political passion? When Dewey imagined he could find in Kant's moral philosophy a preparation for those outrages against the rights of man by which a crazy political movement has shocked the whole world, he failed to observe that he was talking about Kant exactly as the janizaries of the tyrant had also talked. So far as I am concerned, I do not think it the function of philosophy to engage directly in man's battle for the rule of law. All that philosophy can do is to bring the struggle of opinions to a theoretical agreement on rational grounds. Even so, the service it renders to mankind is beyond price; for there can be no assurance of a possible peace among men so long as the division of opinion on ultimate matters cannot be settled. Such a settlement is possible only if those who come to these affairs with reasons can have their reasons heard. The task I had set myself was to make it plain that as regards the reasons Kant puts forward in his doctrine of duty he has not been adequately heard and has not been understood at all.

University of Marburg

George A. Schrader / Autonomy,

heteronomy, and moral imperatives

Immanuel Kant sought to isolate the *pure form* of moral duty
and to account for its possibility. Since the pure form of moral
duty turns out to be identical with the form of pure duty, it
makes little difference whether one begins with duties in general or with moral duty. Whichever route one follows, one
should arrive at the result that duty in its pure form is categorically necessary and, further, that moral duty alone represents duty in its pure form. The implication is that moral duty
is different in kind from all other types of duty and logically
prior to each of them. Moral rules take precedence over social,
political, familial, or religious claims; the latter are related to

Reprinted from THE JOURNAL OF PHILOSOPHY, *Vol. LX, No. 3 (1963), pp.
65–77, by permission of the author and editors.*

the former as the contingent to the necessary, the hypothetical to the categorical.

Not only are all alleged duties subject to the canons of morality—not excepting duties to God—but they have their ultimate foundation in the moral will. This is not to say that every specific duty is *ipso facto* a moral duty; it is to assert that since every duty of whatever sort derives ultimately from the will of the individual, even hypothetical duties have a moral significance. Although hypothetical imperatives have a proximate heteronomous ground, they originate in the autonomous will and owe their necessity to the same will which commands categorically. There is one and only one will, even as there is only one self; it is the source of the necessity of all imperatives, whether hypothetical or categorical.

Kant assumed from the first that duty is essentially a phenomenon of volition. Duty expresses a command and implies a being capable of issuing such a command. From his meticulous analysis of the nature of imperatives Kant became convinced that no command issuing from an *external* source could be unconditionally binding upon the human will. It is this claim, which has been so influential for subsequent moralists, that I propose to examine.

The first step in Kant's argument is to show that duty is the central concept of morality and that moral duty is distinguished from other forms of duty by the fact that it is *categorical*. If there were no categorical imperative there would be, on Kant's view, no such thing as morality. We need not concern ourselves here with the possible circularity of Kant's reasoning. He clearly regarded the claim as a *synthetic* rather than an *analytic* proposition. He intended his analysis to clarify and purify the ideal of duty found in "popular moral philosophy." But, at same time, Kant sought to improve upon popular moral philosophy by stating the principle of duty in the purest possible form.

The language of duty is, as Kant analyzes it, the language of imperatives. Since duty expresses a *necessary* relationship between a moral subject and an object of his volition, it represents a necessity of *freedom* rather than of nature. An imperative may be hypothetical or categorical. If hypothetical, the necessity it expresses is only relative; if categorical, it asserts an unconditional necessity. Since duty involves a practical necessity and pertains only to the volition of free subjects, Kant concluded that it is fundamentally *reflexive* in character. It is the essential reflexivity of duty to which Kant appeals in arguing that duty implies autonomy.

But is Kant correct with respect either to the reflexivity of duty or to its autonomous origin? Does the fact that moral necessity involves the relation of the will of the subject to some end entail that the relationship must be reflexive? Duty can be analyzed in any one or more of the following ways, each of which fulfills the general condition that it be regarded as a phenomenon of volition. We might view it: (*a*) as a command deriving from a source beyond the self, e.g., God, or another person; (*b*) as a demand laid upon the subject through its own act and, hence, reflexive in character; and finally (*c*) as involving the reciprocal demand-response of a subject and one or more beings to which it is related. The first alternative (*a*) would regard duty as essentially heteronomous in point of origin, the second (*b*) as basically autonomous, and the third (*c*) as a combination of the two. The last alternative would allow for the possibility that moral duty can be based upon contractual relationships.

Kant rejects the first alternative and, by implication, the third, in arguing for the unqualifiedly *autonomous* character of moral duty. Since the three alternatives are not necessarily exclusive of one another, the fact that moral duty involves reflexivity does not in itself entail that it cannot be both heteronomous and contractual in nature. In order to rule out (a) and (c), the reasons for regarding duty as autonomous must be sufficient to preclude the possibility that it be either heteronomous or contractual. Otherwise Kant's conclusion simply does not follow.

Kant's reasoning seems to be that an imperative can be no stronger than the end to which it is related. If the end is either arbitrary or only contingently necessary, the imperative that enjoins us to promote it cannot be unconditionally binding. He rejected a theocentric ethics for the twofold reason that (a) God's existence is *problematic*, and (b) the force of a divine imperative depends upon the *acceptance* of God's authority. The second reason is the crucial one since it denies that a categorical imperative could issue from God *even if* His existence were absolutely certain. Granted God's existence, His commandments could be binding upon us only on the condition that we accepted His sovereignty. Hence, a divinely instituted imperative must be regarded as *hypothetical* rather than categorical. In spite of the fact that we should, on Kant's view, regard the moral law *as if* it were the commandment of God, it does not issue directly from God. Nor could it issue from any such source.

This contention of Kant's is worth examining, since it serves for him as the *paradigm* for all cases of heteronomously grounded duties. The fact that we may be less certain of God's existence than of our own—which is by no means self-evident—is not directly relevant to the issue at hand. The question is whether any external being, be it God or another human self, can be the source (as distinguished from the object) of moral duties. It is apparent that, insofar as we are in doubt as to His existence, we must remain uncertain about any possible duties to God. It might be the case, however, that we could be certain of God's existence only in and through the divine imperative— as Kant himself seems sometimes to have believed. The fact that neither the existence nor the necessary existence of God can be established with certainty in no way entails that a divine imperative could not be categorical. If, as a matter of fact, a categorical imperative were possible only on the condition that we establish some being as necessarily existent, we would be in an impossible situation.

It is evident that the divine imperative must be regarded as hypothetical primarily because its *validity* depends upon our volition. No matter what a possible divine being might decree, so Kant argues in effect, it could not give its commands the force of law for our will. Thus, either God's commandments take effect *independently* of human volition and, hence, are *natural* rather than *moral* ordinances, or they depend for their validity upon *human assent*. In the former case they are not properly to be regarded as imperatives and surely not as moral imperatives, and, in the latter case, they are clearly hypothetical. Or so Kant reasoned.

But was he correct? Does the fact that an imperative can be *directed* only to the will of a free agent entail that it can originate only in the will of the agent to whom it is addressed? Did Kant, perhaps, fail to distinguish adequately between the *enunciation* of a command and its *recognition* and *acceptance*? Might God not be the source of an imperative which is unconditionally binding upon man even though His authority were extensively repudiated? We must be careful not to confuse the *hypothetical status* of a possible divine command with the *contingency of its recognition*. An imperative might be objectively necessary even though its observance were highly problematic and uncertain. Such is, indeed, precisely the status of the moral law. It is, then, only the *validity* of the imperative and not its *acceptance* in actual practice that is at issue.

We have seen thus far that the uncertainty of the existence of God does not justify us in regarding a possible divine command as necessarily hypothetical. It is rather because, on Kant's analysis, a divine imperative depends for its validity upon our free response that it cannot be credited with unconditional necessity. But doesn't this argument beg the question? Isn't the hypothetical character of the divine imperative predicated on our *presumed freedom* to accept or reject it? And, if so, doesn't this assume the point at issue? Our response to a possible divine command might be optional in at least two respects: (*a*) it might be our decision whether to acknowledge the sovereignty of God; or (*b*) it might be our option whether or not to honor God's commands. Since the latter option would hold independently of the first, our freedom to repudiate possible divine commands does not in and of itself make their *validity* problematic. Nor does our acceptance of them necessarily establish this validity.

We have now reached a point where we must be clear as to just what Kant means by 'objective necessity.' In what sense and for what reason is it impossible for a divine command to be objectively necessary? In referring to the unconditional necessity of the moral imperative it is clear that Kant meant to emphasize its status as an objective limitation on our freedom. The categorical imperative is unconditional in that it is inescapable; it expresses the law of our being as free subjects. To violate the imperative is to set ourselves in opposition to the law of our own freedom. As an *a priori* condition of our freedom, the law is not itself subject to free choice. We have no more option whether to be subject to the moral law than whether we are to be human subjects. As rational and responsible beings we are liable before the moral law as the inexorable demand of our own rationally informed wills.

The categorical imperative must have a metaphysical foundation. As the supreme law of freedom it conditions all choice and, thus, is objectively necessary. There is more than a tinge of the classical view that rationality is intrinsically good and to be followed for its own sake, in Kant's position. The fact remains, however, that on Kant's view man is a creature under law. The moral imperative is not that which *should* obtain but which *does* obtain; it is the *de facto* 'ought' governing all human actions. All men are subject to the moral law willy-nilly. If this were not so, the moral imperative would be hypothetical rather than categorical.

If the analysis is correct, the moral imperative derives its authority from man's nature as a sensuous though rational being. It is *objectively necessary* in that it is a condition of man's existence as a free subject. Moreover, the primary condition of its validity is *metaphysical* rather than *axiological*. It is not the case that man *should* be a moral being but that he *is* a moral being. Either the moral law is not valid or it is in fact a condition of all human volition.

Although Kant was primarily concerned to delineate the conditions of responsible existence and tended to look upon the moral life as essentially the responsible life, his rationalistic predilections sometimes prompted him to equate *responsibility* with *rationality*. The fact that reason is an essential vehicle for the discovery and promulgation of the moral law does not mean—as Kant sometimes suggests—that it is the sole author of the law. If the primary requirement of the moral life is to be responsible, rationality is neither the sole nor the decisive ethical category. In fact, an excessive stress on rationality can lead to irresponsible conduct. It is a serious limitation in Kant's ethical theory that he did not recognize adequately the positive significance of impulse and emotion for the moral life. As Kant's critics have not been hesitant to point out, too rigid an adherence to a formal principle can lead to disastrous results. If one must heed the voice of reason, one must be sensitive, also, to the dictates of impulse, else human life becomes sterile. In this respect Kant failed to carry out a *Critique* of Practical Reason on a par with his *Critique* of Theoretical Reason. So firm was his confidence in the power of reason to govern human action that he thought it unnecessary to determine "its scope and limits" in moral affairs.

Kant allowed the more basic question: What are the conditions of responsible action? to be supplanted by the quite different question: What are the conditions of rational action? Whereas the first question leaves open the role of reason, feeling, and impulse in the moral life, the latter assumes that reason is the decisive factor in constituting the morally good life. Although Kant recognized that the relation between responsibility and rationality is synthetic, he tended, at times, to treat it as analytic, e.g., in beginning with the idea of a rational will. If, as I believe, the fundamental question of Kant's ethics—as of any ethics, for that matter—is: What are the conditions of responsible action? it must not be assumed that rationality is equivalent to responsibility. Kant's tendency at times to fuse these questions prompted him to assign undue prominence to the role of reason in the moral life. For one thing it led him to place too great an emphasis upon the autonomy of *reason* at the expense of *inclination*. And, in the second place, it occasioned his undue stress upon *universality* as the criterion of morally good action. The supreme imperative of morality is not, I would argue: Be rational! but rather: Be responsible! The validity of the moral law depends upon the fact that it specifies the fundamental conditions of responsible existence.

John Dewey was correct, I believe, in stating that *liability* is the beginning of responsibility. Carrying Dewey's insight somewhat further, we may take note of the commonplace but important truth that to exist at all is a liability and, in that sense, a responsibility. The individual must decide what he is to do with and about the fact of his existence, must answer to himself for what he is and does. Moral responsibility presupposes and expresses this original and continuing liability. Man can have duties to himself only because he is responsible for himself. The 'ought' of the moral imperative has its foundation in man's existential predicament. To be responsible in the *normative* (moral) sense presupposes that he is responsible in a prior *descriptive* (existential) sense. The individual is liable for giving meaning to his action, for choosing which paths to follow, and is, hence, a *legislator* to himself. To be morally responsible means, as Kant so well described it, to act in conformity with one's capacity as a legislator, to follow the "principle of law" in one's action. If moral duty reveals freedom, as Kant correctly maintained, anxiety and dread reveal the responsibility entailed by existence. We have not only to affirm our rationality but, also, our ineradicable irrationality, not only our universality but, also, our concrete particularity. The point I wish to make here is that moral responsibility and the autonomous action it implies are possible only on the foundation of a situation in which the *ought* is also a *must*. Moral liability (responsibility) is the result of a *response* to and determination of an original *existential liability*.

Although Kant did not develop his ethical theory in quite this way, he was aware of the fact that morality has and must have an ontological foundation. If man were not both a rational and a sensuous being he would know nothing of duty. The fact that he has empirical desires is, thus, essential to his nature as a moral being. Yet it is to reason that Kant assigns primacy in establishing the moral imperative. Man cannot escape the moral law because he cannot escape his own rationality. Man's reason makes an inexorable demand upon him at all times, which makes him morally responsible no matter what he may do. Insofar as reason is an original factor in the human situation, moral responsibility for Kant has an explicitly existential or, if you prefer, ontological foundation.

The fact is, however, that man is not, as Kant sometimes suggests, responsible to his reason alone. His task is not merely to endow his appetitive and emotional life with the maximum *rationality* (universality) possible. For he is responsible in an equally basic way to his *appetites* and *emotions*. Reason is, to be sure, the faculty through which, and through which alone, the claims of empirical desire can be either heard or honored. But, insofar as reason heeds the claims of man's sensuous nature, it operates in an *instrumental* and, hence, *heteronomous* fashion. To state this is not, of course, to argue against Kant's emphasis upon autonomy, but only to deny once more that autonomy is to be *equated* with rationality. In a sense, however, responsible treatment of oneself entails heteronomous action. It means to accept oneself as one is empirically given and to credit one's empirical nature as an integral part of oneself, entitled to full consideration in the definition of ultimate purposes. If the role of the moral legislator is unduly stressed, it leads inevitably to a denial and repression of the natural and instinctual. If the categorical imperative has its foundation in human nature, as it most clearly has for Kant, then it must be, I would argue, in man's *totality* as an existing being. Reason's eminence does not derive from the fact that it is the undisputed master of all it surveys but rather from its power to recognize and abide by its own limits. No one knew this better than Kant—to whom we owe so much of our instruction in this matter! Moral responsibility even toward oneself is not, then, exclusively a matter of autonomy—if the latter be construed as giving universal meaning and significance to one's empirical nature.

If the concern about heteronomy with respect to oneself appears to be quibbling, it is surely of greater moment in considering our duties to other persons. The question is whether man's original liability does not refer to other beings, whether animals, other persons, or God. If man's moral duty to himself derives from his original self-relatedness, as I have argued, may not his duties to other persons depend upon another and equally fundamental aspect of the same existential situation? Kant held that we should treat other persons as ends and not as means merely, which is, after all, only to say that we should treat them as persons (subjects-in-themselves). If one asks: Why should we treat other persons as ends-in-themselves? the answer would appear to be quite simple and direct, namely, because they *are* just that. But if such a straightforward answer can be admitted, it would appear that the *primary* ground of the obligation to another person is the person himself. And, if so, it is equally clear that our duty to the other person has a *heteronomous* rather than an autonomous basis. This is, I believe, the truth of the matter. To say this does not entail, however, that our duties toward other persons may not be, also, *indirect*, so as to have their proximate ground in our own will. To deny the claims made upon us by others is, in effect, to negate our own self-responsibility. To be true to ourselves we must be true to others; to recognize our own humanity we must affirm it in other persons. But, at the same time, to make this consideration the *primary* or *exclusive* basis for our duties toward others is seriously to misunderstand the moral situation. Moreover, it is to embrace a form of moral egoism which is none the more palatable for flying the banner of "principle."

If we should help another person who is in need, the primary reason for helping him is that he is in need and not that helping him will add luster to our virtues. We may, indeed, generalize the situation and respond to it in terms of a general maxim about aiding other persons. If we do that, it is partly, at least, because we cannot depend upon the presence of appropriate moral sentiments to motivate an altruistic action. Duty comes to the assistance of wavering sentiments, admonishing us in case of indifference or hostility toward the other person. So far so good! Kant's realism with respect to the moral sentiments of mankind is thoroughly justified. We may dislike our neighbor or simply be insensitive to his need. The moral law instructs us to put aside our peevishness and to concern ourselves with his welfare. With this doctrine we cannot quarrel; to renounce it would be tantamount to rejecting moral rules. The question is not at all whether moral rules are needed to prescribe our duties toward others; nor whether such rules must be formulated by reason as informed by a priori principle. This much of Kant's case must be accepted. What is at stake is the *source* of our duty toward others. Does it derive from one's own rational will or from the concrete reality of the other as a person? (That these alternatives are not exclusive we have already noted.) That both alternatives must be affirmed is the thesis I wish to defend against what is, at least, an overemphasis upon autonomy in Kant's ethics.

There is, of course, no conceivable doubt that Kant recognized our duties toward other persons as equally binding with our duties toward ourselves. My chief objection is that he seems to establish our moral relatedness to others and, hence, our duties to them in a rather artificial manner. Since, so he argues, in affirming our own humanity we affirm humanity in general as an end of action, *by implication* we establish the autonomy of other persons. Because of the shared universality, it would be inconsistent if not absurd for us to treat ourselves as ends and refuse this status to those who are *essentially* like ourselves—possession of a rational will serving as the criterion of essential likeness. Though unimpeachable, this argument is curiously awkward. It seems to stand things on their heads in that it begins with a purely *abstract* relation to others in order to establish a *concrete* obligation. It grants a spurious priority to *possibility* over actuality. Since, so the argument runs, we are committed to pay tribute to rational selfhood in whatever form we may meet it, our neighbor or a resident of China, we are morally obligated to treat any particular person we happen to meet in accordance with this abstract and universal obligation. Not only is this a highly artificial way of establishing moral duties toward others, but it has certain rather perverse implications for morality.

To see the force of this objection, which has been voiced in one way or another by a good many critics of Kant, we need only to consider that our duties to another person presuppose his existence. If there were no other persons, we would have no social obligations. It is, thus, the sheer *fact* of the other's existence in all its concreteness that constitutes the initial ground of our obligation to him. Indeed, the situation with respect to another person is analogous if not strictly parallel to our relation to ourselves. Even as we have an original existential liability to ourselves—of which moral liability is a special case—so, too, we have an original liability toward the other person. He is an item in our world waiting to be acknowledged, capable of judging and acting toward us. If we refuse to acknowledge him, the price may be our own demise. Or, if we refuse to recognize his actual nature, his powers and capacities, it may be to our distress. His *claim* upon us derives from his totality as a person confronting us in our world. It constitutes a responsibility in the most literal meaning of that term, namely, as a liability for answering or responding to the reality of the other. At the point where moral reflection arises we begin to evaluate the legitimacy of claims which we attribute to the other or which he asserts for himself. We should not lose sight of the fact, however, that any possibility of a valid assessment of putative moral claims requires a reference to the concrete reality of the other in the context of our initial relatedness to him. If he is, in fact, a human subject, we are obligated to treat him as such and, hence, not "as a means merely." But, if so, the primary ground of the obligation lies in his person rather than in our own moral will. If so, it is *heteronomously* rather than *autonomously* grounded.

If anyone thinks fit to spare Kant this criticism, let him reflect once more upon the implications of Kant's rejection of a theocentric ethics. If his argument against a theologically determined ethics is sound, it militates with equal force against a heteronomous ethics of a humanistic sort. The other person makes a claim upon us by virtue of his existence. This claim is not *ipso facto* a moral claim, and, in this respect, Kant's argument is sound. But he was mistaken in believing that it is not a *binding* claim and, further, that it is not presupposed in the statement of any *bona fide* moral claim. Moral duties to others not only can have but must have a heteronomous foundation.

It is not that Kant was inclined to ignore or even to slight our obligations to others. He was, however, seriously hampered in his formulation of our duty to others by his initial stress upon rational autonomy. It is true that in our volition we establish for ourselves the autonomy of the other as an end of our action and, hence, give it a reality *for ourselves* which it may not have had previously. The personal reality of the other thus serves both as actuality and ideal. But in dealing with this fact Kant is more than a little embarrassed. If he acknowledges that our action is in any way instrumental in establishing the reality of the other as an end-in-himself, he attributes to moral action an *influence* upon the subjectivity of others which he characteristically denies. But if he fails to acknowledge it, it remains unexplained just how we can treat others as ends rather than means merely. This is no minor dilemma! The only reasonable way out—and one that I am sure Kant accepted in fact if not in explicit theory—is to affirm the twofold status of the other as a person both in actual capacity and in ideal possibility. Had he chosen this resolution of the problem Kant could then have recognized more adequately the full scope of our responsibility toward others. Our concern is, alas, not merely with the *happiness* of the other person but, also, with his *autonomy*, *integrity*, and *moral health*. Our actions toward others are all the more consequential in view of our ability to impair their freedom, to tempt them and contribute to their corruption. Kant was unable to free himself sufficiently of a lingering monadological conception of the self to recognize the true nature of our moral relatedness to others.

One final point remains to be considered, namely, Kant's argument that a claim issuing from a source beyond one's own will cannot be morally binding. He has, as I have tried to show, actually taken a long step toward the qualification of this proposition in holding that we should treat others as ends-in-themselves. If Kant would grant, as surely he must, that this moral requirement depends ultimately upon the fact that they are actual subjects, he has seriously modified his doctrine of autonomy. He might still argue, as he does in fact, that it is our own volition which gives moral force to the claim of the other upon us. This is, as we have seen, qualifiedly true. It is, I have argued, a necessary though not a sufficient condition of moral obligation to others. It must be admitted that only insofar as one has a developed moral consciousness can one recognize the claims of others upon one as morally binding. This does not, however, warrant the inference that our moral consciousness *constitutes* the moral claim of the other *de novo*. The other person deserves and, in this sense, *ought* to be treated as a *subject* whether or not we recognize this fact. When we come to the point of reflection where we are capable of recognizing this claim and making it a principle of our action, we only countenance a liability which was antecedently given. If our statement of obligation does not in fact answer to this prior liability, it must be judged inadequate. Kant's difficulty here stems from the fact that he confuses the *constitution* of a moral claim with its *recognition*. Our recognition of our duty to others first gives it moral significance *for us*. But the duty is categorical *only* because it derives from the undeniable fact of the other's existence.

There are the cases, of course, in which moral action is at least partially self-justifying, e.g., in such moral relationships as friendship and marriage. Whether or not another person is in fact a friend depends in part upon our decision so to regard him. Thus our choice to have him as a friend and our moral obligation to treat him as a friend cannot be divorced. But even so, our volition is not in itself sufficient to constitute him as our friend, for he may not make the appropriate response. Moreover, once he has become our friend, he enjoys a privileged status within our social world. To treat a friend as if he were a total stranger would surely be irresponsible.

A more complete analysis of imperatives would require consideration of contractual relationships between persons. Contractual relationships, whether explicit and formally executed or only implicit and informal, represent the specification of antecedently given relationships between persons. If the *original* relatedness constitutes what might be termed an existential liability, the *freely* constituted relatedness provides a foundation for special duties toward others—e.g., of man to wife, of friend to friend. It is not merely, as Ross points out, that we make promises to others; we establish all sorts of formal and informal contracts with them. Such contracts make up much of the substance of our social, religious, political, and familial life. When specific moral questions arise they appear always within the context of a well articulated social structure. To ask a moral question in a vacuum not only threatens its intelligibility but almost certainly precludes a responsible answer.

In spite of the fact that he recognized the importance of our duties to others and our participation in a community of moral subjects, Kant developed his moral theory too much along monadological lines. Because of his failure to regard our relatedness to others as a *primary fact* of the moral life, he was hampered in providing an adequate social reference for the moral law. If Kant had been clearer in his own mind as to the metaphysical foundation for the categorical imperative, he would have found it necessary to credit heteronomy with a fundamental role in the moral life. Freedom and reason, which Kant properly recognized as necessary conditions of morality, became for him too exclusively ends-in-themselves. It is not my purpose to assess the relative merits of autonomy and heteronomy as ideals for moral striving. I have attempted to establish only the rather elementary point that categorical obligation does not require an autonomous foundation. On the contrary, the same conditions that are *required* to establish the objective necessity of a *reflexively* oriented imperative provide equal support for a *socially* anchored law.

Yale University

Lewis White Beck / Apodictic

imperatives

Relation and modality of imperatives

At the end of § 1 of the *Critique of Practical Reason* there is an extraordinary statement in which Kant distinguishes between the practical rightness and the categoricalness of an imperative, and indicates that the former might be independent of the latter. This is astonishing, because the reader has been led, in the *Grundlegung*, to believe that by establishing a categorical imperative a moral imperative is established. But Kant, in discussing the example, "Never make a deceitful promise," says: "If, now, it is found that this rule is practically right, it is a law, because it is a categorical imperative."

Though Kant says in the *Groundwork* that there is only one categorical imperative, from time to time he calls specific imperatives to do certain actions categorical imperatives. For

Reprinted from KANT-STUDIEN, *Band 49, Heft 1 (1957/58), pp. 7–24, by permission of the author and editors.*

instance, in the *Metaphysics of Morals*,[1] "Obey authority" is called a categorical imperative. I do not know of any instance in which Kant calls an imperative "categorical" and does not regard it as "practically right." But there are indeed imperatives which are formally categorical and yet not "practically right." There are likewise hypothetical imperatives which are morally binding and hence practically right. "Shut the door" is formally categorical, while "If you are married, remain faithful to your spouse" is formally hypothetical. Presumably it would be possible to show that the latter is "practically right" and is in some sense a law.[2] And certainly the former is not "practically right" in the sense required if we are to regard it as a law; it is at most technically practical and not morally practical.[3]

It is clear from these examples that the term "categorical" in Kant's ordinary usage of "categorical imperative" does more than refer to the form of the imperative. And it is worth noting that the distinction among imperatives, when first introduced in the *Groundwork*, is not based on a difference in form of the imperatives themselves, but on their ways of commanding: "All imperatives command either hypothetically or categorically."[4] The distinction between hypothetical and categorical

[1] *Metaphysik der Sitten, Rechtslehre*, Beschluß (Vorländer ed., 206; Akademie ed., VI, 371).

[2] Though Kant explicitly distinguishes "law" from "imperative" and from "rule," he continually uses these words interchangeably, even in § 7 of the *Critique of Practical Reason*, which professes, in its title, to give as it were the official statement of the "law" but in fact states only an imperative.

[3] "Technically practical" and "morally practical" are distinguished in *Kritik der Urteilskraft*, Introduction, I.

[4] *Grundlegung*, Ak. 414; Paton trans., 82 [p. 35 above]. In *Critique of Practical Reason*, Ak. 11, Beck trans., 11, Kant speaks of "problematic, assertoric, and apodictic grounds of determination." In future notes references to the *Grundlegung* will cite two numbers, the first referring to the

imperatives, which seems to be a formal distinction, is derivative from this prior distinction, which is modal.

What is involved in being "practically right" is not the category of relation, but the category of modality. The best name for what Kant called the "categorical imperative" and identified with the "imperative of morality" would seem to be "apodictic imperative." In the *Groundwork* and occasionally in the second *Critique*, terms of modality are used to distinguish among the several imperatives. The technical imperative is called problematic, the pragmatic is called assertoric, and the categorical is called apodictic. But in general the modal division is neglected in favor of the formal. Whereas Paton expresses a certain distrust of the modal division,[5] the purpose of this paper is to justify its use by drawing attention to certain considerations which are neglected as a result of Kant's insistence upon the formal or relational distinction.

The "Table of the Categories of Freedom" in the *Critique of Practical Reason* is regrettably of no help to us in deciding on the propriety of the term "apodictic imperative." This Table is, I may venture to say, one of Kant's less successful productions in the architectonic genre, and it is hard to make heads or tails of it, especially in its division of moments under the dynamic categories.[6] The distinction between hypothetical

---

page number in volume IV of the Akademie edition, and the second, in parentheses, giving the page number in Paton's translation, under the title *The Moral Law* (London: Hutchinson, 1948). References to the *Critique of Practical Reason* will cite, first, the page in volume V of the Akademie edition, and second, in parentheses, the page in my revised translation of this work (New York: Bobbs-Merrill, 1956).

[5] H. J. Paton, *The Categorical Imperative. A Study in Kant's Moral Philosophy* (Chicago: University of Chicago Press, 1949), p. 115.

[6] It seems to have puzzled Kant's contemporaries as much as it puzzles me. Cf. the letter from Schütz to Kant, June 23, 1788 (Akademie ed., X, 541).

and categorical does not appear under "Relation." Under "Modality," corresponding to the moments of necessity and contingency there is "Perfect and Imperfect Duty," while "Duty" itself appears as the member corresponding to the assertoric judgment of existence. According to this Table, an "apodictic imperative" would be an imperative of strict or perfect duty, commanding without exception a definite action (e.g., paying a debt); such imperatives belong to jurisprudence, not to ethics, because they command a specific action without concern with the motive.[7] The contrary of an apodictic imperative is not a prohibition[8] but the imperative of imperfect duty. Such an imperative is not a command to do a certain action, but to act on a certain motive, with room left for the determination of the occasion and the specific kind and direction of the action. Imperatives of imperfect duty belong only to ethics and not to jurisprudence.

In this essay I propose to use the name "apodictic imperative" for all moral imperatives whether they allow *latitudo*[9] in action or not. Imperatives which are not apodictic or necessary will be treated as imperatives which carry no moral weight, according to Kant's estimate. They correspond to the first category of modality in the Table in the *Critique of Practical Reason* and not to the second, which already introduces the concept of duty. But they correspond, in their two species, to the problematic and assertoric modalities in the Table of Judgments of the first *Critique*.

There are two textual justifications for this, apart from

[7] *Metaphysik der Sitten*, *Tugendlehre*, Einleitung, Sec. XVIII (Vorländer, 254; Akademie, VI, 410).

[8] Cf. Richard Barber, "Two Logics of Modality" [in Kant], *Tulane Studies in Philosophy*, III (1954), 41–55 at 46.

[9] *Metaphysik der Sitten*, *Tugendlehre*, Einleitung, Sec. VII (Vorländer, 231; Akademie, VI, 390).

the negative justification of the obscurity of the Table itself. The first is that moral imperatives, whether strict or loose, are necessary—the strict necessitating a specific action, the loose necessitating a general maxim and rendering it a law which yet permits "variety in the rule."[10] As necessary, they are products of reason, which (in its logical use) is the faculty of apodictic knowledge.[11] And, more importantly, we have seen that Kant himself on occasion calls them apodictic imperatives.

Analysis of hypothetical imperatives of the first type

A hypothetical (problematic or assertoric) imperative is one which holds for any rational being under the condition that this being has a certain end or purpose which is believed to be the effect of the action he is told to execute, and which states this condition as the restrictive condition on the validity of the imperative. We shall call these imperatives *conditional imperatives* or *hypothetical imperatives of the first type*, and under them are included two modal types: assertoric and the problematic imperatives.

A full analysis of such an imperative would make the following components explicit:

(*a*) In the protasis:
(I) A conative element: an incentive, impulse, or interest in something (B), which is the purpose of the commanded action; an object or state of affairs the representation of which is one of the causes of its existence through the relation of the representation to the overt action of the subject; expressed in the imperative as "If I want B" or "Because I want B."

[10] *Critique of Practical Reason*, § 1, Remark.
[11] *Critique of Pure Reason*, A 75n. = B 100n.

    (II) A cognitive element: knowledge of the causal relation between the action commanded (A) and the purpose or end (B); equivalent, under condition (I), to "A is a means to B."

    (III) A logical form: "If I fully will the effect [B], I also will the action [A] required for it."[12]

  (*b*) The apodosis: "Do A."

In the technical imperative or rule of skill, the fully expanded form would be: "(I) If you will B, (II) because A is a necessary condition of B, then by (III) do A." Here the problematic element lies in the first conditional: "If you will B. . . ." *If* A is really commanded under this condition, (II) must here be assertoric.[13] In the pragmatic imperative or counsel of prudence, the full exposition would be: "Because you will B (B = happiness), (II) if A is a necessary condition of B, then by (III) do A." Here the problematic element lies not in the antecedent conation, since a rational being having any desires necessarily desires his happiness;[14] it lies in our irremediable uncertainty as to what is the empirical content of B and whether A will in fact lead to it.

Kant tells us that the possibility of these imperatives is easy to establish, because they are, in what concerns the will,

---

[12] *Grundlegung*, 417 (85) [p. 40 above].

[13] There is here no imperative to do A unless A is known or believed to be a means to B. A *purely* problematic protasis could not be the basis for an actual command. Kant in the First Introduction to the *Critique of Judgment* (Cassirer ed., V, 183*n*.) withdraws the name "problematic imperative" as involving a self-contradiction. But the "mixed problematic imperative," one of whose premises is assertoric, does not involve any self-contradiction in its name. The present analysis shows that each of the hypothetical imperatives of the first type may have a problematic and an assertoric antecedent, and that they differ only in the locus of each modality.

[14] *Critique of Practical Reason*, 25 (24); *Grundlegung*, 415 (83) [p. 38 above].

analytical.[15] This is correct, but it requires a little attention to see what it means and why it is true.

It is not entirely clear in what sense an imperative can be either analytic or synthetic. Imperatives are not judgments with a subject and predicate, and so do not fall under Kant's explicit division of the types of judgment. And though for any imperative a set of indicative (but not necessarily factual[16]) statements may be formulated under which the imperative could be derived by a syntactical change of mood, in the case of hypothetical imperatives of the first type, some of the corresponding judgments are themselves hypothetical, and hence likewise fall outside Kant's official rubric for distinguishing analytic from synthetic judgments. It is not entirely pedantic to insist on these points; but the minor infelicities of expression should not permit us to overlook the important point Kant is insisting upon, even though he does it in not entirely suitable language. I shall try to say, therefore, what I think he means.

If we take the statements of the conditions under which the apodosis is regarded as binding and phrase them in declarative statements, e.g., "Under conditions C a rational being will choose A," then the proposition "A rational being will choose A" will follow analytically from this and the proposition, "A rational being is under conditions C." By "following analytically" I mean that a denial of the conclusion will contradict a premise. Thus: "If a rational being fully wills B and knows A to be a necessary condition of B, and if (III) to will fully an end includes willing the means known to be necessary to this end, then the rational being wills A," is analytic in the broad sense in which Kant *here* uses the word "analytic,"

---

15 *Grundlegung*, 417 (85) [p. 39 above].

16 Thus, "Do A" corresponds to the indicative, "You ought to do A," though the two sentences have different roles in moral discourse. "Do A" would not be "practically right" unless "You ought to do A" were true.

since to deny the apodosis is to contradict the protasis. But it is not analytic in the strict Kantian sense, since an analytic proposition for Kant is one whose denial is self-contradictory, and the mere concept of rational being does not analytically "contain" the concept of willing A.

But it is analytic, even in the broad sense, only in what concerns the will. That A is necessary to B is not known analytically, and that the rational being in fact wills B (except perhaps when B = happiness) is likewise not known analytically. All that is known analytically is (III), and this concerns the form of volition and not the contents willed. (III) is not actually a premise,[17] but a rule of practical inference, specifying the relation between the variables A and B. Kant should say, therefore, not that the hypothetical imperatives of the first type are analytic, but that their formal principle, (III), is analytic. "If you wish to have bread, devise a mill" is not, fortunately for most of us, in any sense analytic, but is only a disguised form of the empirical statement, "Mills grind flour, and flour is needed to make bread."

I shall call (III) the formal principle of hypothetical imperatives of the first type.[18] It is indeed analytical, and it alone concerns the will independently of the cognitive content and contingencies of human desire. Not to accept (III) is to fail to be a rational being concerned with desires. It is for this reason that Kant holds even hypothetical imperatives of this type to be objectively valid; they are not persuasive or emotive but ra-

[17] Cf. R. M. Hare, *The Language of Morals* (London: Oxford University Press, 1952), p. 48.

[18] By analogy to Broad's terminology in his discussion of the categorical imperative, it might be called "the supreme principle of conditional imperatives." Cf. C. D. Broad, *Five Types of Ethical Theory* (London: Routledge & Kegan Paul, 1930), pp. 120–121, 123. I call it a principle of conditional, not of hypothetical imperatives, for we shall see that there are hypothetical imperatives which do not fall under this principle.

tional, even though they are relevant to action only under specific conditions which are not true of rational beings as such;
and the conditions they are concerned with are conditions of
him to whom the imperative is directed, not of him who issues
the command.

Since beings like men do not, in fact, always will the
means necessary to their ends, even when they do know the
means, the hypothetical imperative of this type expresses a
constraint. If we were completely rational beings, the maxim
of doing whatever is necessary to the end in view would be
easy to follow; but since we are not completely rational, even
our desires and wishes create constraints and not mere lures
and enticements.

Analysis of categorical imperatives of the first type

By a categorical imperative of the first type I refer to the only
kind of "imperative of morality" to which Kant devoted his
attention. I mean what Kant himself ordinarily called categorical imperatives.

Syntactically, the so-called categorical imperative is
atomic and has no analysis. "Shut the door" is a categorical imperative which means—shut the door. A genetic account of its
utterance can be given, but the reasons for it are not even implicit in the sentence. From the sentence, we cannot reconstruct
the reasons for it. There are indeed reasons for the utterance,
but they are not stated as conditions under which it is imperative that the door be shut. The imperative may be honored for
these or for other reasons, or rejected in spite of them without
any contradiction occurring.

Obviously this is not what Kant means by "categorical
imperative." He means one which not only fails to mention the
conditions, but one which is independent of conditions which

could be stated only in the protasis of a hypothetical imperative and which would concern only our private wants. As to the conative component, the categorical imperative is independent of any "material of desire" or "object of interest," even though they are present in every volition.[19] As to the cognitive component, it is not a condition for the imperative since the imperative does not command us to do anything as a means to an end; indeed, it may not command us to *do* anything, but only to will to do something in a certain way.[20] And as to the third condition, the formal principle does not have the right "logical shape" for an unconditional imperative, since we are not concerned with connecting a variable in (I) with a variable in (II).

Hence it is necessary to look elsewhere than to an analysis of the categorical imperative in order to discover whether it is "objectively right and hence a law."

Whereas Kant told us that the hypothetical imperative was analytic and hence easy to establish, he calls the categorical imperative" an *a priori* synthetic proposition"; "it connects the willing of an action directly with the concept of the will of a rational being as something not contained within the concept."[21] That which would be "contained within it" would be the concept of an object of desire as contained in the concept of the will of a sensuous being like man. The imperative which would follow analytically from such a synthetical concept (the

---

[19] *Critique of Practical Reason*, 34 (34); *Reflexion* 6633.

[20] *Metaphysik der Sitten, Tugendlehre*, Einleitung, Sec. VI (Vorländer, 229; Ak., VI, 388).

[21] *Grundlegung*, 420*n*. (87*n*.) [p. 43*n*. above]. The parentheses in the last sentence of the note indicates that, for a pure or holy will, the imperative would be analytic. Of course it would not be an imperative at all, but only a law; yet in the *Critique* the law is called *a priori* synthetic. I do not know how to resolve this contradiction. Paton (*The Moral Law*, p. 142) suggests that "analytic" here has reference to an analytic *argument*.

concept of will modified by accident) would, of course, be a hypothetical imperative of the first type, conditional upon the empirical character of the specific desires of a finite being with an empirically restricted will.

Yet Kant says immediately thereafter that "the mere concept of a categorical imperative" furnishes "the formula containing the only proposition that can be a categorical imperative." He then goes on to point out the fact which chiefly concerns us in the present essay: to know the formula of a categorical imperative and to know how it is practically right as a law are two very different things. This paragraph contains a number of notions that are a bit obscure, and we must attempt to clarify them.

Kant tells us that the mere concept of a categorical imperative furnishes the formula containing the proposition which can be a categorical imperative. Yet, two paragraphs later, he does not give us what he calls a "formula" but what he calls *the one* "categorical imperative." It is, in fact, a categorical imperative; but the words "maxim" and "law" in it are variables, and it really does state a formula. Broad is correct in calling it "the supreme principle of all categorical imperatives" and in referring to it as a "second-order principle," the first-order principle being a specific imperative fitting this formula.[22]

"Do X" might in one sense be considered a formula for the categorical imperative; but this is not what Kant means by a formula. A formula, he says, determines what is to be done in solving a problem,[23] and "Do X" does not help us in determining the permissible range of values of "X." We must find a formula from which the values of "X" can be determined, independently of any protasis such as (*a*I) and (*a*II), since they are not stated in a categorical imperative.

[22] *Loc. cit.*

[23] *Critique of Practical Reason*, 8n. (8n.)

There seems, at first sight, to be a contradiction in saying that the mere concept of a categorical imperative implies its formula, and in saying that the imperative (or rather its formula, which is the implicate) is synthetic. But it is not really so, at least in Kantian terminology. For him, a proposition which is itself synthetic can be proved analytically; for him, "analytic" is not equivalent to "logically deducible." Mathematical propositions, he at least sometimes says,[24] are synthetical propositions, but can be proved by analysis of synthetic a priori propositions. To be analytical, the contradictory of a proposition must be self-contradictory, and not merely contradictory of some other propositions used in its proof.[25] Hence it is quite possible for Kant to say that the formula follows by analysis of the concept of a categorical imperative, and to say that it is not analytical of any concept contained within it.

Finally, there is the danger we have already noticed in saying that an imperative is *either* analytic *or synthetic*. But if we remember that an imperative is only the mood in which a law is formulated for a being who ought to but does not by nature do what the law says a rational being would do,[26] we can easily enough formulate the law to which the imperative corresponds, and it is this law that Kant means is synthetic. Unfortunately, however, after carefully distinguishing "law" from "imperative" he fails to remain faithful to his distinction,

[24] *Prolegomena*, § 2, c, (2).

[25] Kant's definitions of analytic and synthetic apply strictly only to subject-predicate propositions, though he uses the term much more broadly. To identify "analytical" with "logically deducible" would require the application of the term "analytical" to compound propositions containing an argument. Thus: "If (if *p* then *q*) and *p*, then *q*" might be considered analytical since "If (if *p* then *q*) and not *q*, then *p*" is self-contradictory. But suffice it to say that Kant does not use the terms "analytic" and "synthetic" to apply to such compound propositions.

[26] *Critique of Practical Reason*, § 1.

and says many things about imperatives that can correctly be said only about laws.

All laws are synthetic judgments, and if they are laws in a strict sense (whether laws of nature or laws of morality) they are, for Kant, *a priori*.[27] This is true of the laws which are component (*a*II) in hypothetical imperatives of the first type, though usually we have to be content, in that position, to make do with merely empirical generalizations. The law which the moral imperative expresses, which is the moral law, does not occupy a position in relation to the categorical imperative comparable to that of (*a*II) in relation to the hypothetical. The moral law functions more like the principle (*a*III), with the categorical imperative (or rather *its* formula) being an immediate inference with a change of mood from this law. Factors like (*a*I) and (*a*II) do not function in the determination of the formula, but provide only the variety, content, and occasion of specific first-order categorical imperatives ("rules") under the general formula or principle.

We are now prepared to trace Kant's derivation of the formula of a categorical imperative from the concept of a categorical imperative.

For there to be any imperative which is not merely an unreasoned ejaculation in the imperative mood, there must be a law. The imperative expresses the necessitation of an action, the necessity (either conditional or unconditional) of which is expressed in a natural law. Unless there were such a law, imperatives would be mere prayers or persuasions or ejaculations for which no reason could be given. Even "Shut the door" is a reasonable command only if there is some natural law, or at least an empirical generalization, relating events like shutting the door to other events of a desired kind. Only where there

[27] *Critique of Pure Reason*, A 159 = B 198; *Critique of Practical Reason*, § 3, Remark II.

is a law can the distinction be drawn between valid and invalid imperatives, even on the assertoric and problematical levels.

In a categorical imperative, however, the imperative is not explicitly restricted to any condition such as (aI), and therefore it cannot be the content of a law (aII), as a law of nature, which determines the content of the imperative, i.e., the specific value of the variable "A" which is to be done. For if (aI) is not specified as the condition of the imperative, there is no ground on which a specific law under (aII) can be chosen from all the known laws of nature to give a specific value to this variable. For the content of any specific law that is used in formulating a categorical imperative that is not an unreasoned and indefensible command (*Sic volo, sic jubeo!*) we must substitute the form of a law, and require that that form be a restrictive condition upon the maxim of action, and not require that the content of a natural law (which is not given) be a restrictive condition upon the content of the maxim. That is to say, the categorical imperative commands that the maxim *itself* have the form of universal and necessary law. This form alone must determine the content of the maxim.

Now this determination of the content of a maxim by its form is just what most critics of Kant deny is possible. I believe that this objection is based upon—not a profound misunderstanding but—a simple misunderstanding of what Kant is about. What he is establishing, as we have said, is a principle of categorical imperatives, a formula, a second-order principle, and not an imperative for a specific action. The content of the maxim which is derived from its form is the maxim to act only on maxims that fit the formula; but what these maxims are is not determined, with respect to *their* content, by the formula. The maxims which in fact fit under the formula will have their content determined by considerations of type (aI) and (aII); otherwise the action would have no specificity or overt quality. But the form of universal law serves, in the formula, to determine the second-order maxim, which is the maxim to follow maxims which allow universalization, and to follow them *because* they are universalizable.

It is necessary here to distinguish between the categorical imperative itself and the formula of the categorical imperative. The former is an order to do actions of a certain kind, e.g., let no offense pass unavenged, to treat others fairly, to preserve one's own life, etc. The latter is an order which tells us to choose among these maxims by a certain criterion, to wit, that the accepted maxim be one that at the same time we can will to be a maxim for all rational beings. What Kant ordinarily calls categorical imperatives, such as "Do not make a deceitful promise" and "Obey authority," are imperatives which have passed the criterion of the formula, and they are "practically right." It is these which I call "categorical imperatives of the first type." Categorical imperatives of the second type are those imperatives in the form "Do A" which do not fit under the formula. The categorical imperative—if there is such an imperative which is neither an unreasoned and indefensible command nor an elliptical formulation of a hypothetical imperative —must be to act only on a maxim that can be willed at the same time (i.e., by the very same decision to obey) to be a maxim (i.e., a law) for all rational beings.

A categorical imperative which is "practically right" must be one that commands an action which is motivated by a maxim that fits the formula. Many imperatives of the form "Do A" fail to meet this test. And a man may act on what is, in fact, a maxim that fits this formula, and yet do it without having his action determined by the formula. In this event, his action is legal, but not strictly moral. To show that a maxim to follow the formula can actually be an effective factor in the choice of maxims or imperatives of the first order is the task of showing that the moral imperative is "possible."

Deduction of the categorical imperative of the first type

We have seen that Kant distinguishes between establishing the formula of a categorical imperative—the process we have just traced—from learning how such a law is "possible." To show that a principle is possible is not, for Kant, to show that it is logically possible, i.e., not self-contradictory. It is not even to show that it is "really possible," but to show that it is necessary. "Necessary" in this sense is modal, not logical, for only analytic propositions have logical necessity. Real necessity means "necessity for possible experience," and is shown only by a transcendental deduction, a regression from an experience upon its conditions. To show that the categorical imperative is possible, therefore, is to show that the imperative "really holds" and is unconditionally binding. In the case before us, it is to show that it is "practically right."

Kant says that, in one sense, this deduction cannot be accomplished.[28] Yet in saying this, he is exaggerating the differences between the procedure in the theoretical and in the practical fields. The moral law, "the sole fact of pure reason,"[29] is like the laws of mathematics and natural science in Kant's theoretical philosophy. The synthetic structure of the first and second *Critiques* should not hide from us what is obvious in the analytical procedure of the *Prolegomena* and *Grundlegung*, namely, that morality and our knowledge of nature are the *prius*, the *explicans* and not the *explicate*. To show that a categorical imperative is really possible requires us to show:

[28] *Critique of Practical Reason*, 47 (48).
[29] *Ibid.*, § 7, Remark.

a) That the phenomena of moral constraint are not explicable if all imperatives are conditional upon desires;[30]

b) That the world is such that the commands of the moral law or the formula of the categorical imperative, worked out analytically under (*a*), are in principle performable, i.e., that there is no reason for asserting that the moral law makes impossible demands of us, so that the phenomena of moral constraint would have to be regarded as chimerical. This is shown by the resolution of the antinomy between freedom and natural causation in the *Critique of Pure Reason*.[31]

The connection between the former, which grows out of an analysis of moral phenomena, and the latter, which is metaphysical (in the usual sense of the word), is achieved through the assimilation of the concept of autonomy, as required by genuine moral constraint, to that of freedom as a permissible consequence drawn from transcendental idealism.[32]

In one direction, the reality (binding character) of the moral law is deduced (justified) by being shown to be possible, it being already given as a fact. In the other direction, it is the reality of freedom which is justified by this fact, only the possibility of freedom having been shown in theoretical philosophy.[33]

---

[30] This is performed in *Ibid.*, §§ 1–7.

[31] Cf. especially A 536 = B 564.

[32] It is interesting to note, in this connection, that in the *Critique of Pure Reason*, in the "Canon," Kant has not developed the concept of autonomy, and therefore does not succeed in connecting morality with the concept of freedom developed in the solution to the third antinomy. At the end of the "Canon," therefore, he treats the concept of freedom as an empirical concept and holds that it is independent of the "transcendental" concept. This is inconsistent with the doctrine of the major ethical works. Cf. M. Gueroult, "Canon de la raison pure et critique de la raison pratique," *Revue internationale de Philosophie*, VIII (1954), 333–357.

[33] *Critique of Practical Reason*, 47 (48–49).

The moral law, together with its corresponding imperative, is shown to be synthetical by showing that the mere concept of a rational will does not logically "contain" but "implies" the concept of freedom, and then by showing the law for a free agent to be self-given, i.e., a law of autonomy, expressed in an imperative not conditional upon anything except the freedom of a rational being as such. Hence it follows that a being with a will and a being who can address categorical imperatives to himself are identical, since both concepts are mediated by a "third," that of freedom.

The "Deduction" in the second *Critique* is one of the most obscure and difficult and, in one respect at least, unconvincing, parts of that work. It will not be necessary in this place to point out more than one of the difficulties, one which is characteristic of many parts of Kant's work. This is the difficulty, apparent enough to everyone except seemingly to Kant himself, of sharply distinguishing in many cases between those judgments that are analytic and those that are synthetic. Fortunately, however, the most important steps in his argument do not depend upon specific decisions, made from time to time, concerning analyticity vs. syntheticity. The important thing is not to agree with Kant concerning precisely what is "contained in" and what is only "implied by" the concept of rational being, but to see that Kant is going beyond purely formal considerations of the deduction of the formula from the concept, and is giving some existential status, in a broad sense at least, to the moral judgment. He is trying to show by a general moral, phenomenological, and philosophical consideration, that there are categorical imperatives that are morally practicable as well as logically possible.

But there is nothing in the Deduction that requires that the imperative which meets these requirements shall be categorical in form.

Summary of distinctions among types of imperatives

We have already seen that there are categorical imperatives which are not in fact unconditionally binding, and that there are also unconditionally binding imperatives which are not formally categorical. Those Kant is generally concerned with, however, are put forth unconditionally, in categorical form, as practically right. The various possibilities may be conveniently listed as follows:

(a) Hypothetical imperatives which are conditional, i.e., either assertoric or problematic. These are the only hypothetical imperatives that Kant discusses, and are here called "hypothetical imperatives of the first type." Example: "If you want to be happy, try to develop an interest in some hobby."

(b) Unconditional, i.e., apodictic, categorical imperatives; imperatives that are "practically right" in categorical form. These are the categorical imperative Kant emphasizes, and are here called "categorical imperatives of the first type," but must be distinguished from the *"formula"* of the categorical imperatives, which apply only to this type. Example: "Obey authority."

(c) Conditional categorical imperatives. These are imperatives in categorical form irrespective of whether they are "practically right" or not. They may in fact be only elliptical expressions of hypothetical imperatives, and are here called "categorical imperatives of the second type." Example: "Shut the door."

(d) Unconditional hypothetical imperatives or apodictic hypothetical imperatives. These are here called "hypothetical imperatives of the second type." Example: "If you make a promise, keep it."

It will be noticed that the "first type" under each of the formal divisions is the one that Kant considered, and the "second type" is the one that he neglected.

In the next section, we shall be concerned with the distinction between (*b*) and (*c*), between categorical imperatives of the first and second types, i.e., between categorical imperatives which are apodictic and those which are not. In the final section we shall discuss the distinction between (*a*) and (*d*), between the two modalities of hypothetical imperatives.

Conditional and unconditional categorical imperatives

A recent excellent history of philosophy says: "It is possible to generalize into universal rules all sorts of maxims which nobody (and certainly not Kant) would hold to be obligatory. For instance, I could perfectly well hold that every purchaser of a new book should write his name on the flyleaf when he acquires it. There is nothing self-contradictory about this maxim."[34]

"Write your name on the flyleaf of your book" is a categorical imperative. Why is it not obligatory, and why is it an instance of (*c*) and not of (*b*)? The answer is clear from the formula, which applies to case (*b*) only (and, as we shall see, to case (*d*)). The formula is negative, telling us to act *only* according to a universalizable maxim; it expresses a necessary but not a sufficient condition for the maxim of the action. And in Kant's formula we are commanded to act only on a maxim *through which* and *at the same time* we could will that the maxim should hold for all men.[35] In Mr. Jones' example, there

[34] W. T. Jones, *A History of Western Philosophy* (New York: Harcourt, Brace, 1952), p. 855.

[35] This should be clear from the familiar formula of the *Grundlegung*, but if it is not, the statement in the *Metaphysik der Sitten* is unmistakable: "Der kategorische Imperativ, der überhaupt nur aussagt, was Verbind-

seem to be two separate volitions which are independent of each other, while Kant's formula is that in the very maxim of our action and *because* of it we must take account of its universalizability. The maxim holds for my own action, if it is moral, *only in so far as* I can will it to hold as a maxim for others. Any maxim that passes the test of universalization is legally permissible; there is nothing wrong or unreasonable in my willing to put my name in my book, or indeed in willing that others should do so too. But only the maxim which is a principle of action for me *because* I regard it as binding on rational beings generally is a maxim having moral status.

Under conditional categorical imperatives, therefore, we must distinguish two subtypes: (I) An imperative which, if followed universally, would bring no opposition or antagonism into the relations among personal beings—legal (i.e., legally possible) imperatives; and (II) an imperative which, if followed universally, would bring about such antagonism and opposition—illegal imperatives.

Type (*b*) categorical imperatives are unconditional. They must meet two tests: (I) the test of universalizability, by which they are certified as legally correct, and (II) the test of motive. The latter is the requirement that the motive for their fulfillment shall be found in the fact (or belief) that they are *legal*. An imperative like "Do not lie" constrains me to a moral action and is itself apodictic only when it is addressed to my motive to obey it as valid for and obligatory upon others too. An im-

---

lichkeit sei, ist: Handle nach einer Maxime, welche *zugleich* als ein allgemeines Gesetz gelten kann! — Deine Handlungen mußt du also *zuerst* nach ihrem subjectiven Grundsatze betrachten; ob aber dieser Grundsatz auch objektiv gültig sei, kannst du nur daran erkennen, daß, weil deine Vernunft ihm der Probe unterwirft, durch *denselben* dich *zugleich* als allgemein gesetzgebend zu denken, er sich zu einer solchen allgemeinen Gesetzgebung qualifiziere." (Vorländer, 28; Ak., VI, 224; italics mine.)

perative may bind me legally, i.e., may validly restrict my freedom of arbitrary action, regardless of my motive. In this event
the imperative is external and belongs to jurisprudence and not
to ethics. Other criteria than universalizability may be required
to certify them as "practically right," but in the case of negative imperatives such as *"Do not commit perjury"* the criterion
of universalizability probably suffices. My motive to obey an
imperative like "Write your name in your book" is not expressed in the imperative, as it might be in a hypothetical imperative: "If you want your books returned, write your name
in them." But certainly in this case, the *universal* applicability
of the imperative is not *my* motive for obedience to it.

It is, I think, safe to say that all categorical imperatives
that are in any sense right, and not mere unreasoned and unreasonable commands, either are apodictic or are elliptical
assertoric hypothetical imperatives. The categorical imperatives of the second type, therefore, which are of any philosophical interest, are equivalent to imperatives of type (*a*).[36] This is
because (*a*) and (*c*) are modally alike, and their formal differences are of little or no philosophical interest.[37]

Unconditional (apodictic) hypothetical imperatives

The last type of imperative, (*d*), is the unconditional or apodictic hypothetical, and we must consider it in relation both to the
apodictic categorical and to conditional hypothetical imperatives.

[36] It is in view of this fact that Kant calls the pragmatic imperative a
hypothetical imperative even when the protasis ("Because you want to be
happy . . .") is suppressed. But since "hypothetical" is normally a formal
concept, it would be better to call such an imperative "assertoric" when
it has no explicit antecedent.

[37] They are both called "heteronomous imperatives" by Manfred Moritz,
Studien zum Pflichtbegriff in Kants kritscher Ethik (Lund: C. W. K.
Gleerup, 1951), ch. 2, § 10.

An imperative can be both apodictic and hypothetical if its protasis is itself obligation-creating. Obligation-creating protases state problematically that the person to whom the imperative is directed either (a) has performed a certain kind of action which creates an obligation, e.g., has made a promise, signed a contract, taken a vow, or the like; or (b) is in a certain state or condition which is in part defined by the assumption of special duties and which "contextually implies" specific duties, e.g., is a soldier, a physician, a priest, the only man near the scene of an accident, etc. While the first type of obligation is included under what have been called "*prima facie* obligations" by Ross, I shall refer to the second kind as "*qua*-obligations"; thus, as a soldier, I may have the *qua*-obligation to do certain actions which I am not obligated to do as a citizen. If the state which creates the *qua*-obligation is one freely assumed by a moral act, the two types of obligation merge; otherwise they may differ or even conflict. *Qua*-obligations, like *prima facie* obligations, may not express what I am *in fact* obligated to do.[38]

The hypothetical imperatives discussed by Kant have as their protases statements of conditions which are not obligation-creating but are statements of natural facts. Mr. Singer, who has recently studied such imperatives in Kant's work, concludes that Kant's failure to distinguish between these two dif-

---

[38] It is incorrect to say, as is often said, that Kant cannot take account of so-called "conflicting obligations." They do not arise in the *Grundlegung* and the *Critique of Practical Reason*, for there he is concerned only with the formulae for categorical imperatives, and is not concerned with the casuistical problems which arise only on the level of first-order imperatives. He cites them only as examples. In the *Metaphysik der Sitten* he does discuss the concept of "conflicting duties" and denies that the concept is correct, since in any case it is my duty in fact to do only one thing; but he admits the problem of "conflicting grounds of obligation," and this is the problem often erroneously called that of "conflicts of duties." Cf. *Metaphysik der Sitten*, Einleitung, Sec. IV (Vorländer, 27; Ak., VI, 224).

ferent types of conditions in hypothetical imperatives had the unfortunate effect of causing Kant to shift "from thinking of a categorical imperative as one not conditional upon any purposes of the *agent* to thinking of it as not being conditional upon *anything at all*."[39] Hence one source of Kant's rigorism, as in the essay on the alleged right to lie.

In this essay I do not propose to examine the question of Kant's rigorism directly, or to discuss further, in Kantian terms, the important distinction between *prima facie* obligations, *qua*-obligations, and real obligations. My purpose here is only to point out the manner in which he could have distinguished hypothetical assertoric and problematic imperatives, which he called hypothetical imperatives *simpliciter*, and hypothetical apodictic imperatives, which he did not discuss at all.

In judgments in hypothetical form, we may distinguish between two relations of antecedent and consequent. First, there are judgments in which this relation is real and synthetical: "If there are clouds, it will rain." Second, there are judgments in which the relation is analytic and logical: "If a man is a bachelor, he has no wife." The former can be roughly translated into categorical judgments that are synthetic: "Cloudy

[39] Marcus G. Singer, "The Categorical Imperative," *Philosophical Review*, LXIII (1954), 577–591 at 581. A similar point is made by A. N. Prior, *Logic and the Basis of Ethics* (Oxford: Clarendon Press, 1949), pp. 40–41. Rashdall had earlier written in the same vein: "Kant . . . confuses the inclusion of an exception *in* a moral rule with the admission of an exception *to* a moral rule. He does not recognize that the difference between a rule with an exception and a grammatically categorical rule is often purely a verbal one" (*The Theory of Good and Evil*, Vol. I, p. 116). Mr. Hare (*op. cit.*, pp. 50 ff.) discusses in this connection the difference between "occasional exceptions" and "classes of exceptions." The latter can be specified *in* the rule without affecting its apodicticity, and Mr. Hare says that when so specified the rule is "not looser than it was before, but stricter" (p. 53).

days are rainy days," and the latter can be strictly translated into analytic categorical judgments: "Bachelors are unmarried men."

Similarly, there are two types of relation between antecedent and consequent in hypothetical imperatives. The relation is different in "If you want to keep your feet dry, wear your rubbers," and in "If you make a promise, keep it." Unlike hypothetical judgments of both types, which can be translated into categorical judgments, the former imperative cannot be translated into a categorical imperative having the same meaning and scope of relevance. It does not say, "Wear your rubbers," or, if it says this it does so only to those who do not wish to wet their feet.

The hypothetical imperative of the second type becomes, through only verbal change, "Keep your promises." Now while this imperative is not strictly universal, since it contains "your," its address is not as specific as that of the imperative "Wear your rubbers."[40]

If the imperative "Wear your rubbers" is obeyed, it is not obeyed by anyone because it is a *general* imperative; the reasons why it is obeyed may be stated only in an expanded protasis of the corresponding hypothetical. In this respect, "If you make a promise, keep it" differs from "If you would preserve your good name, keep your promise." The categorical imperative corresponding to the former of these commands is an apodictic imperative under the formula of a categorical imperative; the categorical imperative enunciated in the same sentence (i.e., "Keep your promise") but corresponding to the hypothetical of the first type ("If you would keep your good

[40] Mr. Hare (*op cit.*, pp. 187 ff.), recognizing that no imperative in ordinary English is strictly universal, proposes an "enriched imperative mood," and in this there would be a universal imperative corresponding to "Keep your promise" but not one corresponding to "Wear your rubbers."

name . . .") is not apodictic, does not have the scope of the apodictic, and expresses no necessity.

The hypothetical imperative such as "If you wish to keep your library intact, write your name in your books" has as its antecedent a factual condition, which is related to the consequent only through an empirical causal relation. The declarative sentence reporting obedience to the consequent, i.e., "You do in fact write your name in your books," reports a fact believed to be a causal condition of the end entertained in the antecedent. The fact that a man desires to keep his library intact does not create an obligation to write his name in the book. (He may indeed say, "To keep my books from being stolen, I have been obliged to put my name in each volume," but he does not say, "I have had an obligation to put my name in my books." Wants are not the sort of things that create obligations, though to satisfy them we may be "obliged" to do certain other things. "To be obliged to put my name in each book" merely calls attention to the causal necessity or efficacy of an irksome means to a desired end; but "to have an obligation to put the University book plate in each book" calls attention to a *qua*-obligation of the University Librarian. To be obliged to do something is not, etymology to the contrary notwithstanding, the same as to have an obligation to do it.)

The obedience to the imperative's consequent where the antecedent is obligation-creating is not a means to a state of affairs desiderated or mentioned problematically in the antecedent. The affirming of the consequent by obedience to the imperative is not a means to the accomplishment of the state of affairs envisaged in the antecedent of the hypothetical imperative of the second type; the promise has been made, and we do not say that "fulfilling a promise" is a means to the obedience to the imperative—it *is* the obedience. And certainly fulfilling a promise is not a means to the making of a promise, and the obligation to fulfill a promise is not dependent upon whether the fulfilling of the promise is in fact a means to certain purposes entertained in the original making of the promise.

In all these respects, the relation of antecedent to consequent differs in the two types of hypothetical imperative. Mr. Jackson[41] aptly sums up the differences by speaking of the apodosis of hypothetical imperatives of the second type as being "derivatively practically necessary" while the apodosis in those of the first type, which command a means, he calls "derivatively theoretically necessary." Only moral knowledge is required for the practical derivation of apodosis from an obligation-creating protasis, while theoretical knowledge of the world is required for learning what one must do in order to keep his feet dry or to preserve his library.

Given the imperative, "If you want to keep your feet dry, wear your rubbers," one may intelligently ask, "Why?" and expect an informative answer: "Because the ground is wet, because rubber is impermeable to water. . . ." But, in Mr. Nowell-Smith's idiom, it is "logically odd" to ask, "Why should I keep my promise?" as a response to "If you make a promise, keep it."[42] The protasis here seems to be a sufficient condition for the apodosis, even though it may not *in fact* be sufficient since the apodosis may be *only a prima facie* or *qua*-obligation. But if the question is asked, "I know I made a promise, but why should I keep it?" the question seems to be one that could not be answered by new information on the same level as the fact that a promise has been made;[43] the only appropriate answer to

[41] Reginald Jackson, "Kant's Distinction between Categorical and Hypothetical Imperatives," *Proceedings of the Aristotelian Society,* 1942–43, pp. 131–166 at 143.

[42] Kant would have regarded it as "logically odd." Cf. *Metaphysik der Sitten, Rechtslehre,* § 19 (Vorländer, 86; Ak., VI, 273).

[43] New information on the facts would be relevant only in the decision as to whether the *prima facie* or *qua*-obligation is really binding.

this question would be an exposition of an ethical theory, in which "promise-keeping" would be put under a more general theoretical rubric, etc. Additional reasons to justify this particular apodosis might, in fact, tend to weaken the awareness of the moral connection between promise-making and promise-keeping;[44] and I think this is the principal reason why Kant preferred examples of obligations in which any additional factual information might tend to obscure and impugn the purity of the moral connection between making a promise and keeping it.[45]

I do not say that "You have made a promise" is a sufficient reason for "Keep your promise." Whether I am in fact obligated to keep a promise may depend upon much besides the fact that I have made it, and other facts as well as other obligation-creatings may be relevant to the decision.[46] But that I desire to keep my feet dry is *never* a sufficient reason, and nobody ever believed it was a sufficient reason, for wearing rubbers; and even if I state the sufficient condition, including all relevant facts, the connection between them and the hypothetical imperative "If you wish to keep your feet dry, wear your rubbers" is not like that in "If you make a promise, keep it."

A full theory of apodictic hypothetical imperatives is not to be found in Kant. But it is not difficult to see what some of its features would be. Such imperatives would be first-order imperatives justified by the formula of what Kant called the categorical imperative, but which we have found to be a formula

---

[44] *Grundlegung* 394 (62) [p. 13 above].

[45] I have discussed Kant's examples from this point of view in "Sir David Ross on Duty and Purpose in Kant," *Philosophy and Phenomenological Research*, XVI (1955), 98–107 at 104.

[46] That such considerations are permitted by Kant, how they are evaluated, and what they are in Kant's work have been exhaustively explored by Paton, "An Alleged Right to Lie. A Program in Kantian Ethics," *Kant-Studien*, XLV (1954), 190–203; and by Singer, *op. cit.*

of an apodictic imperative regardless of its grammatical form. This formula would be a criterion of the admissability of various kinds of conditions into the protases of the hypothetical imperative that is apodictic. It would tell us what conditions could legitimately and what conditions could not legitimately be included without destroying the apodicticity. The formula would make it possible for us to answer the Kantian question, "Would I be willing for all men to obey the imperative, 'Do A'?" in the form, "Would I be willing for all men under condition C to obey the imperative, 'If C, do A'?" *without trivialization*, since the range of C could be determined by examining the effect of the various possible C's upon the apodicticity of "Do A."[47] It might permit us to show why, for instance, "If you make a promise and find it inconvenient to fulfill it, don't fulfill it" is not an apodictic imperative, while "If you make a promise and find that an innocent person will die if you fulfill it, don't fulfill it" might be an apodictic imperative.

Though a full theory of such imperatives is not developed anywhere in Kant, the *Metaphysik der Sitten* is filled with clues as to how it could be done; and such a theory is a desirable addendum to the theory that seems to require moral rigidity and is a desirable foundation for his casuistry. The apparent incompatibility of such hypothetical imperatives with Kant's best-known ethical principle vanishes when we realize that "categorical" was not the most suitable adjective for Kant to use in describing the moral imperative.

University of Rochester, New York

[47] Cf. W. I. Matson, "Kant as a Casuist," *Journal of Philosophy*, LI (1954), 855–860.

Paul Dietrichson / Kant's

criteria of universalizability

It might seem that a sufficient number of writers have already explained and criticized Kant's universalizability criteria so thoroughly that nothing new of any importance can be said about this aspect of his thought. His universalizability criteria have not been explained satisfactorily, however, in any of the numerous commentaries and critical works I have read. There is therefore, in my opinion, ample room for further study of this important phase of his moral philosophy. His doctrine is of interest not only to historians of philosophical ideas. Various contemporary philosophers are attempting to work out a satisfactory universalizability criterion for testing maxims of action.

Based on the author's article "When Is a Maxim Fully Universalizable?" KANT-STUDIEN, *Band 55, Heft 2 (1964), pp. 143–170. Printed by permission of the author and editors.*

Judging from my knowledge of their attempts, I would say that these philosophers could profit a good deal from making a more careful examination of Kant's view on the subject.

My purpose in this article is neither to defend nor to attack the Kantian doctrine of universalizability, but simply to clarify certain aspects of it. It might seem that my refutations of certain traditional objections to his doctrine are out of place in a discussion that is meant to be purely interpretive. But they are not. My criticism of certain critics is simply part of my attempt to clarify Kant's meaning, namely by showing that some of the views attributed to him by those critics are not his views. For the purpose of further clarification, I also consider some purely hypothetical objections to Kant's universalizability doctrine and show that such objections would be based on misinterpretations of his position.

It is important to keep in mind that the Kantian universalizability criteria are not criteria for determining whether a person has moral worth (fulfills "the spirit" of the moral law) but only criteria for determining whether an action is objectively correct (fulfills "the letter" of the moral law). Kant insists, of course, that if an action is to be objectively correct and also is to make the agent morally worthy, it must, in addition to being based on a universalizable maxim, be *motivated* in a special manner. In other words, it must proceed, not only "according to duty," but also "from duty." The agent must strive to approximate, to the best of his ability, a motivational ideal of his own pure practical reason, namely the ideal of *making certain* that he adopts as his *sufficient* incentive his pure (merely rationally elicited) interest in obedience based on nothing but his feeling of reverent respect for the moral law. This motivational ideal is transcendent, i.e., humanly unattainable. We are incapable of becoming fully transparent to ourselves, because we are not exclusively rational beings but also sensuously affected beings. We can therefore never *be* absolutely certain that even in a single case we adopt our pure interest in obedience, based on reverent respect for the moral law, as our *sufficient* incentive for acting in conformity with the universalizability requirement of the law. As far as the mental disposition of our action is concerned, our duty is therefore only to *strive* to approximate as fully as we can the transcendent motivational ideal of pure practical reason. According to Kant, a persistent *striving* of this kind is not a *means* to purity of heart; it *constitutes* purity of heart, fulfillment of the requirement to act "from duty." I shall not attempt to discuss how we are to determine whether we are in the process of developing such purity of heart.

The above comments on Kant's doctrine of moral motivation are very sketchy. I have, however, in a separate article explained what Kant means by the requirement to act "from duty" and how one, according to him, is to determine whether one is satisfying this motivational requirement.[1] My present purpose is therefore to explain Kant's procedure for determining whether an action proceeds "according to duty" (i.e., in conformity with the universalizability requirements of the moral law).

I *The moral law and the typic*

One point that should be stressed at the outset of any analysis of Kant's conception of acting "according to duty" is this: even if a person has a crystal clear awareness of the universalizability requirements of the moral law, such insight by itself does *not* enable him to judge whether a given maxim satisfies the law. In other words, the moral law as such cannot be applied

[1] "What Does Kant Mean by 'Acting From Duty'?" *Kant-Studien*, Band 53, Heft 3 (1961/62), pp. 279–288.

directly as a standard for determining whether or not our maxims are of a morally legitimate kind. The reason for this is quite simple. The moral law (the categorical imperative) springs from our *pure* reason, i.e., from our reason in that mode of its operation which is not to any extent conditioned by *empirical* (material) factors. Issuing as it does from pure reason, the moral law is therefore by necessity a merely *formal* paradigm, an *abstract* norm, completely *indeterminate* in so far as reference to the empirical dimension of reality is concerned. Our *maxims*, on the other hand, which need to be tested in some way or other by this prescriptive law, are *material* principles, *concrete* principles, namely *empirically determinate* (and subjective) rules of voluntary action.

The categorical imperative is formulated as follows in the *Foundations:* "*Act only on such a maxim that you could also want it to become a universal law.*"[2] I do not have an applicable criterion for testing my maxim, however, unless—in addition to knowing that I should be able to want my maxim to be a universal law—I also know *what* such a universal law would be a universal law *of*. The same categorical imperative is stated

---

[2] *Grundlegung zur Metaphysik der Sitten*, Cassirer ed., Vol. IV, p. 279. Cf. Thomas K. Abbott's trans., *Kant's Critique of Practical Reason and Other Works on the Theory of Ethics* (6th ed., London: Longmans, Green and Co., 1909, reprinted 1954), p. 38. Cf. also Lewis W. Beck's trans., *Immanuel Kant: Critique of Practical Reason and Other Writings in Moral Philosophy* (Chicago: University of Chicago Press, 1950), p. 80 [p. 44 above].

The translations in this paper are my own, based on the Ernst Cassirer edition of Kant's work: *Immanuel Kants Werke*, Vols. I–XI (Berlin: Bruno Cassirer, 1912-22). (I use italics where extended type is used in the original. Words in bold type in my translation correspond to words printed in extra-bold type in the original.) As far as the argument for my interpretation of Kant's ideas is concerned, I could have adhered to any one of the standard translations of the passages I cite. I believe, however, that where my translation differs from the standard ones (e.g., from Abbott's and Beck's) it gives a more precise rendering of the original.

in a somewhat different manner in the second *Critique:* "So act that the maxim of your will could any time hold also as principle of a universal law-giving."[3] Again, the problem is that the completely abstract categorical imperative of my pure practical reason in no way defines the nature of that system of things to which I should be able to want to give a universal law modeled on the principle of my maxim.

So far, then, I have no concretely applicable criterion for determining whether a given maxim is or is not of a morally legitimate kind (universalizable as prescribed by the categorical imperative). In the form in which it issues from my pure reason, the categorical imperative provides me with no directive as to what *sort* of universal law I should be able to want to become modeled on my maxim of action. Nor do I get the needed directive from my moral feeling: my feeling of reverent respect for duty. If by some applicable rational criterion I could know that my subjective behavioral rule *is* a legitimate (universalizable) one, my feeling of reverent respect for the categorical imperative could serve as an *incentive* for *acting* on that rule. But my feeling of reverent respect, pure and elevated though it be, can, of course, not serve as a criterion for judging whether my subjective rule of action (my maxim) is in principle objectifiable in such a manner as to have the kind of universal validity that is demanded by the moral law. "This feeling (under the name of moral feeling) . . . does not serve for estimation of the actions nor, indeed, as the foundation of the objective law of duty itself, but merely as the *incentive.* . . ."[4] So the important question as to how we are to go about *applying* the purely formal, abstract, existentially indeterminate moral law as a criterion for evaluating the *material*

[3] *Kritik der praktischen Vernunft*, Cassirer ed., Vol. V, p. 35. (Abbott, p. 119; Beck, p. 142.)

[4] *Ibid.*, p. 84. (Abbott, 169; Beck, 184.) My italics.

maxims of our particular actions in the concretely existing phenomenal world is still left unanswered. My pure practical reason commands me to act in a certain way, namely on maxims that are fully universalizable in principle. But it does not inform me how I might determine whether or not any given maxim satisfies this requirement of universalizability (moral legitimacy).

There is obviously a need for some principle of *mediation*, whereby the purely abstract moral law can be made concretely applicable as a standard for determining whether such-and-such a material maxim of voluntary action is morally legitimate. Kant meets this need; what he calls the *"type"* (*Typus*) of the moral law is precisely a concretizing of the moral law, namely a restatement of the abstract moral law in a symbolically concrete form. If one is to get a clear understanding of the overall structure of Kant's moral philosophy, it is important, therefore, to understand what he means by the typification-procedure he calls the "typic" (*Typik*). It is surprising that Kant's commentators and critics have not devoted more attention to the typic. Its nature and function is not explained satisfactorily in any work on Kant that I am familiar with.

Before I attempt to develop my interpretation of the typic, however, I shall try to clear up a rather persistent misunderstanding of Kant's view as to the relationship between the moral law and maxims of action.

It is sometimes maintained that Kant's moral philosophy is absurdly formalistic, nothing but a philosopher's pipe dream, because (so the argument runs) he claims to be able to deduce moral maxims from the moral law, i.e., from a purely formal normative principle. If he had in fact made such a claim, his moral philosophy would, of course, be palpable nonsense. For, as he himself has pointed out repeatedly, no material principle can be deduced from a purely formal principle, or from any number of purely formal principles for that matter. So if our morally legitimate maxims were to be deduced from the moral law, we would end up with maxims completely devoid of determinate empirical reference—devoid of material content. Our moral maxims would in that case be merely *formal* (devoid of empirical reference) and, therefore, contradictions in terms. A maxim is a practically useful subjective rule of voluntary action in the empirical world. It describes a person's subjective behavior policy in a certain type of empirical circumstances. A maxim containing no reference to any material factor, i.e., no reference to any object of volition (such as, e.g., under such-and-such conditions developing one's talents or letting them rust, giving truthful or deceptive promises, helping people or remaining inactive in respect to their needs), could not possibly be of any practical use to us. In other words, it would not *be* a maxim of action. But the point is that Kant does not say that moral maxims can be *deduced* from the purely formal paradigm that he calls "the moral law." What he says is merely that our maxims are not morally legitimate unless they *conform* to this purely formal paradigm. He makes clear that it is possible for us to be quite arbitrary when we decide to *adopt* this or that maxim as our subjective principle (private rule) of voluntary action in such-and-such a type of empirical circumstances. What *cannot* in any way be an arbitrary matter, however, is the moral *appraising* of our maxim. Such appraising, i.e., our testing whether or not the maxim is of a morally legitimate kind, is to be done in a strictly *rational* manner. For we are to appraise the maxim in terms of a formal principle of our own pure practical *reason*, which prescribes that the maxim should be fit to serve as the model for a universal type of law-giving. As Kant puts the matter, "maxims of actions might be *arbitrary*, and are only *subject to the restricting condition of fitness* for a universal law-giving, which is a formal principle of actions."[5]—So what Kant is saying is, not that we can *deduce* material maxims from the formal principle called the moral law, but that we can, and should, *appraise* our actual material maxims and our contemplated material maxims in terms of that formal principle. There is a big difference between deducing and appraising. And what is more, he insists that it is impossible for us to make any practical use of the purely abstract principle of the moral law as a standard for appraising our material maxims, unless we first express the principle in the form of a *type*. So any objection to the effect that Kant claims to deduce moral maxims from the moral law is a completely stillborn objection.

As for the moral law itself, Kant certainly does not claim to have invented it. "But who would want to introduce and, as it were, first discover a new principle of all virtue? just as if the world before him should have been ignorant or in thorough-going error as to what duty was."[6] To have worked out, as Kant claims to have done, a *new formula* for the commonly recognized moral principle might seem like a trifling philosophical contribution. "But whoever knows what it means to a mathematician to have a *formula* which defines completely accurately and prevents one from mistaking what is to be done in order to work a problem, will not regard a formula, which does this in respect to all duty as such, as something insignificant and superfluous."[7] Kant does not believe, then, that one needs any special philosophical training or acumen in order to recognize the standard of moral obligation: ". . . no science

---

[5] *Die Metaphysik der Sitten*, Cassirer, VII, 199. (Abbott, 300.) "Subject to the restricting condition of fitness" italicized by me.

[6] *Kritik der praktischen Vernunft*, p. 8n. (Abbott, 93n.; Beck, 123n.)

[7] *Ibid.*

and philosophy is required in order to know what one has to do to be honest and good, indeed even wise and virtuous."[8] In the first section of the *Foundations* he shows, at least to his own satisfaction, that ordinary people have a sound working knowledge of the moral law and make moral judgments in terms of it (even though he recognizes, of course, that they do not conceive this law in the technically precise form in which he expresses it in his philosophy). That he is able to show that ordinary people have such a knowledge should not, he thinks, come as a surprise to anyone. "One might indeed have presumed in advance that the knowledge of what every man is obliged to do, and therefore also to know, would be within the reach of even the commonest man. Here we cannot but regard with admiration how great an advantage the practical faculty of judgment has over the theoretical in common human understanding."[9] According to Kant, then, common sense is perfectly capable of making a practical application of the normative law (categorical imperative) of pure practical reason. But Kant maintains, it will be remembered, that it is impossible for us to *make* a practical application of the law of pure practical reason unless we think this law in terms of some concretizing principle. He should therefore be able to show that his "typification of the moral law" is nothing but a technical and more precise formulation of a concretized version of the moral law employed in moral judgments by common sense.

It seems to me that the best approach to an understanding of what the typic is, and of what it is not, is to recall a mediation-procedure that Kant explained in the first *Critique*, namely the mediation-procedure he called the *schematism*. A good

[8] *Grundlegung zur Metaphysik der Sitten*, p. 260. (Abbott, 20; Beck, 64 [p. 23 above].)

[9] *Ibid.* [pp. 23–24 above].

deal of misguided criticism of Kant's ethics has resulted from a failure to see sufficiently clearly how the typic is—and why it *has* to be—in *kind* different from a schematism.

It will be recalled from the first *Critique* that the transcendental categories of the understanding could not be applied *directly* to the raw data of sensory intuition. A category is formal and universal; a sensory manifold is material and individual. If those heterogeneous entities are to be synthesized, some appropriate mediating factor must be provided. In other words, a *schematization* had to be worked out in order to explain how the purely abstract, existentially indeterminate categories could be applied to concrete individual sensory contents so as to organize and structure those contents and enable us to know actual and possible objects of a phenomenal world. Since the function of the schemata is to serve as a mediation between the categories and sensory manifolds, the schemata must have something in common with the universality of the categories as well as with the individuality of the sensory contents. Kant finds, of course, that one of the pure (i.e., non-empirical) a priori forms of sensory intuition in general, namely the pure form of temporal intuition, can serve as the basis of such a mediation-procedure. The pure form of temporal intuition is individual but has universality in that it characterizes all our empirical intuition, i.e., is a form of all actual and possible inner and outer sense perceptions. It can be said to be particularizable, namely in the sense that it contains various modes of possible time-determinations (time-series, time-content, time-order, time-scope) pertaining to diverse objects of possible experience. Our transcendental productive imagination "collects," so to speak, the raw data that are intuited by inner and outer sense and casts those data in its own mold of the form of time. Inner and outer sensory data thereby become presented to us in a temporally schematized manner.

Our transcendental productive imagination also supplies each of the twelve categories of the understanding with a special time-schema: a transcendental determination of time in accordance with a rule appropriate to the given category.—The common form of inner and outer phenomena in accordance with the three categories of *quantity* is number. Transcendental productive imagination can represent numerical unities, pluralities and totalities as constructions of the time-series itself and thereby schematize the categories of unity, plurality and totality. Kant finds that the three remaining triads of categories can also be cast in appropriate schemata of the form of time. When we make cognitive judgments concerning the nature and existence of phenomenal objects, we *literally impose* the *schematized* categories upon intuited inner and outer sensuous manifolds, which are themselves cast in a general time-schema. The important point to note about the cognitive mediation-procedure that Kant calls a "schematism," then, is this: the schemata become *constitutive* of the categorized sensory manifolds; i.e., of all appearances (phenomena) that are actually known by us, and of all appearances that can come to be known by us. The schemata *literally* become *properties of the objects of nature.*—So much for the schematism.

The *moral law* (the law of pure practical reason) is an empirically empty principle, a purely *formal* principle, namely a norm prescribing that I should always act on such a maxim that I could also consistently want a universal law to become modeled on it. A *maxim*, on the other hand, is an empirically determinate principle, a *material* principle, namely a specific subjective rule of action in the phenomenal world. Any human maxim of voluntary action is of the following structure: when I am in such-and-such a type of empirical circumstances, I will adopt such-and-such a rule as my policy of action. It is obvious that the completely formal (empirically empty) law of pure practical reason is not a standard of evaluation that can be applied directly to our material (empirically determinate) rules of action, any more than the universal, completely formal categories of transcendental understanding are frameworks of cognition that can be applied directly to our particular material manifolds of sensory intuition. As already suggested, some kind of *mediation-procedure* has to be worked out. It might seem reasonable to suggest that what is needed is a schematizing of the moral law (i.e., of the categorical and universal normative rule of pure practical reason), so that "what is asserted in the rule universally *(in abstracto)* . . . [could be] applied to an action *in concreto.*"[10]

It would certainly be convenient if a schematism would once again do as a mediation-procedure. But if there is anything Kant is emphatic about, it is that *the moral law cannot be schematized.* It is important to understand clearly his reasons for insisting on this point.

The moral law is not, and cannot be made to function as, a law of the world of *nature*, i.e., a law of necessary causal sequences of events. It is a law of a non-empirical (supersensory) realm, which Kant calls the realm of *freedom*. It is a law of freedom, even of the freedom of a holy being. The freedom of a holy being would be no mere *capacity* to act autonomously, i.e., in complete unison with pure reason's conception of the good. Its freedom would be *absolute* autonomy, namely in the sense that such a being would *inevitably* act autonomously. (Cf. Augustine's conception of the freedom that will be bestowed on those who are elected for heavenly bliss: *non posse peccare.*) In other words, it would be impossible for a holy being to *avoid* acting on maxims that could be consistently willed to hold as universal laws.[11] In its own right, the moral

---

[10] *Kritik der praktischen Vernunft*, p. 75. (Abbott, 159; Beck, 176.)
[11] Cf. *Ibid.*, p. 37. (Abbott, 121; Beck, 144.)

law is not a prescriptive law. It is a *descriptive* law, a law descriptive of the freedom of a holy being, namely the following law: every maxim of a completely perfect volition is grounded exclusively in reason and is capable of being consistently thought and consistently willed to hold as principle of a universal law-giving.

Our freedom is of a limited kind: not absolute (incorruptible) autonomy, but merely an *ability* to act autonomously. We can decide to act on such maxims that we could consistently want them to become universal laws. We can also decide to act on maxims that do not have such universal validity. (Even when we act on fully universalizable maxims, we might do so in a manner that is *motivationally* heteronomous, namely for the sole sake of attaining certain personal advantages or escaping certain personal disadvantages.) But even though our freedom is in kind different from that of a holy being, the moral law is still a law of *our* freedom as well as of the freedom of a holy being. We are rational agents affected by sensuous impulses and we have an innate propensity to evil. It is therefore unavoidable that we will sometimes be tempted to act on maxims of such a kind that we could not consistently want them to hold as principles of a universal law-giving. In other words, we are sometimes tempted to act on maxims which would not conform to the law that is descriptive of the actions of a holy being. When we become aware of the law of holiness, then, we cannot help but feel respect and reverence for it; as temptable beings we come to recognize that we always *ought* to act on the kind of maxims on which a holy (purely rational) being would *inescapably* act. We therefore unavoidably come to regard the descriptive law of moral holiness as subjecting our freely choosing nature to an unconditional *imperative*. In short, we find that we have to regard the moral law as a *prescriptive* law of our limited kind of freedom.[12]

[12] Cf. *Ibid.*, p. 90. (Abbott, 175; Beck, 189.)

Freedom is according to Kant a supersensory efficacy. The moral law is therefore *a law of the noumenal realm*, namely a law of free noumenal agents. The nature of our freedom is not capable of being grasped by our introspection, which is dependent on sensory intuition; but the reality of our freedom (*that* we are free) is guaranteed by our consciousness of being duty-bound to conform in our actions to the moral law which is revealed to us by our own pure practical reason. According to Kant, we must therefore assume that our deliberately chosen actions, as observed by us through inner and outer sense, are phenomenal manifestations of our free agency as noumenal beings.[13]

I need to make the abstract moral law concretely applicable as a standard for appraising the specific material maxims that I, as an empirical being, act on or might consider acting on. I must therefore in some manner restate the empirically empty moral law in terms of *some principle of the empirical realm*. However, if I were to attach such a concretizing principle to the moral law as a literal *schema* of that law, I would be making an untenable claim, because I would be claiming that a principle of the empirical realm can become a *constitutive part* of a law pertaining to *non*-empirical beings, namely free noumenal beings. So when I am to reformulate the moral law in terms of the *typic*, I must realize clearly what the limited function of the typic is supposed to be. The only function it can properly serve is to supply the moral law with a *non-constitutive*, purely heuristic, illustrative mediation-principle enabling me to make use of the moral law as a practical standard for appraising my material maxims. The gap between the

---

[13] For the purpose of the present inquiry, it is not necessary to make any further analysis of Kant's controversial and complex conception of man's ability to make free decisions. I prefer to deal with that subject in a separate discussion.

abstract moral law and my material maxims of actions cannot be bridged, then, by a literal schematizing of the moral law. What is needed is a merely *figurative substitute* for a schematization of the moral law, i.e., a *typification*.

The problem of expressing the principle of the abstract moral law in terms of a *Typus* is analogous to that of a playwright who wants to portray a certain virtue in a morality play.

A purely formal idea of a certain moral virtue has no concreteness as an idea for dramatic presentation in a play. The playwright therefore devises an artistic construct in the form of a fictional character (a *dramatis persona*) which in a symbolically concrete manner *typifies* the abstract principle of the virtue he wants to portray. In other words, he develops a heuristic dramatic construct which serves as its *type*, without thereby in any way implying that he is describing any *actual* person when he characterizes the *dramatis persona*. The *dramatis persona* is simply a practical device for symbolizing concretely the abstract idea of the virtue in question.

I have to proceed in a similar manner if I am to succeed in concretizing the abstract principle of the moral law.

The purely formal principle of the moral law has no concreteness as a criterion for appraising my material maxims. I therefore devise a rational construct in the form of a fictional idea which in a symbolically concrete manner *typifies* the abstract principle of the moral law I want to apply. In other words, I develop a heuristic philosophical construct which serves as its *type*, without thereby in any way implying that I am describing any *actual* state of affairs when I characterize the typified moral law. The typified moral law is simply a practical device for symbolizing concretely the abstract principle of the moral law.

My practical device must be of a rational kind, because it

is to serve the function of concretizing a categorical command of pure *reason*. I am commanded by my pure practical reason to act as though the maxim of my action were to become, by my wish, a universal law. As already mentioned, when I ask, *What* would such a universal law be a universal law *of*? I find that no answer can be gleaned from the abstract formula of duty. I therefore have to reformulate the abstract categorical imperative in a manner that symbolizes it concretely without distorting the principle of the imperative itself. The idea I am to use for the practical purpose of making the abstract categorical imperative concretely applicable as a standard for appraising my empirical maxims in the sensory world must be a fiction, but a fiction of a rational kind. The only device I can use is to restate the abstract principle of the categorical imperative so as to make it include reference to the idea of a purely *hypothetical* world of *nature*. The kind of world I shall have to conceive of—and conceive of as though I were a part of it—is one that would be like ours but capable of being arranged according to purely hypothetical *causal* laws (i.e., *natural* laws, *descriptive* laws). According to the thought-experiment that I need to conduct, my actual maxim in the phenomenal world is to serve as a principle on which would be modeled a universal causal law holding for all persons in a counterfactual system of nature of which I am to envisage myself as though I were a part. My action proceeds "according to duty" (i.e., satisfies the "legality" requirement of the moral law) if and only if I could consistently want an *objective law*, namely a universal causal (natural) law, to become modeled on the principle of the *subjective rule*, the maxim, of my action. Such a hypothetical causal law would be a universal causal law of *voluntary action*, namely a natural law according to which everyone, whenever he is in circumstances of the *kind* I in fact now happen to be in, would invariably (by causal necessity) act on the same subjective rule as the one I now in fact act on. That any imaginable person (including myself) in such-and-such circumstances—*within the hypothetical world* that I have to envision—would act in conformity with a causal law of volition patterned on the principle of my maxim, would be just as certain as it is, in the actual world, that any stone under such-and-such conditions will move in such-and-such a manner in accordance with the law of gravitation.

Having worked out the device of thinking in terms of a system of nature capable of being arranged according to hypothetical causal laws, I am no longer left with a completely abstract and for practical purposes useless categorical demand to act as though the maxim of my action were to become by my wish a universal law. Just as the medieval author of a morality play typified the abstract idea of a particular virtue by inventing a dramatic construct in the form of a hypothetical person, I have typified the abstract principle of the categorical imperative by inventing a practical construct in the form of a hypothetically constituted natural world. I have developed a concrete and practically useful typification of the abstract categorical imperative. The *typified* categorical imperative, then, is this:

"*Act as though the maxim of your action were to become by your volition* **a universal law of nature.**"[14]

The abstract cognitive categories of our pure theoretical understanding had to be *schematized* before they could be (constitutively) applied to the material manifolds of our sen-

---

[14] *Grundlegung zur Metaphysik der Sitten*, p. 279. (Abbott, 39; Beck, 80 [p. 45 above].) For textual support of my interpretation of the typic of pure practical judgment, see *Kritik der praktischen Vernunft*, pp. 75–79; cf. especially end of 4th paragraph. (Abbott, 159–163; Beck, 176–179. The 4th paragraph in Cassirer ed. is 5th paragraph in Beck's translation.)

The words "universal law of nature" are printed in extra-bold type in the German text; the rest of the words of the sentence are printed in extended type.

sory intuitions. The abstract moral law of our pure practical reason had to be *typified* before it could be (normatively) applied to the material maxims of our voluntary actions. According to Kant, then, we cannot make any practical use of the categorical imperative as a standard for appraising our material maxims in the *actual* sensory world unless we think the idea of a purely *hypothetical* sensory world.

It might seem that this symbolic concretizing of the abstract principle of the moral law is a far-fetched, highly complicated procedure and that it would be very cumbersome to appraise our maxims by reference to the typic. As already suggested, however, Kant is convinced that any rational moral appraisal of maxims in everyday life—however quickly and almost automatically it be made—involves, directly or indirectly, reference to the symbolic expression of the moral law that he calls "the type *(Typus)* of the moral law." His statement of the *Typus* is, according to him, simply a precise and systematic formulation of the principles involved in a concretizing mediation-procedure of a heuristic kind employed in moral judgments at the level of common sense. The common-sense employment of this heuristic device is occasionally quite explicit. "Thus people say: What if *everyone* allowed himself to deceive when he thought it to his advantage, or held it justified to shorten his life as soon as he happened to feel thoroughly weary of it, or regarded with complete indifference the need of others, and you belonged to such an order of things, would you, indeed, be in it with the consent of your will?"[15] According to Kant, then, when people at the level of common sense make moral appraisals, they sometimes quite explicitly think in *universal* terms (". . . everyone . . ."). They also make use of the idea of a world of *nature* capable of being ordered in a *hypothetical* way (". . . *if* everyone allowed himself to . . .

[15] *Kritik der praktischen Vernunft*, p. 77. (Abbott, 161; Beck, 178.)

[act on such-and-such a maxim] . . . and you belonged to *such an order of things* . . .") . And the point is that they use the idea of such a hypothetically structured societal world as a *practical device for testing maxims of action* (". . . would you, indeed, *be* in . . . [such an order of things] . . . with the *consent* of your *will?*"). In short, what may be called *a common-sense version of the typic* is being employed as a standard for appraising maxims in respect to the requirement of legality.

It will be noted that the opening phrase of the above cited passage is, "*Thus people say.*" If one were to focus attention on this phrase and attempt to show that Kant's justification of the principle he calls "the typic of pure practical judgment" is really based on an appeal to ordinary language usage, one would not get very far. Kant's point is not that the typic is to be established by an appeal to ordinary language usage. His point is rather that people who have learned to speak often say the sort of thing he has mentioned, because they have a *pure faculty of judgment (Urteilskraft)*. He maintains that it is impossible for people to make a rational, moral appraisal of maxims unless they, at least in some implicit manner, think in universal terms and by reference to the idea of a hypothetically structured world of nature. And because their own pure power of judgment makes it necessary for them to *think* in that manner when they make moral evaluations of maxims, they often quite explicitly *express* themselves accordingly. So the ordinary language pattern he has referred to is, not a *proof* of the correctness of the typic, but a *manifestation* of the typic that their own *pure power of judgment requires them to use.*

The ability to make practical úse of pure reason is by no means a prerogative of philosophers, according to Kant. As a matter of fact, he points out repeatedly that ordinary people are *more* apt to arrive at a sound understanding of morality than most philosophers are. The majority of those technically trained philosophers who have attempted to explain the origin and nature of moral principles have become preoccupied with and enamoured by *empirically conditioned* reason's inherent tendency to claim that it provides, not only technic-practical principles, but also moral-practical principles. The result has been that a large majority of moral philosophers have ended up with the view that moral principles are *a posteriori* principles. They have used a good deal of intellectual ingenuity and subtlety in an effort to substantiate that claim, which to Kant is a preposterous one.

Kant does not maintain that every single moral appraisal in everyday life involves a direct and explicit reference to what might be called the common-sense typic of pure practical judgment. When a geometrician on one or more occasions has assured himself by his own reason that certain geometric procedures are correct, he does not find it necessary to reassure himself on that score every time he employs those procedures. His use of them becomes very soon a matter of *habit* to him. Likewise, when on certain occasions, *by reference to the* (common-sense) *typic of our pure practical judgment*, we have—in a more or less reflective manner, and perhaps by some intellectual guidance from others—assured ourselves that certain maxims are morally legitimate, we do not on subsequent occasions need to go through fresh acts of reflective moral judgment to reassure ourselves that maxims of that kind are morally sound. In daily living, the majority of our moral appraisals are so much a matter of habit that hardly any effort of reflection is required. If those habits were not at some time or other initiated or at least approved by our own pure judgment employing the typic, however, we would, according to Kant, be amoral imitators rather than morally responsible agents. When Kant at the end of the second *Critique* works out the program of moral education that he calls "the methodology of pure practical reason," he comments at length on the natural development and the importance of moral habit formation.[16] He insists, however, that, for the purpose of technical philosophy, it is necessary to formulate very precisely the principles involved in the fundamental type of moral judgment without which habit patterns of moral appraisal could not be formed.

In the version employed by common sense, the typified moral law might be stated as follows: your rule of action in a given set of circumstances should be such that you could want to live in a world where *everybody* in circumstances of that kind would act on that rule. As Kant points out, common sense usually employs this version of the *Typus* by raising a question involving a moral challenge: "What if *everybody* allowed himself to . . . [act in such-and-such a manner in such-and-such circumstances] . . . and you belonged to such an order of things, would you, indeed, be in it with the consent of your will?" In a form like this, the question is usually precise enough for the practical purpose of making moral judgments. For the purpose of technical philosophy, however, it is important to explicate certain principles that common sense in an implicit manner has recourse to: If there were a *universal law of nature* according to which everybody in such-and-such empirical circumstances would *necessarily* act in such-and-such a way, and you belonged to such a causally arranged system of things, would it be at all *possible* to think consistently that a rational and sensuously affected being, such as you, might, any time whatever, want such a natural law to prevail without exception?—If one wants to state the typified moral law in the manner in which it is involved in this more precise version of the moral question-technique used by common sense, one will probably find that Kant's formulation (which has already been

[16] Cf. *Kritik der praktischen Vernunft*, pp. 171–172. (Abbott, 257–258; Beck, 256.)

cited) is sufficiently precise: *"Act as though the maxim of your action were to become by your volition a* **universal law of nature."**

Let us assume that the principle of a certain maxim of mine is such that I cannot possibly conceive of it as becoming raised to the status of a universal law of nature, because the very principle of the maxim would *contradict itself* if it were to serve in such a universal capacity. In other words, a universal law of nature patterned on the principle of my maxim would be a self-contradictory law and therefore no law at all. It would then be clear to me that my maxim would violate the categorical imperative. My reason tells me that if it were morally legitimate for *me* to act on my present subjective rule in the type of circumstances I am in at present, it would be morally legitimate for *everyone* to act on the same type of rule in the same type of circumstances. It should therefore be possible at least to *conceive the idea* that everyone would do so; for it should be possible to conceive the idea that everyone in circumstances like mine would, with the regularity of events conforming to natural law, act in a *morally legitimate manner*. If the principle of the maxim on which I act is such, then, that I cannot consistently conceive of it as becoming raised to the universality of a law of nature, I am acting in a morally illegitimate manner: exempting myself from the categorical demand which *my own reason* makes clear to me.

But (and this point is crucial to Kant's moral philosophy) even if the principle of my maxim should happen to be such that it *is* possible to conceive of it as becoming raised to the status of a permanent universal natural law of voluntary action, my maxim might *still* be a morally illegitimate one. In other words, my maxim must be able to pass also a *secondary* test of universalizability.

The *primary* test is whether I can consistently think the

idea that the principle of my maxim could *become* a permanent and universal natural law of voluntary action. The *secondary* test of universalizability is whether I can conceive of myself, at any time, as *wanting* the principle of my maxim to become such a universal law. Let us assume that my maxim is such that I find it impossible to think the latter idea consistently— impossible in the sense that if I were to want my maxim to become raised to the status of a universal law of nature, my very *wanting* would *contradict itself*. In other words, as a sensuously affected being wanting happiness for myself, I would have to take into account a type of situation in which—in order to want my maxim to become a universal law of nature— I would have to want precisely the *opposite* of what I would want in that type of situation. It would then be clear to me that my maxim would be a morally impermissible one. For my own reason tells me that if it *were* morally legitimate for everyone in circumstances essentially like mine to act on the rule I now propose to act on, it should be logically possible for me to want everyone to act invariably on that rule in circumstances of such a type; i.e., it should be possible to think the idea that I would *want* everyone in such circumstances to act invariably in a *morally legitimate manner*. So if a certain maxim on which I act is such that it would be logically impossible for me to want the principle of that maxim to hold as a permanent universal law of nature, I am in fact doing what *my own reason* recognizes to be morally impermissible: making myself an exception in my own favor.

We have seen why the categorical imperative, as originally revealed to us by our own pure reason, needs to be concretized symbolically before it can be of any practical use to us as a standard for making a moral appraisal of our material maxims in respect to the requirements of legality. We have also found out why a schematism will not do as a mediation-procedure for making the abstract imperative concretely applicable. We have seen what Kant means by the typic of pure practical judgment and how he argues that the typified moral law is, at least implicitly, employed in common-sense moral judgments. And, finally, we have seen what he means by the primary and secondary universalizability criteria that are contained in the typified categorical imperative. So far my discussion has been general. To make my interpretation more specific, I shall in the following section give examples of maxims and examine how they are to be appraised in terms of Kant's primary and secondary universalizability tests. A careful examination of all of Kant's examples of maxims would require a very lengthy discussion. I shall therefore restrict my analysis only to those points that seem to me important for getting a clearer understanding of his universalizability criteria. I shall discuss one maxim that fails to pass even the primary universalizability test, and one that passes the primary but fails to pass the secondary. When I examine the latter type of maxim, I shall also have an occasion to discuss briefly some maxims that pass the secondary (and, thereby, also of course the primary) test.

II *Examples of applying the typified moral law*

I

One of Kant's well-known examples of a maxim can be paraphrased as follows: "When I find myself in need of money and become convinced that no one will lend me the money unless I firmly promise to repay it at a specified time, I shall from self-love give such a promise even though I intend not to keep it, and know that I shall never repay the money."[17]

---

[17] Cf. *Grundlegung zur Metaphysik der Sitten*, p. 280. (Abbott, 40; Beck, 81 [pp. 45–46 above].)

The principle of the maxim, then, is that of giving false promises in order to get oneself out of a financial difficulty, or to get oneself out of some other difficulty (Kant generalizes his original example). It would not necessarily be *imprudent* for a person to adopt this principle of self-love as a subjective rule (maxim) of action. "Now this principle of self-love or one's own advantage might well be compatible with my whole future well-being. . . ."[18] (A sufficiently clever person might be able to amass a fortune by giving false promises. When his creditors in one community become suspicious or troublesome, he could move to some other community far away, etc., etc.) But even though it might be compatible with enlightened self-interest, one can according to Kant easily show the principle of the maxim to be incompatible with morally correct conduct. The *principle* of the maxim is, of course, not self-contradictory; but if the principle were to become a universal law of nature, such a law would be a *self-contradictory law*. Because the very principle of the law would contradict itself, the law in question would be no law at all.—If the world were to be such that everybody who makes promises in order to get out of a difficult situation would, according to a *natural law* of voluntary action, be absolutely incapable of keeping those promises, no one would take their so-called promises seriously. Such "promises" would be known to be worthless and would therefore not be regarded as *promises*. A universal law of nature modeled on the principle of the maxim in question would be a law according to which everybody in a certain type of situation would have to *do the impossible*: make promises which he *intends* to be deceptive, even though he *cannot* intend them to be deceptive, namely because he *knows* that his so-called promises are absolutely incapable of deceiving anybody. Thus the law would be a law of non-deceptive deceptive promise-making, i.e., no law at all. It is impossible, then, to think that a universal law of nature

18 *Ibid.* [p. 46 above].

(a universal natural law of voluntary action) could be modeled on the principle of the maxim. The maxim is therefore quite clearly a morally impermissible one, according to Kant.

Various critics have correctly pointed out that innumerable maxims that would obviously be morally *wrong* ones would still be such that their principles could, without contradiction, be thought to hold as universal laws of nature. (To match some of the grim examples conjured up by such critics, one might imagine that some woman has arbitrarily adopted the following maxim: "If I give birth to a baby weighing less than six pounds, I shall do everything in my power to kill it." One can consistently conceive the idea of there being a law of nature according to which every mother would try to kill any baby of hers weighing less than six pounds.) Such critics have therefore insisted that what Kant considers to be a sufficient test for determining whether a maxim is morally acceptable or not is by no means a sufficient test, and that his moral philosophy therefore breaks down miserably.

What such critics have failed to recognize, of course, is that Kant himself is most insistent on the point that his primary test is by no means a *sufficient* test for determining whether a maxim is universalizable in the *full* sense that is demanded by the typified moral law. It is difficult to understand how readers of Kant can have missed this point, because Kant states it repeatedly, and very explicitly—as, e.g., in the following passage: "Some actions are of such a nature that their maxim cannot, without contradiction, even be *thought* as a universal law of nature. . . . In other actions, that intrinsic impossibility is not involved, to be sure, but it is nevertheless impossible to *wish* that their maxim be raised to the universality of a law of nature, because such a wish would contradict itself [*sich selbst widersprechen*]."[19]

[19] *Ibid.*, p. 282. (Abbott, 41–42; Beck, 82–83 [47–48 above].)

The critics in question have therefore either failed to recognize that Kant has developed both a primary and a secondary universalizability test, or they have failed to recognize that the secondary test contains a highly important additional requirement. (If one were to make a successful criticism of Kant's primary test, one would have to come up with one or more maxims that would clearly be of a morally *permissible* kind but would *fail* to pass the primary test. I shall not in this article attempt to settle the question of whether it is possible to conceive of such maxims.)

II

Another of Kant's examples of maxims is as follows: Someone "for whom things go well, while he sees that others (whom he could very well help) have to struggle with great hardships, thinks: what concern of mine is that? let each one be as happy as heaven wills, or as he can make himself; I will take nothing away from him and not even envy him; only I have no desire to contribute anything to his well-being or to his assistance in distress!"[20]

This maxim for behavior toward people in need of one's help is certainly not a maxim for benevolent action but neither is it a maxim for malevolent action. It is a maxim for non-benevolent action toward them. Kant does not say that it would necessarily be *imprudent* for a person to adopt such a principle of action. Even if *I* act on the maxim of never going out of my way to help others, and thereby save myself much work and inconvenience, it is still possible that others might on the whole act in a benevolent manner toward *me*. It could even happen that various people might show unusual benevolence toward me in an effort to make me change my way of acting.

So it is possible that some person would find it quite pru-

20 *Ibid.*, p. 282. (Abbott, 41–42; Beck, 82–83 [47 above].)

dent—in line with his enlightened self-interest—to act on a maxim of non-benevolence. The question is whether a maxim of this kind satisfies the universalizability requirements of the typified categorical imperative. Kant points out that it passes the primary test. One can without contradiction think that the principle of such a maxim could *hold* as a universal natural law of voluntary action. If there were such a law, nobody would be able to go out of his way to contribute to the well-being of others or to their assistance when they are in distress. But the human race could still continue to exist under such conditions, "and undoubtedly even better than in a state where everybody babbles about sympathetic participation and benevolence and even occasionally exerts himself to practice them while, on the other hand, he also cheats when he can, and sells, or otherwise violates, the right of men."[21] So the maxim of non-benevolence passes the primary universalizability test; i.e., its principle could hold as a universal law. But "even though it is possible that a universal law of nature patterned on this maxim might well endure, it is nevertheless impossible to *want* such a principle to hold everywhere as a law of nature."[22]

When Kant gives examples of applying the secondary universalizability test, he presupposes, and needs to presuppose, the principle of self-love (that every person desires happiness for himself) and the auxiliary principle that every person at times desires some type of help from others in order to satisfy his desire for happiness. Some critics have insisted that Kant thereby contradicts himself by incorporating two merely a posteriori principles in his ethical system, even though he claims it to be a purely a priori system. To the best of my knowledge, no one has shown this seemingly devastating criticism to be invalid, but it is. Even though Kant himself does not explic-

[21] *Ibid.*, p. 281. (Abbott, 41; Beck, 82 [47 above].)
[22] *Ibid.*

itly demonstrate the a priori nature of the principle of self-love and the principle that persons desire some help from one another to satisfy their self-love, I shall show that these two principles are in fact a priori conditions of Kant's conception of moral obligability.

Kant, of course, affirms it to be a fact that the vast majority of human beings (namely "persons")[23] are, and know themselves to be, morally obligated agents. The moral law is, according to him, the one and only *fact* of pure practical reason. (If one were to justify the moral law on non-moral grounds, one would, of course, get nowhere; and if one were to justify it on *moral* grounds, one would be assuming what one sets out to justify.) We could not *be* morally obligated agents, however, unless we were sensuously affected beings with a *self-love* which (in conjunction with an innate propensity to evil) could *tempt* us to act contrary to the paradigm of holiness. So when Kant in connection with the secondary universalizability test makes use of the principle that any "person" has self-love, he does not need to argue for this principle on *empirical* grounds. He is entitled to assert the principle to be *a priori*: at least all human beings who come to recognize themselves as being under moral obligation (i.e., all "persons") *must* be assumed to be sensuously affected beings with a desire to attain happiness for themselves.[24] And what is more, if human beings as indi-

---

[23] For his distinctions between the original predisposition to *animality*, *humanity*, and *personality*, see *Die Religion innerhalb der Grenzen der bloßen Vernunft*, Cassirer, VI, 164–167. Cf. Theodore M. Greene's trans., *Religion Within the Limits of Reason Alone* (Chicago: The Open Court Publishing Company, 1934), pp. 21–23.

[24] Self-love can of course be manifested in perverted forms. A masochist desires his peculiar brand of happiness. A misanthrope who does not feel himself in the least deprived—and unjustly deprived—of happiness would probably be a contradiction in terms, as would a suicidal person who does not find his desire for happiness in the least unfulfilled. So the principle that "persons" desire happiness—though in need of no a posteriori support—can easily be supported a posteriori.

viduals were *completely self-sufficient* in satisfying their desire for happiness, instead of needing and desiring some help
from one another, it would be *impossible* for them to be *morally obligated* to one another. That they can recognize that they
are morally obligated to one another, however, is according to
Kant a fact of pure practical reason.

A morally obligated being, i.e., a "person," is therefore
necessarily so constituted that he wants to be happy, and so
constituted that the preservation and furtherance of the happiness he desires for himself are at least at certain times to some
extent dependent on some form of benevolent treatment from
others. In a situation where somebody would want others to
treat him benevolently it would of course be impossible for him
to want everybody to be *incapable* of acting benevolently. A
"person's" nature being what it is, then, he would at various
points of his life career *inevitably* find himself in situations
where he could not consistently want for there to be a universal
law of nature modeled on the principle of a maxim of non-
benevolence. If there were such a universal natural law of
behavior, he would in the above-mentioned type of situations
want for there to be *exceptions* to that law. In short, if a "person" claims that a maxim of non-benevolence satisfies the
secondary universalizability requirement of the categorical imperative, he is in effect making the following self-contradictory
claim: As a "person," I would want my maxim of non-benevolence to hold as a universal law of nature even at those times
when I would not, and could not, as a "person," want my maxim
of non-benevolence to hold as a universal law of nature!

Such a desire (or wish or volition) would be self-contradictory, then, and hence no desire (or wish or volition) at all.
When Kant—in a passage I have already cited—states that
"such a wish would contradict *itself*" (*sich selbst*[25] *wider-*

---

[25] "Itself" (*sich selbst*) is not printed in extended type in the original. If
Kant could see today how his view has been misunderstood on this essen-

sprechen), there is no reason for assuming that he is using the post-Kantian dialectical jargon of Hegel & Co. That is to say, when in this passage, and in a number of other passages to the same effect, he explicitly states that a "person's" desire for the principle of a certain maxim to hold as a universal law of nature would contradict *itself*—would conflict with itself—there is no reason for taking him to mean merely that the desire in question would conflict with some *other* desire or conative tendency of the "person." Kant's point has to do with *self-contradiction* in the old-fashioned and ordinary sense of the term. He is speaking of the self-contradiction involved in an idea to the effect that a desire for a certain maxim to *hold* as a universal law of nature would at the same time be a desire for this very maxim *not* to hold as a universal law of nature.

The maxim of non-benevolence passes the primary universalizability test, then, but fails to pass the secondary test. So according to Kantian principles, it is *demonstrable* that the maxim of non-benevolence is a morally impermissible one. A maxim of *malevolent* behavior is of course not universalizable as demanded by the categorical imperative of our pure reason. A maxim of *benevolent* behavior, on the other hand, satisfies both the primary and secondary universalizability requirements and is therefore clearly a morally permissible one. But since the only other alternative maxims—the maxims of non-benevolence and malevolence—are morally impermissible maxims, we are on rational grounds entitled to conclude that, when we recognize somebody in need of help whom we are in a position to help, it is not only morally *permissible*, but morally *obligatory* for us to act benevolently, i.e., to adopt a maxim of benevolence.

---

tial point, however, he might well have wanted some of his works on ethics reprinted for the sole purpose of getting the words *sich selbst*, as used in the above context, printed in capital letters—and in extra-bold type at that!

What, then, is the maxim of benevolence that I am duty-bound to adopt as my rule of action? It could hardly be a subjective rule of acting so as to *produce good will* in others; because I cannot have a duty to do what I am incapable of doing. If anything is exclusively a freely choosing individual's own task, it is to develop in himself the character pattern of good will. But since I cannot have a duty to accomplish what is beyond my power, the maxim of benevolence could not even be a subjective rule of always so acting as to *produce happiness* in others. For even my best effort to make someone else happy—or contribute to his happiness—might in some instances fail (due, then, to no fault of my own). My duty to act benevolently can therefore be no more than a duty to *strive*— to the best of my ability[26]—to contribute by my action to the happiness of others (*provided*, of course, that my striving is compatible with my acting on maxims of such a type that I could at any time consistently want them to be raised to the universal status of natural—causal—laws of voluntary behavior).[27] What I would have as the aim of *my* dutiful striving, namely to produce happiness in others (to the extent that such

[26] I have in my above-mentioned article explained how one according to Kant is to understand the phrase "to the best of my ability." For the purpose of the present discussion it is not necessary to restate that explanation.

[27] The proviso stated in the above parentheses is highly important. (It is the essence of the deontological character of Kant's ethics.) Because of that restricting condition, I do not, according to Kant, have a duty *always* to strive as best I can to contribute to what I judge would be the greatest happiness for the greatest number of people. I might believe —and be correct in my belief—that by pushing my rich miserly grandmother into the deep well on her estate and convincing everybody concerned that she tripped and fell in and that I did my best to rescue her when I discovered the accident, I would contribute more to the happiness of mankind than I would by letting her remain alive or by actively protecting her life. If I were supposed to consider *only* the principle of maximizing happiness, I might well find myself having a duty to send the old lady on her way. On Kantian principles, however, I would be duty-bound

striving would be compatible with acting on fully universalizable maxims), would be precisely the same as the fundamental
aim of the natural inclinations of *others* for whom I strive. For,
as already shown, it must be assumed a priori that every "person" (i.e., every morally obligated agent) has self-love, a natural inclination to obtain happiness for himself. The aim of my
dutiful behavior towards another "person" would therefore be
one he could always wish for me to have, in that it would coin-
cide with his own fundamental natural inclination to obtain
happiness for himself. My duty to act benevolently—which is
demonstrable by testing the alternative maxims in terms of the
rational universalizability criterion of the categorical imperative
—can therefore equally well be expressed in the following
form: "*So act that you treat human nature, whether in your
own person or in the person of anybody else, never as a means
only but at any time also as an end.*"[28] It is fairly easy to see,
then, how one can make the transition from Kant's first formulation of the typified categorical imperative to the second formulation of it. And the third formulation is of course nothing
but a combination of the first (the idea of a *universal natural
law*) and the second (the idea of a person), namely the idea of
a universal lawgiver: regarding oneself as though one were to
be the *giver* of *universal laws of nature* through all the maxims
of one's actions.

---

to *abstain* from any action of that kind—however great its *utility* might
be—because the maxim of that kind of action is not such that I could,
any time, consistently want it to hold as a universal natural law of human
behavior. It is a mistake to assume that Kant's ethics is absolutely nonteleological. His ethics *involves* teleology—the duty to strive for the happiness of others (and, by the way, also the duty to strive to perfect one's
own natural talents)—but his nonteleological (deontological) universalizability requirements impose a most important *restriction* on this moral
teleology.

[28] *Grundlegung zur Metaphysik der Sitten*, p. 287. (Abbott, 47; Beck, 87
[54 above].)

For the sake of clarifying the Kantian universalizability principle even further, it might be of value to discuss briefly two ways in which the secondary universalizability criterion might be misinterpreted, and to consider also a certain view that Kant advocated at the end of his life.

One might make the claim that Kant's secondary universalizability test is in fact reducible to a merely *prudential* calculation of a peculiar kind. The argument for such a reductionistic interpretation can be stated as follows: "I am asked by Kant to conceive of myself *as though* I had the power to raise the principles of certain maxims to the universality of laws of nature by simply *wishing* for those principles to hold in that universal capacity. Kant recognizes that it would not necessarily be imprudent to adopt the maxim of non-benevolence as one's rule of action in the *actual* world. It must therefore be granted that it is a mistake to assume, as some critics have, that his secondary universalizability test is reducible to a calculation as to what is *actually* prudent. But his testing procedure is *still* reducible to a merely prudential type of calculation, namely to a calculation based on principles that might, for lack of a better term, be called principles of *counterfactual prudence*. For the sake of making a correct appraisal of my maxim I am supposed to think of the world as though it were such that the principle of my maxim would become a universal law of nature by my mere wanting for it to happen. But the point is that, within the framework of such a hypothetical world, *for purely prudential reasons* I would not *wish* for my maxim of non-benevolence to hold as a permanent universal law of nature. For if I did, the consequence would be that no one in such a world could possibly act in a benevolent manner towards *me*. So within a hypothetical world-order where the principle of my maxim would become a universal law of nature by my mere wishing for it to serve in that capacity, I would for strictly pru-

dential reasons find it unwise to wish, and would in all likelihood not wish, that the principle of my maxim of non-benevolence would hold as a universal law of nature. Kant's secondary universalizability test is therefore reducible to a test based on principles of a counterfactual type of prudence: my maxim must be such that—within the counterfactual world that I am supposed to envisage according to the typic—I would find it compatible with long-range prudence to want the principle of my maxim to hold as a universal law of nature."

An objection of this type misses completely the point of Kant's secondary universalizability requirement. Kant's point is, not that for *prudential* reasons I *would* not, but that for strictly *logical* reasons I *could* not wish that the principle of non-benevolence would hold as a universal law of nature. Within the counterfactual type of world-order that I explicitly or implicitly have to envisage myself as a part of if I am to make a moral appraisal, it would, at certain times, be, not *imprudent*, but simply *impossible* for me to want the principle of non-benevolence to hold as a universal law of nature—impossible because (as already explained) in certain situations, I, as a "personal" being, would then have to wish precisely the *opposite* of what I in those situations unavoidably would wish as a "personal" being. In short, the idea of wishing, at any time, that the principle of non-benevolence would hold as a universal law of nature would be an idea of a self-contradictory wish and hence not an idea of a wish.

An objection of a somewhat similar type would run as follows: "Kant maintains that if it should happen that someone at a certain time as a matter of psychological fact would be willing to have the principle of his maxim become a universal law of nature, then that maxim is to be considered as being *ipso facto* a morally legitimate one. It is perfectly possible, however, that even though someone acts on a morally *impermissible* maxim, he might still in fact be willing to have its principle raised to the status of a universal law of nature. Kant's moral philosophy is therefore reducible to an unacceptable type of subjectivism—to arbitrariness and irrationality—in spite of all his talk about the need for being objective, impartial and rational when one makes a moral appraisal of one's maxims."

Certain contemporary ethical theories setting forth a requirement to act on universalizable maxims are in my opinion open to this very criticism, because they contain nothing corresponding to Kant's secondary universalizability requirement.[29] But it would be futile to level this particular criticism against Kant's doctrine, because Kant's universalizability test has nothing whatsoever to do with whether someone might happen to be in such a frame of mind that he would want his maxim to become universalized. Kant's point is a *logical*—not a *psychological*—one. According to his view, the question is, not whether a "person" psychologically *would* want (or believes he would want), but whether he logically *could* want the principle of his maxim to hold as a universal law of nature. A "person" might honestly say that he would be perfectly willing to see the principle of a certain maxim hold as a universal causal law of a system of nature of which he himself would be a member. It might still be true, however, that if he were to reflect further on the matter he would find that he was mistaken, namely in the sense that he would have to assume himself to be able to accomplish something contradictory in order to be willing to have the principle of that maxim raised to the universal status of a law of nature: be able to think of himself

[29] Anything like a careful analysis of such theories would require a separate study.

as being at one and the same time both willing and unwilling to have the principle of his maxim serve as a universal law of nature.

If one is to be successful in working out a refutation of Kant's secondary universalizability criterion, one would have to proceed in a different manner. One would refute his criterion if one could formulate some maxim that is clearly of a morally *impermissible* kind but still such that one could always consistently want its principle to hold as a universal law of nature. Another line of refutation would be to formulate some maxim that is clearly of a morally *permissible* kind but still such that one *could not* consistently want its principle always to hold as a universal law of nature. I shall not in this article attempt to determine whether it is possible to conceive of a maxim that satisfies the one or the other of these two conditions.

It is interesting to note, however, that Kant at the end of his philosophical career considered certain maxims to be morally correct even though it is difficult to see how they would satisfy the requirements he himself laid down when he explained the categorical imperative and the typic.

Towards the end of his life, he was criticized by Benjamin Constant for going "so far as to affirm that to tell a falsehood to a murderer who asked us whether our friend, of whom he was in pursuit, had not taken refuge in our house, would be a crime."[30] Kant responded to the criticism by stating flatly that one has no right to be dishonest in one's declarations, even in an extreme situation of that kind: ". . . the duty of veracity . . . is an *unconditional duty* which holds *in all circumstances*."[31]

---

[30] Immanuel Kant, *On a Supposed Right to Tell Lies from Benevolent Motives* (this essay is not included in the Cassirer edition; my quotations are taken from Abbott's trans.), Abbott, 361. (Beck, 364.)

[31] Abbott, 364 (Beck, 349); "in all circumstances" italicized by me.

"To be *truthful* (honest) in all declarations is . . . a sacred unconditional command of reason, and not to be limited by any expediency."[32]

I doubt seriously that Kant at this point sees clearly the full implications of the principles he himself laid down in his previous works on ethics. To make the example unambiguous, let us assume that my house is such that it would be impossible for my friend to escape from my house except through the door where I am confronting the murderer. At the outset, let us consider Kant's *second* formulation of the typified categorical imperative. There is every reason to believe that my friend will be killed if in some way or other I let the murderer know or come to suspect that my friend is hiding in the house. I could therefore hardly be said to treat my friend as an *end* if I make no attempt to deceive the murderer: let him know the truth and thereby aid him in his search for my friend. It seems to me that in that case I would be treating my friend as a means only. I would be sacrificing, not only my friend's future happiness, but his life, in order to enable myself to adhere to an abstract principle of absolutely unconditional veracity in my declarations. This point should have given Kant pause for further reflection.

Let us consider the first formulation of the categorical imperative and assume that I act on the maxim of attempting to *deceive* the murderer in order to save my friend's life. Whether I attempt to deceive him by telling the truth or by telling a lie is immaterial to the case. The point is that I am being *dishonest*, am doing my best to *deceive* by any means I see fit. I might give the murderer the impression that I know what he is up to, tell him please to come into the house and that I have hidden my friend there. My hope would then of course be that he would assume I am telling a lie. The situation might on the other hand be such that I find it wisest to give the murderer, at least initially,

[32] Abbott, 363. (Beck, 348.)

the impression that I do not know what he is up to, and tell him that I saw my friend hurrying up the street a few minutes ago. The general principle of my maxim is that of attempting to deceive for the sake of preventing a murder from taking place. The particular way in which I might attempt to deceive is not part of the general principle of the maxim. If the world were such that the general principle of my maxim would hold as a universal law of nature, it would still not be a matter of common knowledge *how* someone in a situation like mine would attempt to deceive: by telling a lie, the truth, or a half-truth of some kind. Even if all murderers inquiring concerning the whereabouts of their prospective victims would know that anybody they asked who happened to know the answer would invariably attempt to deceive them, a murderer might still decide to make such inquiries. He might not know whether the person he approaches happens to know where the prospective victim is. If on the other hand he is sure the person knows, he might still decide to ask his question in an attempt to outwit that person, namely by attempting to detect the way in which that particular person is attempting to deceive him. So it is perfectly possible to think consistently the idea of a world in which the principle of my maxim would hold as a universal law of nature.

It might be objected that, even though the maxim satisfies the primary universalizability requirement, it does not satisfy the secondary. For (so the objection would proceed) it is possible that *I* might some day be in the position of searching for a person I intend to murder. In such a case I would not wish to be deceived as to the whereabouts of my prospective victim. So if in such a situation I were to wish that there would be a universal law of nature modeled on the maxim of attempting to deceive to prevent a murder, such a wish would, at the same time, have to be a wish for such a law of nature *not* to prevail. In short, my wish for the principle of that maxim to hold as a universal law of nature would be a *self-contradictory* wish, which is to say that it would be no wish at all. It might be highly unlikely but it is at least possible that I would at some time be in a situation where I would search for a person to murder him. Since such a situation is possible, it is one that I *must* take into account when I am to determine whether the maxim of attempting to deceive to prevent a murder satisfies the secondary universalizability requirement of Kant's categorical imperative. I arrive, then, at the following conclusion: it is *impossible* to conceive of anyone wishing, at any time, that a universal law of nature be modeled on the maxim of attempting to deceive to prevent a murder—impossible because one *has* to take into account a type of situation in which such a wish would contradict itself. The maxim in question is therefore a morally impermissible one according to Kant's secondary universalizability criterion.

This objection to the maxim of attempting to deceive to prevent a murder might seem to be of the same kind as the previously described objection that one cannot consistently conceive the idea of wishing, any time, that a universal law of nature were modeled on the maxim of non-benevolence. I shall attempt to show, however, that the two objections are different in *kind* and that the maxim of attempting to deceive to prevent a murder *does* satisfy the secondary universalizability requirement of the categorical imperative (at least as I find it reasonable to interpret the requirement).

In order for me to be able, at any time whatever, to wish consistently to live as a "person" in a world in which a universal law of nature would be modeled on the maxim of non-benevolence, a certain condition pertaining to my conative being would have to be satisfied, namely the condition that I would at no time want anybody to make any effort at all to further my welfare. It is impossible, however, for such a condition to be satisfied. As already shown, I could not possibly be a "person" if I were not a sensuously conditioned agent desiring to avoid unhappiness, desiring to attain happiness, and wishing for some form of benevolent treatment from others to further my innate desire for happiness. In other words, the idea of anyone, at any time, wishing that there were a universal law of nature patterned on the maxim of non-benevolent action is *incompatible with the idea of being a "person":* a rational agent who, because he has a sensuously conditioned self-love that can tempt him to act contrary to the paradigm descriptive of holiness, comes to regard himself as morally *obligated* by this paradigm. So only on the condition that I would cease to be a "person"—a morally obligated self—would it be possible for me, at any time, to want the maxim of non-benevolence to hold as a universal law of nature. It is absolutely impossible, then, that a "person" should be able, at any time, to wish consistently for there to be a universal law of nature modeled on the maxim of non-benevolence—impossible in the sense that such a wish would *necessarily* contradict itself at certain times, because a "person" is necessarily so constituted as to have self-love and to wish for some form of aid or considerateness from others, even if it be only the considerateness of leaving him alone to fend for himself, at certain times. When one examines Kant's secondary procedure for testing maxims in respect to universalizability one finds, then, that what he takes to be a "person's" a priori demonstrable desire to attain happiness and desire to be aided in some way by others play an *essential* part in the testing procedure.

The considerations pertaining to the maxim of attempting to deceive to save a life are in kind different from those pertaining to the maxim of non-benevolent action. The idea of being able at any time whatever to wish for there to be a universal law of nature modeled on the maxim of attempting to deceive to prevent a murder is by no means incompatible with the idea of being and remaining a *"person,"* a morally obligated agent. Such a wish is incompatible only with wishing to commit a murder or wishing for a murder to be committed, i.e., incompatible with wishing to act or wishing for somebody else to act on a morally illegitimate maxim, namely a maxim of malevolent action. An incompatibility of that kind, however, constitutes no moral objection to the maxim of attempting to deceive to prevent a murder. For Kant's secondary universalizability requirement is of course not reducible to the following piece of nonsense: Your maxim of action is morally legitimate if and only if it is possible to think that you at any given time could want its principle to hold as a universal law of nature and that you *also* at some time could want to act on a maxim (namely a morally illegitimate maxim) which would be an *exception* to that type of universal law of nature. His universalizability requirement is the following: Your maxim of action is morally legitimate if and only if, without having to disregard any condition indispensable to your being and remaining a *"person,"* it is possible to think that you, any time whatever, could consistently want the principle of the maxim to hold as a universal law of nature.

To want to escape misery and attain happiness and to want at various times some type of benevolent treatment from others for the sake of furthering my own well-being are indispensable conditions of my being a "person" (a rational-and-sensuous agent conscious of being under moral obligation). *Qua* "person," I *must* therefore take those conditions into account if I am to make a rational test of my maxims by the criterion of universalizability. To happen to be, however, at a certain time in such a frame of mind as to strive to commit murder or want someone else to commit murder is *not* an indispensable condition of being a "person," because it is perfectly possible to think the idea of a "person" who is never in such a frame of mind. To determine whether the idea of remaining a "person" is consistent with my idea of wishing, any time whatever, that there were a universal law of nature patterned on the maxim of attempting to deceive to prevent a murder, I do not, of course, need to take into account any factors *incidental* to my being a "person," but only factors *essential* to my being a "person." A desire to murder or for a murder to be committed is not an essential condition of my remaining a "person," because as a "person" (an agent recognizing myself as being under moral obligation) I might or *might not* come to have such a desire. When I test my maxim by the criterion of universalizability, I am therefore not required to take into consideration the contingency of coming to have such a desire. As shown above, however, the desire to attain and preserve happiness for myself and the desire at certain times to get some form of help from others are indispensable conditions of my remaining a "person" (a morally obligated being). My thinking the idea of being able, at any time of my life career, to wish that there were a universal law of nature modeled on the maxim of attempting to deceive to prevent a murder is not incompatible with thinking the idea that my nature would continue to satisfy the conditions essential to being a "person."

In spite of Kant's latter-day claim to the contrary, I contend, then, that the maxim of attempting to deceive to prevent a murder is a morally legitimate maxim in the sense of satisfying the secondary (and thereby of course also the primary) universalizability criterion of the categorical imperative. The maxim of *not* attempting to deceive in such a situation—or stated in a more general form, the principle of being absolutely honest in all one's declarations *regardless of circumstances*— does not as far as I can see satisfy the secondary universalizability requirement of the categorical imperative.

It might be interesting to speculate as to why, late in life during his controversy with Constant, Kant defended the view that, in all declarations, one has a duty to be truthful regardless of circumstances. The traditional senility explanation is at least somewhat controversial. What seems to me to be uncontroversial, however, is that the principle Kant insisted on during the Constant controversy—namely that the type of empirical circumstances in which the given action takes place must be considered irrelevant to a moral appraisal of the subjective principle of the actions—is out of keeping with almost everything else he wrote about the concept of duty and about the categorical imperative as a criterion for testing the moral legitimacy of maxims. When Kant in his major works on ethics gives specific examples of maxims and shows how they are to be tested in terms of the primary and secondary universalizability criteria of the categorical imperative, he almost invariably makes it unambiguously clear that the idea of *the type of empirical circumstances* in which a given action would take place *is to be regarded as an essential constituent of the maxim of action* that is to be tested. (By way of illustration of this point, it is sufficient to make a brief reference to a few of Kant's own examples of maxims: the idea of taking one's life *when one has become reduced to despair by a series of misfortunes and feels wearied of life;* the idea of giving a false promise *for the sake of getting oneself out of a financially difficult situation or out of some other situation that frustrates one's self-love;* the idea of remaining inactive in respect to others *when they are in need of assistance and one is capable of helping them.*) I maintain, then, that my interpretation of the universalizability criteria of the categorical imperative as being criteria for testing the moral legitimacy of subjective principles of voluntary actions *considered in their given types of circumstances* is, not only compatible with, but strongly supported by almost everything Kant, in his major works on ethics, has written on the principle of universalizability as a means of testing maxims.

It should be noted, however, that there are in Kant's major ethical writings a few exceptional passages in which he does not make clear that the type of circumstances in which an action takes place must be taken into account when one appraises the subjective principle of the action by the universalizability criteria. It is therefore conceivable that, prior to his controversy with Constant, he wavered somewhat on this fundamental point. If one were to maintain that Kant's real intention all along was to say that empirical circumstances of action are morally irrelevant, one would have to insist that he, by sheer inattentiveness, in numerous passages happened to say precisely the opposite. If such an extreme interpretation were acceptable, I would say that the philosophical merit of Kant's major writings on universalizability would be found in his persistent misstatement of the view he intended to convey.

University of Washington

Jonathan Harrison / Kant's

examples of the first formulation

of the categorical imperative

I do not know of any commentator who has given an accurate account of all of Kant's examples of the first formulation of the categorical imperative, and though some have given an accurate account of some examples, there are other examples of which no-one has given an accurate account. Accounts of the first formulation of the categorical imperative have frequently been vitiated by the assumption that what he says in dealing with one of his examples—a different one in the case of different commentators—can be taken as showing, without consideration of the other examples, what Kant meant by the first formulation of the categorical imperative. Commentators have frequently been misled in their account of Kant's argu-

Reprinted from THE PHILOSOPHICAL QUARTERLY, *Vol. VII, No. 26 (Jan. 1957), pp. 50–62, by permission of the author and editors.*

ment in the examples not only because they have assumed that Kant always does what one would expect him to do from what he says about the categorical imperative generally, but because they have found a certain argument in one of the examples, and then seen it when it was not there in one or more of the other examples. Kant's treatment of his four examples is extremely wayward and sometimes inconsequential, and each one of them must be considered independently both of the others and of Kant's remarks about his own programme.

Kant divides duties into perfect and imperfect duties, and into duties to self and duties to others. If you combine these two divisions, four classes of duty result, (a) perfect duty to self, (b) perfect duty to others, (c) imperfect duty to self, and (d) imperfect duty to others. Kant gives one example of each of these four classes. It does not appear to me that there is any noticeable difference between Kant's treatment of duties to self and duties to others. There is obviously, however, a great deal of difference between his treatment of perfect and imperfect duties. It is alleged to be *impossible* for everybody to adopt the maxim which I adopt when I infringe a perfect duty. It is not impossible for everybody to adopt the maxim which I act on when I infringe an imperfect duty; it is merely impossible for me to will that everyone should adopt this maxim. Before going on to a detailed consideration of Kant's four examples of the application of the first formulation of the categorical imperative, there are some general comments I wish to make.

1) In the first formulation of the categorical imperative, Kant was attempting to put forward the supreme principle of morality, and in this respect the first formulation of the categorical imperative is similar to the principle of utilitarianism. He is not just telling us that what is right for me is right for any similar person similarly placed, which would not tell me

what was right for me; nor is he laying down certain conditions (for example, that they should be of unrestricted generality) to which a principle must conform if it is to be a moral principle, from which, of course, no moral principle could be deduced. These are things which Kant takes for granted, but they are not what he is trying to prove. To hold that this is all that Kant is saying is to replace views which are exciting and important, if erroneous, by certain harmless platitudes, which would make ridiculous the fanfare of trumpets with which Kant heralded them.

2) Kant did not use the first formulation of the categorical imperative to test whether certain alleged moral principles really were moral principles, or even to test whether they were acceptable moral principles. He does not use it to test the morality of moral principles at all, but the morality of maxims. For the same reason, it cannot be held that Kant is dealing with a problem which has received a good deal of attention recently, the problem of the universalisation of moral judgements and the universalisation of moral reasons. It has been held, I think rightly, that any moral judgement gives rise to a moral principle, on the ground that if a particular moral judgement is true of a given action, then the same moral judgement must apply to all similar actions performed in similar circumstances, and it has also been held that if a certain statement is a good reason for coming to a certain moral conclusion, then the same statement must give rise to the same moral conclusion in all similar cases. Kant is not, however, discussing the universalisation of moral judgements or of reasons for moral judgements, but the universalisation of maxims, e.g., he does not consider the moral judgement "It is right for me to borrow this money, though I know I cannot pay it back" but the maxim "Whenever I believe myself short of money, I will borrow money and promise to pay it back, though I

know that this will never be done." Nor is he saying that if a maxim is right for me, it is right for everyone, but that if it is not possible for everyone to act on it (or not possible for me to will that everyone should act on it) it is not right for me to act on it.

The following points about maxims should be noted: (*a*) A maxim is a subjective principle of action, that is, a principle on which a man in fact acts. It seems to me that by this it is meant that a maxim is a rule which a man makes for himself. If I make it a rule to rise at seven, then to rise at seven is my maxim. If I make it a rule to make promises which I cannot keep, whenever I need a service which I cannot obtain in any other way, then to make such promises is my maxim. (*b*) Maxims can be formulated, but what the words which formulate them express cannot properly be said to be true or to be false. My maxim will be expressed in words such as "to turn the other cheek" or "always to declare my full income." It does not make sense to say that "to turn the other cheek" expresses a truth or a falsehood. (*c*) Maxims may be "legislated." In more ordinary English, maxims are rules which I make for myself, and I may make it a rule to turn the other cheek, or I may not. Whether I make this my rule or not is something which I personally decide. (*d*) Maxims are not moral principles, as has already been said. It may well be a valid moral rule that the other cheek ought to be turned, but my maxim or rule is not that the other cheek ought to be turned, but to turn the other cheek. Maxims or rules can be "made," but moral principles cannot. I can make it a rule to declare my full income, but I cannot make it a rule that men ought to declare their full incomes. To talk of making this a rule does not make sense. (*e*) Though maxims are not identical with moral principles they can accord or fail to accord with moral principles. My maxim always to tell the truth conforms with a moral principle if it is in fact the case that the truth ought to be told, whereas, on the same hypothesis, my maxim to lie when it suits me does not. (*f*) Maxims apply only to the person who makes them. I can make it a rule for myself always to rise at seven, but I cannot make this a rule for Jones, or, if I do—let us suppose I am Jones's wife—the rule I make for Jones is not a maxim, but some other sort of rule.

3) Kant holds (*a*) that a maxim is not morally acceptable and must not be adopted (ought not to be adopted) if it cannot be universalised; (*b*) that it may be adopted (it is false that it ought not to be adopted—not to be confused with saying that it ought to be adopted) if it can be universalised. He may also have thought (*c*) that a maxim must be adopted (ought to be adopted) if what I shall loosely call its "contradictory" is not universifiable. (*a*) and (*b*) are logically independent of one another. (*c*) would follow from (*a*) together with the additional premise, which I see no reason to cavil about, that if it is our duty not to do A, then it is our duty to do non-A.

4) A maxim is not universifiable if (*a*) it is impossible for everyone to act on it, or (*b*) it is impossible for anyone to will that everyone should act on it. When formulating the categorical imperative, Kant only mentions the impossibility of willing that everyone should act on a given maxim. Perfect duties, therefore, would only fall under Kant's first formulation of the categorical imperative if we can assume that, if it is impossible for everyone to act on a given maxim, it is impossible for anyone to will that everyone should act on it. I shall assume that what Kant means by saying that we cannot will that a maxim should become a universal law is that, if it were within our power to bring about a state of affairs in which everyone acted on our maxim, we could not bring ourselves to do it, or, what comes to the same thing, that if, as a result of our acting on a given maxim, it became a law of nature that everyone

acted on that maxim, we would not act on it. The statement that, if it were within my power to bring about a state of affairs in which everyone acted on a maxim which infringed an imperfect duty, I could not do it, is a hypothetical proposition with a false antecedent, and there are difficulties enough about these. The statement that, if it were within my power to bring about a state of affairs where everybody acted on a maxim which infringed a perfect duty, I could not do it, is, on Kant's view, a hypothetical proposition with a logically false antecedent; for if it is logically impossible for everyone to act on a given maxim, it must be logically impossible for me to have the power to will that they should. I do not know how one decides what one could or could not bring oneself to do in the event of some state of affairs being realised, the realisation of which is logically impossible.

5) There is no logical difficulty whatsoever in deducing whether or not a maxim is morally acceptable from Kant's first formulation of the categorical imperative, as there would be if he were merely saying that what is right for me is right for anyone or that moral principles must be unrestrictedly general. We simply argue syllogistically as follows: A maxim is not morally acceptable, if it is either impossible for everyone to act on it or impossible for the person whose maxim it is to will that everyone should act on it; it is either impossible for everyone to act on this maxim or impossible for me to will that everyone should act on it; therefore this maxim is not morally acceptable.

6) There certainly are maxims which it is logically impossible for everyone to act on. For example, I may make it a rule to be first through every door, but not everybody could successfully make this their rule. I am not convinced that there are any maxims which I could not, if I made a supreme effort, will that everybody should adopt (supposing this to be in my

power) but there certainly are maxims which I would be unlikely to act on, if I knew that as a result of my acting on them
everyone else would adopt and act on them. I may make it a
rule to consume without producing, but I should be unlikely
to make this my rule if I knew that, as a result of my making
this my rule, everyone else would make it their rule.

The first maxim the universalisation of which Kant considers is one which enjoins suicide. Kant states the maxim as
follows: "From self-love I make it my principle to shorten my
life if its continuance threatens more evil than it promises
pleasure," but he is quite wrong to state it in this way. The
phrase "From self-love I make it my principle" has nothing to
do with my maxim, but only with the motives which cause me
to adopt the maxim. These words should be omitted, therefore,
in which case my maxim will be simply "to shorten my life if
its continuance threatens more evil than it promises pleasure."
It is perhaps a little odd to speak of this as a rule—I have maintained that to adopt a maxim is to make so-and-so a rule. It is
a little odd to say that I make it a rule to commit suicide, for I
can only do this once, but this limitation does not spring from
the nature of my maxim, but from matters of fact extraneous
to it, so perhaps it can be ignored.

What, then, is the contradiction which would result if this
maxim were to be universally adopted? There must be such a
contradiction, of course, because suicide is alleged to be a perfect duty, not an imperfect one. It is natural, I think, to suppose from what Kant says in other places—he says, for example, that it is inconceivable that a maxim which infringes
perfect duty should be universalised—to look for a contradiction in the conception of everybody's acting on this maxim: to
look for a contradiction in the bare statement that everybody
is acting on it. It is obvious to the meanest intelligence, how-

ever, that there is no contradiction whatsoever in the idea of everyone's committing suicide if they would be happier dead, and, what is more, Kant makes no attempt whatsoever to show that there is such a contradiction. What he does try to show is, not that the statement that everybody acts on this maxim is self-contradictory, but that it contradicts another statement, a statement of fact, namely that the purpose of self-love is "to stimulate the furtherance of life," which I shall take to mean—I don't think it affects my argument if I am wrong—that the purpose of self-love is to prevent people from committing suicide.

Either something can have a purpose which it usually does not fulfil—as my watch usually does not fulfil its purpose of telling time—or it cannot. In the first case, there is obviously no contradiction between the statement that self-love usually prompts people to commit suicide, and the statement that the purpose of self-love is to stop people from committing suicide. Is there a contradiction in the second case? Perhaps there would be if the universal adoption of my rule to commit suicide if I should be happier dead would mean that self-love usually led people to kill themselves, but it does not mean this. My rule— and Kant almost seems to forget this—is not simply to commit suicide, but to commit suicide if I should be happier dead. Since it is not unreasonable to suppose that those people who would be happier dead are in a minority, the universal adoption of my maxim would not mean that people usually committed suicide, and not mean, therefore, that self-love usually (or even frequently) caused people to commit suicide.

It is not sufficient, of course, for the statement that everybody acts on my maxim to commit suicide if I shall be happier dead to contradict the statement that the purpose of self-love is to stimulate the furtherance of life. It is also necessary for this to be a true statement. To consider whether it is a true statement or not, however, is not a problem for a moral philosopher.

Let us now pass to Kant's second example—one of perfect duty to others. The maxim the universalisation of which he considers is this: "Whenever I believe myself short of money, I will borrow money and promise to pay it back, though I know that this will never be done." Kant argues that, though it is possible for me to adopt and act on this maxim, it is not possible for everybody to adopt and act on it; for, were they to do so, no-one would trust anyone who made a promise to keep it, hence no-one would be able to obtain a service by making a promise, hence no-one would make any promises, hence no-one would be able to act on the maxim in question.

On this argument I have the following comments to make:

1) Kant is obviously not considering the universalisation of the maxim he says he is considering, which concerns only obtaining money by promising to pay it back. The universalisation of this maxim would not lead to a cessation of promise-making in general, but only to a cessation of promising to pay back loans. However, I see no reason why we should not be charitable to Kant in this, if in no other, instance, and substitute for the maxim he states the more general rule to promise anything to obtain any service, even when I know I cannot keep my promise.

2) Kant claims that the statement that everybody acts on this maxim is self-contradictory, "that this maxim can never rank as a universal law and be self-consistent." He has not shown that this statement is self-contradictory, however. He has at most shown that it is impossible for everyone to act on my maxim to obtain services by making promises which I know I cannot keep, given that certain contingent statements are true. The contingent statements in question include at least

the following: (*a*) People frequently find themselves in circumstances when they need a service which they can only obtain by making a promise they cannot keep. Unless this statement were true, the universal adoption of my maxim would not lead to much dishonest promise-making, and so promise-making would not cease to be a human practice. (*b*) People usually remember when in the past other people have made promises they cannot keep. If people always forgot this, then people could quite happily go on obtaining services by making promises they could not keep, and promises would not cease to be made. (*c*) People are sufficiently egotistical not to provide a service for someone, in return for a promise to perform a future service, unless they think there is a reasonably high probability that the promise is one which can be kept. I am not disputing the truth of any of these statements. What I am doing is pointing out that they are contingent statements, and that if the universalisation of my maxim is only impossible given the truth of certain contingent assertions, its universalisation is not logically impossible.

3) I am willing to grant that if everyone acted on the maxim in question, promise-making would die out. This, however, does not mean that it is impossible for everybody to act on my rule to obtain services by making promises I know I cannot keep. For my rule is hypothetical: If circumstances arise in which you can obtain a service by making a promise which you know you cannot keep, make that promise—and there is a perfectly good sense in which everybody can make this their maxim, even if, as will be the case if everybody does make it their maxim, circumstances never do arise in which they can obtain a service by making a promise they know they cannot keep.

4) You would expect Kant's treatment of promise-making to be parallel to his treatment of suicide, since they are both

cases of perfect duty. They are not parallel, however, as they would be if he said something like "Everybody cannot make promises they know they cannot keep, for the purpose of some motive, e.g. enlightened self-interest, is to prevent people making such promises."

I shall now depart from the order in which Kant considers his examples, and consider the fourth before the third, for a reason which will be apparent later. The third and the fourth examples, of course, are examples of imperfect duties, so there is no impossibility in my maxim's being universally adopted. What is impossible is that I should be able to will its universal adoption, or that I should be able to act on the maxim, if I knew that as a result, by some queer freak of nature, it would be universally adopted.

Kant states his fourth maxim in an extremely rhetorical way, which I shall not repeat. It appears, however, that the maxim or rule in question is "Never to help others in distress." Kant argues that, though I can adopt the maxim, I cannot will its universal adoption, and the reason why I cannot will its universal adoption is that, if it were universally adopted, no-one would help me when I was in distress.

Again, I have the following comments to make:

1) It has often been alleged that Kant is appealing to self-interest in this particular example. This is not the case. He does not argue that it is wrong to adopt the maxim of not helping others in distress, because as a result no-one would help me when I was in distress, which would consist in an appeal to self-interest. It is not the consequences of my adopting the maxim which are contrary to my interest, but what would happen if everybody adopted it. Since there is no suggestion that my adopting the maxim would actually cause others to adopt

it (i.e., the condition in the hypothetical statement, "if everyone adopted my maxim, no-one would help me when I was in distress," is unfulfilled) there is no suggestion that the action is wrong because it has unfortunate consequences for me.

2) The reason why it is wrong for me to make a rule never to help anyone in distress is that, if I were to will that everyone acted on this maxim, my will would be at variance with itself. I take this to mean that, though there is a motive for willing the universal adoption of my maxim, for if my maxim were universally adopted, I should not have the disagreeable task of helping others in distress, there is also a motive against, for I would in this case not have the agreeable experience of being helped by others. I am not sure whether or not it is Kant's view that it is the same motive which militates both for and against the universal adoption of my maxim, or whether it may be one motive which militates for, and a different motive which militates against. Nor am I sure that Kant's view is not that there would be motives for and against the universal adoption of my maxim, but that the same motive which would make me want to adopt the maxim myself would make me want it not to be universally adopted. Or perhaps his view is that, though there is a motive for adopting the maxim myself, there is some other motive for not wanting it to be universally adopted.

3) It should be pointed out that to say that a will which willed the universal adoption of my rule not to help others in distress would be at variance with itself, is not to say that it is impossible for me to will the universal adoption of my maxim. I often do things in spite of motives impelling me not to do those things. From the fact that my will would be at variance with itself if it willed the universal adoption of my maxim it does not follow that I cannot will the universal adoption of

my maxim. All that does follow is that I cannot will it whole-heartedly.

Kant's third example, which I am taking last, of a maxim which cannot be universalised is "neglect to develop my natural gifts." The reason why, though a man can adopt and act on this maxim himself, he cannot will that everyone should adopt and act on it, is that "as a rational being he necessarily wills that all his powers should be developed, since they serve him, and are given him, for all sorts of possible purposes."

My comments are as follows:

1) The reason why I took the fourth example before the third was that I wanted to point out a lack of similarity in Kant's treatment of the two cases. If Kant's treatment of the third example had been analogous to his treatment of the fourth, what he would have said, presumably, would have been that, though I can act on the maxim "neglect my talents" my-self, I cannot will that everyone should make this their maxim, for in that case I should be deprived of any benefits accruing to me from other people's developing their talents. It is obvious that I do benefit from other people's developing their talents. However, what Kant in fact says is, not that I cannot will the universalisation of my maxim because other people's talents are useful to me, but that I cannot will the universalisation of my maxim because my talents are useful to me.

2) If the fact that a man's talents are useful to that man is not sufficient to prevent him from neglecting to develop them —as it obviously is not, for people do neglect to develop their talents, in spite of the fact that these are useful to them—it is not going to stop him from willing the universal neglect of talent-developing. For Kant's argument to have any sort of plausibility, it would have to be the case that the fact that my talents were useful to me was a better reason for not willing

that everybody should neglect their talents than for not willing that I should neglect my own talents. The case is quite the opposite, however. That my talents are useful to me is a much better reason for not neglecting my own talents than it is for not willing universal neglect of talents.

3) I am somewhat at a loss to know what is the import of the phrase "as a rational being" in "For as a rational being he necessarily wills that all his powers should be developed. . . ." This statement cannot be equivalent to the statement which you would get if you omitted the phrase in question, which is "He necessarily wills that all his powers should be developed." For it is absolutely obvious that this statement is false, and Kant must have known that it was obvious. Perhaps "As a rational being he necessarily wills that all his powers should be developed" means "If he were a completely (instead of a partially) rational being, he would necessarily will that all his powers be developed." The most this statement would prove would be that a completely rational being could not will neglect of his own talents. It would not prove, what Kant claims he is trying to prove, that I, who am not a completely rational being, cannot will universal neglect of talents. In any case, as has often been pointed out, if "rational being" means "being who always wills what is right," you could not deduce that talent-neglecting was wrong from the fact that a rational being could not will it. All you could do would be to deduce that a rational being could not will talent-neglecting from the prior fact that it was wrong.

I now want to make some general comments relevant to Kant's four examples of the application of the first formulation of the categorical imperative:

1) Only in one case, the third, does Kant make any mention of the actual consequences of my adopting a given maxim

in order to show that it is one which ought not to be adopted. In dealing with the third example, Kant does point out, as we have seen, that my talents are useful to me, i.e., that adopting the maxim of talent-neglecting would have bad consequences for myself. Only this is not a utilitarian argument, for Kant is not saying that my adopting the maxim would be harmful to society as a whole, but that it would be harmful to me, the agent. Furthermore, this is not held to be the reason why my maxim is a wrong one. The reason why it is wrong is that I cannot will its universal adoption, and that it has harmful consequences for me is—allegedly—the reason why I cannot will its universal adoption.

2) Not only is there no appeal to the actual bad consequences of my adopting a given maxim, alleged to be wrong; there is no appeal to the fact that the consequences of everyone's adopting the same maxim would be bad. There is, of course, mention of what would happen if everyone were to adopt my maxim, but this is not the same thing as an appeal to the bad consequences of what would happen, if everyone were to adopt my maxim. It is quite clear, of course, that, in all the four cases Kant considers, the universal adoption of the maxim in question would be bad; but Kant never appeals to this as a reason for thinking the maxim a wrong one. Furthermore, it is sometimes the case that the adoption of a given maxim by n people would be more than n times worse than the adoption of this maxim by one person alone. In such cases some philosophers have argued that I ought to take account of the bad consequences of the universal adoption of the maxim as well as or instead of the bad consequences of the adoption of the maxim by myself only. I should like to point out that in the case of Kant's second example, concerning the making of promises, the consequences of the adoption of the maxim "Obtain services by making promises you know you cannot keep"

by n people would quite clearly be more than n times worse than the consequences of the adoption of this maxim by one person. In the case of suicide and talent-neglecting it is arguable that the same would be true, though they are less obvious cases. Only in the case of not helping others in distress does it seem pretty clear that the consequences of the adoption of the maxim by n people would not be more than n times worse than the adoption of the maxim by one person. These, however, are just facts about Kant's examples. Kant himself makes no use of them, though the theory that does has a distinctly Kantian flavour.

3) There is an occasional reference to purpose in Kant's examples. In his third example, Kant says that our talents are given us for all sorts of possible ends, though this is not alleged to be the reason why it is wrong not to develop them, but to be the reason why, as a rational being, I cannot will that everyone should neglect to develop them. In Kant's first example there is a reference to the purpose of self-love, which is said to be to stimulate the furtherance of life, though, again, this is not held to be the reason why it is wrong to commit suicide, but to be the reason why it is impossible that everyone should act on my maxim enjoining suicide in certain circumstances. In Kant's second example there is a reference to the purpose of promising, but I interpret this not as being a reference to the purpose of promising itself—compare "the purpose of the liver"—or to the purpose some transcendent being has for promising, but to ordinary human purposes in making promises. On these references to purposes I shall allow myself one brief comment. If Kant were arguing—and I have just pointed out reasons for thinking he is not—that suicide from self-love and talent-neglecting are wrong because this is to use self-love and talents for purposes other than those which they have, or for which they were intended, then, if this argument

were valid at all, its conclusion would follow immediately, without any reference to the universalisation of suicide from self-love or to the universalisation of talent-neglecting.

4) There are a number of maxims which are such that what might be termed the "natural" or "normal" purpose— though not just any purpose—of anyone's adopting them would be defeated if they were adopted by everybody. It is clear that the maxims Kant considers in his last three examples are all of this sort. If my purpose in making it a rule to make promises I cannot keep is to obtain services from others without doing anything in return, my purpose will be defeated if everyone adopts my maxim. If my purpose in making it a rule to neglect my talents is to live on the fruits of other people's labour without myself contributing anything, my purpose will be defeated if everybody adopts my maxim. If my purpose in making it a rule not to help others in distress is to benefit from the help of others without doing anything in return, then my purpose will be defeated if everyone adopts my maxim. This is not true of suicide, however. My purpose in making it a "rule" to commit suicide if circumstances arise in which I shall be happier dead will not be defeated if everybody makes this a rule. Furthermore, only in the case of neglecting to help others in distress does Kant actually use this as a reason for thinking that I cannot will the universal adoption of my maxim. In the case of talent-neglecting we could scream with frustration and bafflement because he does not argue in this way. He may be arguing in this way, in the case of making promises you cannot keep, and this may be what he means when he says "the universality of a law, that everyone believing himself to be in need may make any promise he pleases with the intention not to keep it, would make promising, *and the very purpose of promising*, itself impossible. . . ." Only this is a case of perfect duty, so Kant should be trying to prove that the universalisation of

my maxim is impossible, not that I cannot will it, though, of course, there is no reason why he should not try to prove both.

5) Up to now I have considered the relation between the categorical imperative and the morality of maxims. So far, however, I have not said anything at all about the morality of individual actions. Let us suppose, for the sake of argument, that Kant has provided us with a satisfactory criterion for deciding upon the morality of maxims. It is quite clear to me that Kant thinks that, by doing this, he has automatically also provided us with a criterion for deciding upon the morality of actions. For example, he seems to think that, from the fact that my maxims or rule to commit suicide if I should be happier dead cannot be acted upon by everybody, it follows that the action of committing suicide, which would be performed on this maxim, is wrong. I think this is a howler. A maxim may be wrong, although an individual action performed upon it is right. Let us suppose, for example, that a promise is extracted from me by means of force. I may make it a rule to break promises which it is inconvenient for me to keep, and so break my promise. It is arguable that it is impossible for everybody to act on this maxim, and pretty clear that the maxim is a wrong one, whether it is possible for everybody to act on it or not. But the fact that my maxim was wrong would have no tendency whatsoever to show that my action, of breaking a promise extracted from me by means of force, was wrong. To suppose that it does is to commit a fallacy analogous to that of denying the antecedent in the *modus ponendo ponens*. If my maxim is right, it will follow that every action performed upon it is right, but if my maxim is wrong, it will not follow that every action performed upon it is wrong. In other words, the relation between the morality of maxims and the morality of actions is more complicated than Kant seems to have supposed. I am inclined, fairly tentatively, to say that a maxim is right if

and only if every action it could conceivably enjoin is right, and is wrong if some action it could conceivably enjoin is wrong. It does not follow that because a maxim enjoins a right action it is right, nor does it follow that because a maxim is wrong, the action which it enjoins is wrong. (I should also add that for every right action there is at least one, and possibly more than one, right maxim which would enjoin it, and that for every wrong action there are a large number of maxims which would enjoin it.) In other words, you may have: maxim right, action enjoined right; maxim wrong, action enjoined wrong; maxim wrong, action enjoined right; but you cannot have: maxim right, action enjoined wrong. This suggests that, instead of arguing that, because my maxim cannot be universalised, the action it enjoins must be wrong, Kant would have done better to argue that, because my maxim can be universalised, the action it enjoins must be right. In this case, though an action is shown to be right if a maxim can be found for it which can be universalised, it is not shown to be wrong because a maxim can be found for it which cannot be universalised. It is only shown to be wrong if every maxim which would enjoin it cannot be universalised. Is it the case that, if an action is wrong, no maxim which would enjoin it can be universalised? Against this there is a very formidable objection, which I am not sure can be answered. It is this: Given any wrong action, you can find a maxim for it which is so specific that it enjoins that action and no other. For example, my action of killing my mother-in-law would be enjoined by my maxim to kill anyone with purple hair (we will assume my motives are aesthetic ones). If she is the only purple-haired person, it would seem that my maxim can be universalised, in Kant's sense, without contradiction. It is, nevertheless, very wrong of me to kill my mother-in-law.

I want to end by making some very brief remarks on some of

the ethical theories which a consideration of Kant's examples of the first formulation of the categorical imperative might suggest.

1) I have a slight inclination to agree that, if my maxim is such that not everybody can successfully act on it, then it is a wrong maxim—though, as I have pointed out, it does not follow that every action it enjoins is wrong. I do not know how to prove this, however, and I am very far from being sure that it is true. There is an alleged proof of a different statement, namely that, if a maxim is such that not everybody can successfully act on it, it cannot be a maxim on which it is my *duty* to act. The proof is as follows: If it is everybody's duty to act on a maxim, it must be possible for everybody to act on it. Hence if it is not possible for everybody to act on a maxim, it cannot be a duty for everybody to act on it. What is not a duty for everybody is not a duty for anybody. Therefore it cannot be anybody's duty to act on a maxim on which everybody cannot act. I must confess I have some doubt about the premise: What is not a duty for everybody cannot be a duty for anybody, which I suspect some philosophers have confused with the different statement that what is not a duty for me cannot be a duty for anybody else in the same circumstances. I am inclined to think that "What is not a duty for everybody cannot be a duty for anybody" really means "What is not a duty for anybody, if everybody else is doing the same, is not a duty for anybody, even where not everybody else is doing the same." This is not self-evident, for, from the fact that it is not anybody's duty to do something in one set of circumstances, it does not follow that this is not anybody's duty in another different set of circumstances.

2) I have very little tendency to agree that, if I should be more reluctant to will the universal adoption of my maxim than to adopt it myself, this shows that the maxim in question

is wrong. A murderer who was also a hangman might be very reluctant to will that everybody should make it a rule to hang murderers, but this would not show that the maxim is a wrong one, though it might be wrong for other reasons. I make one exception to this expression of disagreement with Kant, however. If the reason why I am reluctant to will the universalisation of my maxim is that I should be horror-struck at the spectacle of everybody's acting on a wrong maxim—Kant nowhere says that this is the reason—then the fact that I feel this horror does indicate that the maxim in question is wrong. But I do not think you can argue from the fact that I would feel horror at the universalisation of my maxim to the fact that it is wrong —though you can argue from this to the different fact that I think it is wrong—for unless I first thought it was wrong, I should not feel horror at its universalisation, and if I mistakenly thought it was right, I should feel no such horror, and hence contemplating its universalisation would not enable me to correct my mistake.

3) Lastly, I am very strongly inclined to think that the fact that my maxim would have bad consequences if everybody were to adopt it would show it was wrong, even if my adopting it alone had no bad consequences, but this view has enormous difficulties, with which I have no space to deal adequately. Perhaps the worst of them, however, has already been mentioned. If I make my rule sufficiently specific, so specific that it enjoins simply one action, which itself has no bad consequences, then no bad consequences would result from its universalisation. I should like, if I can, however, to get over the difficulty in the following way. If my maxim is to break my promises, where this has no bad consequences, provided that I happen to be a person with webbed feet—we will assume that I have webbed feet, and that I am the only person who has —everybody else could adopt this maxim without harm re-

sulting. But not everybody could adopt this sort of maxim without harm resulting, for if I can argue that I may break my promises where promise-breaking has no bad consequences because I have webbed feet, someone else may argue that he may break such promises because he is over nine feet high, and someone else that he may break such promises because he is unique in having blood-group Z. But if everyone argued in this sort of way, harm would result. The problem is: What is the difference between arguing in this sort of way, which is not admissible, and arguing in other sorts of ways, which are? But I hope I have already said enough to show that, though Kant's theory is not tenable as it stands, there are implicit in it numerous suggestions which it would be profitable to consider at greater length on another occasion.

University of Durham

J. Kemp / Kant's examples of

the categorical imperative

In his article on "Kant's Examples of the First Formulation of the Categorical Imperative"[1] Mr. Jonathan Harrison has combined an exegesis of some of Kant's views with a criticism of them. My purpose here is to express certain doubts about his exegesis; the criticisms will be referred to only incidentally.

The difficulties begin with the title: what *is* the "first formulation"? It would be natural to suppose that it is what Paton, in *The Categorical Imperative*, refers to as Formula I: "Act only on that maxim through which you can at the same time will that it should become a universal law."[2] But this for-

Reprinted from THE PHILOSOPHICAL QUARTERLY, *Vol. VIII, No. 30 (Jan. 1958), pp. 63–71, by permission of the author and editors.*

[1] *The Philosophical Quarterly*, Jan. 1957, pp. 50–62.

[2] *Grundlegung*, 52 [p. 44 above]. It is highly desirable that agreement

mula has, in the *Grundlegung*, no examples at all; and the examples which Harrison discusses all belong to what Paton calls Formula Ia: "Act as if the maxim of your action were to become through your will a universal law of nature." Nor is this just a piece of pedantry, for the two formulae differ in meaning and in the method by which they are applied. The "universal law" of Formula I is a law (of freedom, not of nature) to the effect that everyone ought to, or may, act in a certain way: the "universal law of nature" of Formula Ia is a law to the effect that everyone necessarily does, or is able to, act in a certain way. And the arguments in Kant's first, third and fourth examples,[3] at least, would not even begin to make sense in terms of Formula I; for they depend on the concept of nature, to which that formula makes no reference. The law of nature, in fact, is used by Kant as a "type" or illustration of the moral law; "for if common sense did not have something to use in actual experience as an example, it could make no use of the law of pure practical reason in applying it to that experience."[4] The formula of the law of nature is thus intended as a practical criterion (or, more strictly, as the formal statement of a criterion which ordinary people actually use) for judging the morality of actions. Harrison is therefore in error in saying

should be reached on a systematic way of referring to Kant's works. The simplest procedure, here adopted, is to follow the practice of Kemp Smith with the *Critique of Pure Reason* and of Paton with the *Grundlegung*, and quote the pages of the original editions, where necessary denoting the first and second editions by "A" and "B" respectively. In cases where the use of this method alone might cause difficulties, I have added a reference to the pages of an easily accessible English translation, although my quotations are not always taken from the translations referred to.

[3] As for the argument of the second example, see pp. [236–239] below, especially n. 16.

[4] *Critique of Practical Reason*, A 123. Abbott's trans., . . . *and Other Works on the Theory of Ethics* (London: Longman's Green and Co., 1909), pp. 161–162.

that, in this formula, Kant was attempting to put forward the supreme principle of morality.[5] Even in the *Grundlegung*,[6] Kant makes it clear that autonomy, not universality, is the supreme principle of morality; and in the *Critique of Practical Reason*, just before the passage quoted above, he states also that the comparison of one's maxims with a universal law of nature is not the "determining ground" of one's will (as the supreme principle of morality would presumably be), but merely a useful example of a universal law which we can employ by a kind of analogy, as a criterion.

Before he proceeds to discuss Kant's examples in detail, Harrison makes some preliminary remarks (mostly about maxims), one of which requires comment. "I shall assume," he says,[7] "that what Kant means by saying that we cannot will that a maxim should become a universal law is that, if it were within our power to bring about a state of affairs in which everyone acted on our maxim, we could not bring ourselves to do it, or, what comes to the same thing, that if, as a result of our acting on a given maxim, it became a law of nature that everyone acted on that maxim, we would not act on it." Kant's conception of being able, or unable, to will that a maxim should become a universal law of nature is admittedly at first sight obscure—although some, at least, of the obscurity is due to the fact that the English verb "to will" is used far less commonly and naturally than the German *wollen*. But it is quite clear that Harrison's interpretation will not do. The inability to bring oneself to do something is quite irrelevant; a man may be unable, for various reasons, to bring himself to do his duty, but this neither means nor implies that he is unable to will it. Nor

[5] Harrison, p. 50 [p. 209 above].
[6] Cp. especially *Gr.* 87–88 [67 above].
[7] P. 52 [212–213 above].

is the notion, contained in Harrison's interpretation, of a maxim becoming a law of nature as a result of someone's acting on it to be found in Kant.

It is clear from Kant's own arguments that the impossibility of willing certain types of maxims to be universal laws of nature is due to, or at least connected with, the fact that it would be irrational (not impossible) to set oneself to act accordingly. It is impossible for a man to will a universal law of nature that all men let their talents rust because "as a rational being he necessarily wills that all his powers should be developed, since they serve him, and are given him, for all sorts of possible ends"[8] i.e. it is irrational to set oneself to produce such a state of affairs, because it is inconsistent with purposes which one necessarily has. And it is impossible to will a universal law of nature to the effect that nobody helped anybody else, because "a will which decided in this way would be at variance with itself [*würde sich selbst widerstreiten*]."[9] The essential point is that irrational willing, in this sense of the word, is for Kant a contradiction in terms; whereas setting oneself to act irrationally is always possible for human beings, but is, in his technical language, a manifestation of *Willkür*, not of *Wille*.[10]

As not infrequently happens, Kant expresses himself more clearly in the corresponding passage in the *Critique of Practical Reason*. He there argues that men do in fact use the formula of the universal law of nature as a criterion for judging actions: "People ask, 'If you belonged to an order of things in which everyone would allow himself to deceive when he thought it to his advantage . . . , would you assent of your own will to

---

[8] *Gr.* 55–56 [47 above].

[9] *Gr.* 56 [47 above].

[10] For this distinction see *Metaphysik der Sitten*, Introduction AB 5. Abbott 268.

being a member of that order? [*würdest du darin wohl mit Einstimmung deines Willens sein?*]' "[11] This cannot of course mean "Would you like, or enjoy, being a member of that order?" for liking or enjoyment can never in Kant's view function as a criterion of morality. Nor can it mean "Could you bring yourself to remain if you had a chance of leaving?" for you might be able to bring yourself to remain, from love of pleasure or idleness, against your better judgment. The question is rather, "Would you freely (i.e. rationally, independently of the pressure of your desires or other empirical factors) assent to your membership?"

We can now turn to consider Harrison's discussion of the examples themselves.

I   Suicide

Kant's explanation of the wrongness of suicide rests on a teleological assumption about the function of the instinct of self-love. A system of nature (*eine Natur*) in which everyone who felt tired of life was led by self-love to kill himself "would contradict itself and consequently could not subsist as a system of nature,"[12] because the function of self-love is to stimulate the furtherance of life. Now this argument is obviously open to criticism in various ways; one might, for instance, object to basing any duty on a belief about the purposiveness of nature or, less sweepingly, one might say that Kant has failed to distinguish the instinct of self-preservation (a blind tendency to preserve one's life at all costs) from the principle of self-love (a calculated desire for pleasure and aversion from pain). But Harrison's objection to the argument is different and is, I

[11] *Critique of Practical Reason*, A 122–123. Abbott 161.
[12] *Gr.* 54 [45 above].

think, based on a misunderstanding of Kant's meaning. What Kant is trying to show, he thinks, is that the statement that everybody acts on the maxim of killing himself when the continuance of life promises more pain than pleasure contradicts the (true) statement that the purpose of self-love is to stimulate the furtherance of life. But this misses the point of Kant's argument. What is in question is not a mere statement to the effect that everyone acts on a certain maxim, but a law of nature to the effect that everyone necessarily acts on it, and this, Kant is saying, in effect, contradicts another law of nature according to which the function of self-love is to preserve life. This failure to distinguish between a statement that people as a matter of fact always, or usually, behave in a certain way and a law of nature to the effect that people necessarily behave in that way is at the root of Harrison's objections to Kant on this point. There are, he thinks, two possible interpretations of the contention that it is the purpose, or part of the purpose, of self-love to prevent people from committing suicide. (*a*) The purpose referred to may be one which is usually not fulfilled (as some watches usually fail to fulfil the purpose of telling time.) In this case, he says, "there is obviously no contradiction between the statement that self-love usually prompts people to commit suicide, and the statement that the purpose of self-love is to stop people from committing suicide."[13] This is true, but completely irrelevant to anything Kant actually says. (*b*) The purpose may be one which cannot remain as a rule unfulfilled. But on this assumption also, Harrison thinks, the contradiction alleged by Kant does not occur. "Perhaps there would be [a contradiction] if the universal adoption of my rule to commit suicide if I should be happier dead would mean that self-love usually led people to kill themselves, but it does not mean this. My rule—and Kant almost seems to forget this

[13] P. 54 [215 above].

—is not simply to commit suicide, but to commit suicide if I should be happier dead. Since it is not unreasonable to suppose that those people who would be happier dead are in a minority, the universal adoption of my maxim would not mean that people usually committed suicide, and not mean, therefore, that self-love usually (or even frequently) caused people to commit suicide." Once again, the connection of Kant's notion of universality with the word "usually" is a mistake. It does not matter how many weary people commit suicide—it is as wrong for one as for a million, and as possible for a million, or for the entire human race, as for one. Kant is not saying that it is impossible for self-love to lead everybody to commit suicide, still less that it is impossible for it to lead all those who are weary of life to do so; what he *is* implying is that such a state of affairs could not form part of a system of nature which also contained the law that the purpose of self-love is to promote the furtherance of life. For a system of nature is *ex hypothesi* rationally ordered, and it would be irrational if one and the same principle or instinct could lead to diametrically opposed types of behaviour. (One might, of course, conceive of a system of nature which included beings in whom some sort of death-wish was the guiding force, though they would obviously not form part of this system for long; but nature is not, in Kant's view, like that.)

II *False promises*

Here the maxim which Kant considers cannot become a universal law of nature is "Whenever I believe myself short of money, I will borrow money and promise to pay it back, though I know that this will never be done."[14] "Kant argues," Harrison says, "that, though it is possible for me to adopt and

14 *Gr.* 54 [46 above].

act on this maxim, it is not possible for everybody to adopt and act on it; for, were they to do so, no-one would trust anyone who made a promise to keep it, hence no-one would be able to obtain a service by making a promise, hence no-one would make any promises, hence no-one would be able to act on the maxim in question."[15] But what Kant says is, not that it is impossible for everyone to adopt and act on this maxim, but that a law that everyone is able[16] to do so would contradict itself; and thus the impossibility of everyone adopting the maxim cannot be a merely causal impossibility, as Harrison's version would allow it to be. But the chief error here, a not uncommon one, lies, I think, in a misunderstanding of Kant's statement that the universality of the maxim in question "would make promising, and the very purpose of promising, impossible." Kant's use of the word *machen* here is taken by Harrison to indicate a causal relationship: if the maxim were universally adopted, then a causal consequence would be that the practice of promise-making, or at least of making promises in connection with loans, would soon die out, because it would be seen to be pointless (cp. Harrison, p. 55 [217 above], "I am willing to grant that if everyone acted on the maxim in question, promise-making would die out"). And if this were Kant's meaning, the argument would indeed be as unsatisfactory as Harrison maintains. It may well be true, for instance, that if everyone cheated at bridge, it would soon result that no-one would play it; but this result is in no way inconsistent with the universalised maxim to cheat whenever it is to one's advantage. For the

[15] P. 54 [216 above].

[16] Paton here mistranslates *könne* by "may"; and also, presumably by an oversight, omits the phrase "of nature" after "I then see straight away that this maxim can never rank as a universal law," thus creating the misleading impression that Kant is talking about a law of morality, not a law of nature.

maxim does not assert or imply that everyone plays bridge, but only that, if and when they play bridge, they will cheat whenever they think it is to their advantage.

What Kant actually says, however, is not that the maxim of making false promises could not exist as a universal law of nature for very long (which is what Harrison's interpretation amounts to, for there would obviously be a time-lag), but that it could not exist at all as a universal law of nature without contradiction. And if he really means this, it is clear that the relation designated by the verb *machen* must be one of logical or quasi-logical, not causal consequence. The argument has the effect of a *reductio ad absurdum*. If, *per impossibile*, there were a universal law to this effect, then there would not be and would never have been any promises[17] (the "if . . . then" indicating an entailment-relation); but the statement that there is such a law of nature also entails that there are promises. Hence it has contradictory implications—i.e. it is self-contradictory.

It is worth noticing that Kant is careful to distinguish the concept of self-contradiction from that of being self-defeating or self-destructive. In the passages of the *Grundlegung* under discussion, whenever a putative universal law of nature is rejected as being inconsistent with itself, Kant says (and, I have argued, means) that it is self-contradictory, using always the phrase *sich widersprechen*. But when he wishes to say, of a putative universal law of morality, that it would be inconsistent with itself, he uses different terminology—such a law

[17] People might have used the expression "I promise," but they could not (logically) have used it for the purpose of making a promise; for you cannot (again logically) make a promise if nobody will believe you. Although you could say "I promise to repay the money," it would be only a statement of intention, not a promise, which requires the existence of a promisee as well as a promisor.

would annihilate itself, *sich selbst vernichten* or *sich selbst aufreiben*.[18]

III *Developing one's talents*

Harrison here makes the mistake of supposing that Kant's argument to show that willing the universal neglect of talents is impossible involves a reference to prudential considerations. "If Kant's treatment of the third example had been analogous to his treatment of the fourth, what he would have said, presumably, would have been that, though I can act on the maxim "neglect my talents" myself, I cannot will that everyone should make this their maxim, for in that case I should be deprived of any benefits accruing to me from other people's developing their talents. It is obvious that I do benefit from other people's developing their talents. However, what Kant in fact says is, not that I cannot will the universalisation of my maxim because other people's talents are useful to me, but that I cannot will the universalisation of my maxim because my talents are useful to me."[19] In this last sentence, as in some other places, Harrison says "says" when he means "means"; but even as an interpretation of what Kant means it is, to say the least, hazardous, for there is nothing in the *Grundlegung* to suggest that the ends which the development of my talents may help me to achieve are selfish ones. This interpretation is, indeed, hardly consistent with Kant's original description of the situation, in which he refers to a man with a talent, the cultivation of which "would make him a useful man [*not* "would be useful to him"] for all sorts of purposes."[20] In the *Metaphysik der*

[18] Cp. *Critique of Practical Reason*, A 50. Abbott 115.

[19] P. 57 [220 above].

[20] *Gr.* 55 [46 above].

Sitten, when Kant comes to expand his views on the development of talents and faculties, he expresses himself quite unmistakably. Man's duty to develop his faculties, he there says, is not dependent on any advantage their development may bring him; indeed, the advantage might turn out to be in favour of Rousseau's noble, but uncultivated, savage. "On the contrary, it is a command of morally practical reason, and a duty of a man towards himself, that he should cultivate his capacities (one rather than another according to the diversity of his objectives), and be a man who, from a practical point of view, is well adapted to the purpose of his existence."[21]

The key to the understanding of this third example lies in its last sentence: "For as a rational being he necessarily wills that all his powers should be developed, since they serve him, and are given him, for all sorts of possible ends."[22] What chiefly distinguishes man from the rest of creation, according to Kant, is his possession of freedom; this in turn depends on his possession of reason, not in the sense that he is capable of theoretical activity, but in the sense that he can set ends or purposes before himself (whereas the rest of creation can merely fulfil passively the purposes of nature).[23] And this gives its point to the expression, which Harrison finds obscure, "For as a rational being he necessarily wills . . . ." Whatever a man's private aim or purpose in life may be, the fact that he

21 *MdS, Tugendlehre*, A 111. J. W. Semple's trans., *The Metaphysic of Ethics* (3rd ed., Edinburgh, 1871), pp. 261–262. (This translation of Semple's is full of inaccuracies and should be used with great caution.)

22 *Gr.* 56 [47 above].

23 Cp. *Critique of Judgment*, B 399. J. H. Bernard's trans. (New York: Hafner, 1951), p. 361. "Only in man, and only in him as subject of morality, do we meet with unconditioned legislation in respect of purposes, which therefore alone renders him capable of being a final purpose, to which the whole of nature is teleologically subordinated."

has such a purpose is a sign of his rationality, even though all men, being imperfectly rational, have some purposes which they would not have if they were perfectly rational, and fail to have some which they would then have. Now any human purpose requires the exercise of some talent or capacity for its fulfilment; for a talent or capacity just is the ability to take appropriate means to given ends. Man's ability to conceive of purposes would be of no value, and his freedom would be incomplete, if he were not also endowed with the capacity for discovering and adopting the best means for the attainment of those purposes. Hence to refuse to develop *any* of one's talents would be irrational; it would be failing to take rational means to the achievement of any of one's aims or purposes, and all of us must have some such aims or (as we should more naturally say) desires. But why, it might be asked, should I not restrict my efforts to developing those talents which will enable me to live a more pleasant life; why should I worry about developing my moral capacities or increasing my ability to help others? Because, Kant would reply, you are a man and a rational being, and to restrict the development of one's capacities to those which provide an increase of pleasure for oneself is to put oneself on a level with the beasts, to behave in an inhuman and irrational way. It is because of this that a man cannot rationally assent to being a member of an order of nature in which self-development was universally neglected. Moreover, the use of reason, as manifested in the deliberate cultivation of one's talents, in order merely to promote one's own happiness is unlikely to be successful, human nature being what it is: "the more a cultivated reason concerns itself with the aim of enjoying life and happiness, the farther does man get away from true contentment."[24]

[24] *Gr.* 5 [14 above].

IV *Helping others in distress*

All that need be said under this head is that Harrison once again seems to misunderstand Kant's use of the words *Wille* and *wollen*. He points out that people sometimes do things in spite of motives impelling them not to, and concludes "From the fact that my will would be at variance with itself if it willed the universal adoption of my maxim, it does not follow that I cannot will the universal adoption of my maxim. All that does follow is that I cannot will it wholeheartedly."[25] But although it does not follow that I cannot set myself, whether whole-heartedly or not, to achieve its universal adoption, it does, in Kant's terminology, follow that I cannot *will* its universal adoption; for the notion of a will at variance with itself is self-contradictory, even though the notion of human efforts at variance with one another is not. *Wille* and *wollen* always include the notion of rational effort; and inconsistency, whether of judgment or of volition, is a sign of irrationality.

Harrison concludes his article with some more general comments. Of these, the only one I wish to discuss concerns the relation between the morality of maxims and the morality of actions. Kant is alleged to have committed a howler in supposing that his criterion for deciding upon the morality of maxims automatically provides us with a criterion for deciding upon the morality of actions; in supposing, for example, that the impossibility of willing that the maxim of committing suicide if one would be happier dead should become a universal law entails that the action of suicide in itself is necessarily wrong. Even if a maxim is wrong, Harrison thinks, some individual actions performed in accordance with

25 P. 57 [219–220 above].

it may be right. "Let us suppose, for example, that a promise is extracted from me by means of force. I may make it a rule to break promises which it is inconvenient for me to keep, and so break my promise. It is arguable that it is impossible for everybody to act on this maxim, and pretty clear that the maxim is a wrong one, whether it is possible for everybody to act on it or not. But the fact that my maxim was wrong would have no tendency whatsoever to show that my action, of breaking a promise extracted from me by means of force, was wrong."[26]

Now the whole question of the relation between actions and their maxims is somewhat obscure, and Kant does not give us as much help in elucidating it as we should have liked: serious difficulties, in particular, arise from the fact that we can apparently extract maxims from actions at varying levels of generality. And if I have performed an action, and tell someone what its maxim was, it is easy to imagine a situation in which he might wish to challenge my statement, but not at all easy to formulate the grounds on which such a challenge might be supported or resisted—disagreement about the maxim of an action is not the same as, though it may be connected with, disagreement about its motive. Nevertheless, I do not think that Kant has committed a "howler" in this instance, however obscure, and perhaps mistaken, his general account of maxims may be. Harrison's impression that he has done so seems to be due to the misleadingly abstract sense in which he, in contrast with Kant but in common with most contemporary British philosophers, uses the word "action." For Kant, the use of the principle of universality is to test, by examining the nature of its maxim, the totality consisting of action-on-this-maxim; whereas Harrison argues as if examination of the maxim will provide a criterion of the action, even when this action is con-

[26] P. 60 [225 above].

sidered quite independently of the maxim examined, i.e. as if the wrongness of action on a certain maxim entailed the wrongness of any action which, even though performed on a different maxim, was otherwise identical with it. In Kant's view, the assessment of actions in the narrower sense, considered independently of their maxims, concerns, not their morality, but their legality—quite a different matter.[27] The impossibility of universalising the maxim of breaking promises whenever it is inconvenient to keep them shows, not that breaking promises is always wrong (if Kant had held that it did he would have been mistaken), but that breaking promises just because it is inconvenient to keep them is wrong. It is true, of course, that Kant took a very rigorous view of the obligation to keep promises, as of that to avoid telling lies, whatever the circumstances. But it is important to distinguish Kant's personal opinions on moral matters from the principles of his moral philosophy; for there are some of the former which are not entailed by anything in the latter.

University of St. Andrews

[27] For this distinction between *Sittlichkeit* and *Gesetzmässigkeit* see *MdS*, Introduction, AB 27. Abbott 282.

Jonathan Harrison / The categorical

imperative

I cannot hope to deal with all the points raised by Mr. Kemp in his scholarly criticism of my paper; on the other hand, I cannot forbear from commenting on the following somewhat arbitrary selection.

On "willing"

Talk about whether or not we could will that our maxim should become a universal law is queer not, I think, because "will" is an unusual verb, but because it is difficult to see what volitional attitude we could take up to something so utterly outside our power to achieve as the universalisation of our

Reprinted from THE PHILOSOPHICAL QUARTERLY, *Vol. VIII, No. 33 (Oct. 1958), pp. 360–364, by permission of the author and editors.*

maxim. This is presumably the reason why some commentators use "desire" and "wish" instead of "will," and it is why I talk about what we could choose, if we had the power, or what we would choose, if the universalisation of our maxim should by some miracle be the consequence of our action. Again Mr. Kemp's view that willing should be defined not simply in terms of choosing, but in terms of rational choosing, the following objections may be raised.

(1) The trouble with using what a rational being can or cannot will as a test of right or wrong is that in the ordinary sense of "rational," rational beings are as capable of immorality as anyone else, and that in its technical, capital-letter sense it tends to be a criterion of a Rational Being that he never chooses immorally; hence you have to know what is immoral first in order to know what a Rational Being would choose, and so cannot deduce that it is immoral from the fact that a Rational Being would not choose it.

(2) Kant [*Grundlegung*, Akademie ed., 403; p. 22 above] states that I can will to lie, and clearly means decide or choose to lie.

(3) In the passages we are discussing there is an obvious antithesis between the *objects* of my choice, i.e., the action and its universalisation. According to Mr. Kemp, there is also an antithesis between two sorts of choice, ordinary choice and rational choice (willing). If this were correct, we would expect to see Kant contrasting being about to *choose* an action with being unable to *will* (rationally choose) it, and being able to *choose* the universalisation of our maxim with being unable to *will* it; in fact he never does this. On my view, the contrast between being able to choose the action but unable to will its universalisation is a straightforward antithesis between two different objects of choice. On Mr. Kemp's view, it is a clumsy because simultaneous contrast of object of choice and nature

of choice, i.e., between being able to choose the action, but unable rationally to choose its universalisation.

On "law" in formula I

If Mr. Kemp is right in thinking that "law" in Formula I means "moral law," Formula I may mean one of (at least) two things. (A) Act only on that maxim which you could cause to become a moral law, if you had the power. (B) Act only on maxims which you are satisfied accord with moral laws.

(1) A would be the most natural interpretation of Kant, given that "law" means "moral law."

(2) B would have the advantage of being true; I surely ought to consider whether my maxims accord with moral law before I adopt them. B has the disadvantage, however, that it does not tell me what the moral law is to which my maxims ought to conform.

(3) On neither A nor B is Kant right in supposing Formula I equivalent to Formula Ia, for they mention my attitude to laws on which people ought to act, whereas Formula Ia mentions my attitude to laws which describe how people actually do act. There might be many things that I could will to be a law that people ought to act on, so long as I thought that it would not become a law (of nature) that they act on them, e.g., the debtor of the parable might well be able to will it to be a moral law that everyone ought to imprison their debtors, but unable to will it to be a law of nature that everyone did imprison their debtors.

(4) On A, however, consideration of what it would be like if my maxim became a law of nature might be one of my motives for deciding whether or not to make it a moral law. Perhaps I cannot will it to be a moral law that no-one ought to help others in distress (or should the moral law be that

anyone may refrain from helping others in distress?), because in that case no-one would help anyone else in distress, and then no-one would help me. And perhaps there are other maxims which I could not make moral laws had I the power because, as a legislator, I must wish to make practicable moral laws, and the worst sort of impracticability in a moral law is the logical impossibility of its being acted upon by everybody.

(5) On this view, of course, I am not subject to laws which I make, but subject to laws which I could have made, had I the power.

(6) What, on this interpretation of Kant, I am asked to do (i.e., consider what moral laws I could make, had I the power), must not be confused with something different (i.e., considering what positive laws I could make, had I the power). The notion of making moral law is such a very odd one, that I think anyone trying to put himself in the former position is likely to succeed in putting himself only in the latter. The difference is important, for there might be many things that he might wish to make illegal, which he did not wish to make immoral (and, perhaps, vice versa).

(7) In deciding what moral laws one could make, I think it would be important to avoid moral considerations. Of course, if one were considering what positive laws to make, it would be natural and proper to allow moral arguments to weigh with one—e.g., if one were considering whether to make homosexual intercourse illegal, one would naturally, though I hope not exclusively, be influenced by whether or not one thought it immoral. But I think that in imagining oneself as a moral-law giver, one cannot properly do this, for if one has to decide what the moral law is *via* a consideration of what moral laws one could legislate, one must not suppose it to be already determined what it is, in order to decide what moral laws one could legislate.

(8) If I am right in supposing that the only reason why one could not will one's maxim to be a moral law would be consideration of what would happen if this moral law were acted upon (i.e., consideration of what would happen if one's maxim became a law of nature), then if there are immoral maxims which one could will to be laws of nature, one could also will them to be moral laws, so any difficulties with Formula Ia would also be difficulties with A above.

(9) It must not be supposed that "law" in Formula I must mean "moral law" because Ia mentions the law of nature explicitly. It could mean (as I had supposed it did) "law in general" (i.e., that of which moral laws and natural laws and logical laws are all species). If it does, Formulas I and Ia are much more nearly equivalent than if it means "moral law," for a law of nature is a species of law in general, though it is not even a species of moral law.

Suicide

(1) I take it that to say a system of nature contradicts itself is to say that the statements involved in its description are contradictory, nor do I know what it means to say that *laws* contradict one another if it does not mean that the statements which formulate these laws contradict one another. Mr. Kemp himself finds the contradiction which he thinks is involved in the universalisation of promise-breaking in a contradiction between statements.

(2) To point out that the universality of suicide among *men who would be happier dead* does not even imply that suicide is usual among *men* (without restriction) is no more to misunderstand what is meant by universality than is to point out that men are not usually hanged to fail to appreciate that murderers always are.

False promises

(1) Mr. Kemp accuses me of attributing to Kant the view that the universal making of promises which one has no intention of keeping is only causally impossible; what I actually say is that though Kant thought it was logically impossible, it is in fact (at most) only causally impossible—and not even this in a universe where people's memories are very short.

(2) Mr. Kemp agrees with Kant that the universal making of promises one has no intention of keeping is logically impossible, for, if the maxim in question became a universal law, then there would both be and not be promises. Three questions arise: (i) Would the universalisation of Kant's maxim entail that all promises were false promises? (ii) If all promises were false promises, would this entail that no promises would be "believed"? (iii) If no promises were believed, would this entail that there were no promises?

(i) Even if we ignore—as I believe we may—the fact that Kant's maxim relates only to promises to obtain money, and substitute the maxim "make false promises when it suits me," the universalisation of this maxim does not entail that all promises are false promises, unless we add the additional dubious premise that it never suits me to make any promises except false promises. If we drop the qualification "if it suits me," the result is a maxim which is absurd, and does not in any case entail that I never make any other sort of promises. The maxim which would entail that all promises were false promises, "*Only* make false promises," is not Kant's, and would not in any case entail that there *were* promises, which is a necessary step in Mr. Kemp's argument.

(ii) That all promises are false promises does not in itself entail that no promises are believed, but only in conjunction with certain other empirical propositions about people, e.g. that they are all possessed of a certain (admittedly low) degree of acumen, not given to superstitions about the integrity of certain limited classes of people.

(iii) It is certainly not necessary that any given promise should be believed either by the promisee or by anybody else. Why then should it be necessary that at least one, or a good many, *other* promises should be believed? I suspect that the truth is that uttering the words "I promise" (or an equivalent) cannot accomplish the making of a promise if they are greeted with open ridicule by the promisee. The proposition that if no promises were believed, all promises would be greeted with open ridicule by the promisee is an empirical proposition. I do not know whether or not it is true.

Developing one's talents

(1) My concern was not to criticise Kant morally (for appealing to self-interest, which I don't think he does), but logically for seeming to suppose that the effects of my talent-neglecting on my interest, which are features of an individual case of talent-neglecting, were reasons for my being unable to will the universalisation of talent-neglecting. Mr. Kemp may be helping Kant's character, but not his logic, by suggesting that he regarded my talents as something useful to everybody, for that my talents are useful to everybody is just as much a feature of the individual action as that my talents are useful to me, and so no better a reason for being unable to will the universalisation of talent-neglecting than that my talents are useful to me.

(2) Mr. Kemp's positive interpretation turns on taking "talent-neglecting" to mean "neglecting to develop one's capacities for achieving any of one's purposes." That talent-ne-

glecting does not mean this is shown by the fact that the South Sea Islanders neglected to develop their talents; yet I understand they cultivate their capacities for achieving some ends quite assiduously. The contradiction found by Mr. Kemp (between having purposes but not developing one's capacities for achieving them) has nothing to do with universalisation, and would make Kant's mention of this irrelevant.

Helping others in distress

(1) Surely there is nothing in the least irrational about willing things—one's duty, for example—in spite of having motives impelling one not to will them.

(2) I am inclined to think we are both wrong in the meaning we attribute to "at variance with itself."

Kant's howler

Mr. Kemp's remarks raise questions too general to be considered here. I call the fallacy I attribute to Kant a howler, because it is analogous to the fallacy of denying the antecedent. It does not follow that if a rule is wrong—because there are some cases in which it would lead one astray—it has led one astray in this case.

University of Durham

Robert K. Shope / Kant's

use and derivation of the

categorical imperative

Kant tried to prove that one of man's duties is to obey the categorical imperative, "Act only according to that maxim by which you can at the same time will that it should become a universal law."[1] Kant also believed that the categorical imper-

Professor Shope's essay appears for the first time in this volume.

[1] I shall consider the categorical imperative as formulated in terms of universalizability but not as formulated with reference to a kingdom of ends or to men as ends in themselves.

The following abbreviations have been used for English editions of Kant's works:

DV *The Doctrine of Virtue: Part II of the Metaphysic of Morals*, trans. M. Gregor (New York: Harper & Row, 1964).

F *Foundations of the Metaphysics of Morals and What Is Enlightenment?* trans. L. W. Beck (New York: Bobbs-Merrill, 1959). These references are to the pages above in the present edition.

FC *Critique of Pure Reason*, trans. N. K. Smith (New York: St. Martin's Press, 1963).

ative is obeyed (1) by any morally good man, (2) by any man who fulfills any moral obligation, and (3) by any man who does any morally valuable action. Kant provided arguments in support of these claims and thought that common-sense moral opinion concurred with his conclusions. I shall show, however, that Kant's arguments for these claims are not satisfactory and shall suggest that requirements (1) and (2) are actually contrary to common sense while (3) is at least not supported by common-sense convictions. Thus, in want of more convincing arguments to support his claims this part of Kant's theory of the categorical imperative must be rejected. I shall even show that Kant failed to provide satisfactory proof that there is a duty to obey the categorical imperative. Yet I shall then sketch an argument which Kant did not employ but which might show that there is a duty to obey the categorical imperative in a certain way. Even if this argument is satisfactory, however, there still is no reason to suppose that the categorical imperative can be used in quite the way Kant intended.

The first section of this paper explains what Kant views as obedience to the categorical imperative and how he thinks this obedience is connected with the good will, with morally valuable actions, and with doing one's duty and fulfilling one's obligations. The second section reviews Kant's arguments on behalf of his doctrines about the categorical imperative. The third section discusses the relations of doctrines (1), (2), and (3) to common sense, and considers whether they suggest any

LE   *Lectures on Ethics*, trans. L. Infield (New York: Harper & Row, 1949).
MJ   *Metaphysical Elements of Justice*, trans. J. Ladd (New York: Bobbs-Merrill, 1965).
R   *Religion Within the Limits of Reason Alone*, trans. T. M. Greene and H. H. Hudson (New York: Harper & Row, 1960).
SC   *Critique of Practical Reason*, trans. L. W. Beck (New York: Bobbs-Merrill, 1956).
TC   *Critique of Judgment*, trans. J. H. Bernard (New York: Hafner, 1951).
The page references in parentheses are to the English editions, those in brackets to the Akademie edition.

insights even while remaining themselves unacceptable. It also outlines a possible proof, different from those which Kant gave, of the claim that there is a duty to obey the categorical imperative.

I

Kant not only believes that the way to *test* the moral validity of one's maxims is by checking them for universalizability—he also maintains that the categorical imperative commands men to *will* the policy of choosing only universalizable maxims. A good man must *use* the criterion of universalizability as *his* standard when he acts, as his basis for rejecting certain practical principles and for accepting others as his maxims. This means that obedience to the categorical imperative involves adopting as one's higher-order maxim what Kant calls the *principle of autonomy:* "To act only according to that maxim by which I can at the same time will that it should become a universal law." The fact that another spectator could see that my particular maxim, e.g., the maxim "To tell the truth," is universalizable is not sufficient for me to have a good will; rather, I must use the principle of autonomy as a way of choosing among more particular practical principles, as a way of choosing only certain ones as maxims.[2] Thus, a good man

[2] The content of a *practical principle* specifies a line of conduct pursuable by a moral agent, and can include an indication of circumstances and conditions governing the conduct. Such a principle has either the form "To do *x*" or the form "To do *x* if . . ." where doing *x* is a type of action. A supposedly immoral practical principle which Kant mentions is "To shorten my life when by a longer duration it threatens more evil than satisfaction" (cf. F 45 [422]). A morally valid practical principle would be "To pay my debts."

Another way in which practical principles can be stated is in the form "I will do *x*" or in the form "I will do *x* if . . ."; for example, "When I believe myself to be in need of money, I will borrow money and promise

has at least two principles of volition or two maxims when he performs some intentional phenomenal action, namely, a principle with that kind of phenomenal action as its content, such as "To tell the truth," and the further principle "To act only according to that [subordinate] maxim by which I can at the same time will that it should become a universal law." The agent chooses his more specific maxims so that they conform to the policy indicated by the principle of autonomy, which itself is the *ultimate* maxim of a good human will. Kant believes that if a man tells the truth because the ultimate maxim of his action is "To tell the truth" then his decision does not show that he has a good will, nor does his action even have moral value. His action has moral worth and manifests his good will only when it is done from duty, and that requires him to have the principle of autonomy as the ultimate maxim governing his action. This requirement is what the categorical imperative demands of a man.

Some commentators believe that Kant did *not* claim that the categorical imperative requires an agent actually to adopt the principle of autonomy as a principle of volition.[3] But Kant's remarks in his later ethical writings leave little doubt on this point.

In *Religion Within the Limits of Reason Alone* Kant states that any given man has some one principle which he has

---

to repay it, although I know I shall never do so" (cf. F 46 [422]). This way of phrasing them indicates that the conception of a practical principle is not only the conception of a line of conduct but can itself be involved in the process of willing. Kant believes that when we act rationally we act from particular practical principles, whose conception guides our action and each of which is then called a *maxim*, "the principle which the subject himself makes his rule (how he chooses to act)" (*DV* 25 [225]).

[3] Cf. S. Körner, *Kant* (London: Penguin Books, 1955), p. 135, and A. R. C. Duncan, *Practical Reason and Morality* (London: Thomas Nelson and Sons, 1957), pp. 71, 115, 154.

adopted as the supreme guiding policy controlling all his actions: "The disposition, i.e., the ultimate subjective ground[4] of the adoption of maxims, can be one only and applies universally to the whole use of freedom" (R 20 [25]). This disposition is an "inner principle of maxims" (R 18n. [23–24n.]) and this ultimate subjective ground of the will is itself "a rule made by the will for the use of its freedom, that is . . . a maxim" (R 17 [21]). It is the "supreme maxim of the free will" (R 34n. [39n.]). This ultimate maxim of the will may be good or bad. In the case of an evil disposition, in order "to call a man evil, it would have to be possible . . . to infer from several evil acts . . . an underlying evil maxim; and further, from this maxim to infer the presence in the agent of an underlying common ground, itself a maxim of all particular morally-evil maxims" (R 16 [20]). The moral law is to be the maxim by which all

---

[4] Kant's notion of the subjective determination of the will is connected with his notion of a *determining ground* of the will. For Kant not only says that by adopting practical principles as its maxims the will can causally influence the phenomenal world and that "rational beings . . . have a will, i.e., faculty of determining their causality through the conception of a rule . . ." (SC 32 [32]); he also speaks of the will as itself causally determined, of "a cause determining the will" (F 90n. [459n.], cf. SC 34–35 [34]), of what acts as an "effective cause, i.e., as determining the will" (F 92 [462]). This notion of a cause determining the will is connected with that of a determining ground of the will by means of Kant's notions of *incentive* and *interest*: "by an incentive . . . we understand a subjective determining ground of a will whose reason does not by its nature necessarily conform to the objective [moral] law [i.e., a "non-holy" will] . . ." (SC 74 [72]). "From the concept of an incentive there comes that of an interest . . . it indicates an incentive of the will so far as it is presented by reason" (SC 82 [79]). "Interest is that by which reason becomes practical, i.e., [becomes] a cause determining the will" (F 90n. [459n.]). Thus, when X is the determining ground of the human will, practical reason exerts a causal influence on the will through its conception of X. But since "will is nothing else than practical reason" (F 34 [412]), the causal influence which determines the will comes from the will itself (also cf. DV 10 [213]).

particular morally good maxims are to be adopted, the supreme principle of morality, and the supreme maxim of a morally good man (cf. *R* 19–20 [24]).

Likewise, in the *Metaphysics of Morals* Kant maintains that it is the characteristic property of ethical legislation to command us "to make the principle of duty itself the sufficient motive of our choice" (*DV* 19 [220]). This principle is a *single* principle, which unites all other moral principles into a system; there can be only one true system of philosophy from principles "no matter in how many different and even contradictory ways men may have philosophized about one and the same proposition. So the *moralist* is justified in saying that there is only *one* doctrine of virtue—that is, one single system that connects all duties of virtue by a principle . . ." (*DV* 3 [207]). Thus there is "only one formal element of moral choice (one virtuous attitude of will [i.e., disposition]), which is, however, valid for all actions" (*DV* 41 [383]). There is "only *one* virtuous attitude of will, as the subjective ground determining us to fulfill our duty" (*DV* 73 [410]). The principle guiding this formal element of moral choice is "the formal principle of duty [which] is contained in the categorical imperative: 'So act that the maxim of your action could become a universal law.' Ethics adds only that this principle is to be conceived as the law of *your own will* and not of will in general . . ." (*DV* 48 [389]). "Like anything *formal*, virtue considered as the will's firm resolution to conform with every [subordinate] duty is always *one*" (*DV* 55 [395]). Thus, "the *resolution* to practice virtue must be made all at once and in its entirety . . ." (*DV* 149 [477]). In fact,

> Man's greatest moral perfection is to do his duty and this *from a motive of duty* (to make the law not merely the rule but also the motive of his actions) . . . the law, here again pre-

scribes[5] only the *maxim of the action*: a maxim of seeking the ground of obligation solely in the law and not in sensuous inclination . . . the maxim of striving with all one's might to

5 In the *Metaphysic of Morals* (cf. DV 20–21 [222]) Kant attempts to distinguish *laws* from *imperatives* by saying that a law merely states that an action is necessary, while an imperative also constrains a non-holy will to conform with the imperative. To conform with an imperative need not be actually to *do* the action in question, for Kant notes that in ethics "the law can prescribe only the maxim of action, not actions themselves" (DV 49 [390]). Thus, the moral imperative "You ought to make this or that (e.g., the happiness of another) your end" (cf. DV 48 [389]) does not require the person to perform any individual act of doing this or that, e.g., any act of promoting another's happiness; rather, it constrains one to will a policy of action, e.g., to adopt the principle "To seek the happiness of others" as a maxim. There can be a plurality of such moral imperatives, for "in relation to the obligatory *end* of action or what one ought to make one's end . . . there can be many virtues. And since obligation to the maxim of such an end is called a duty of virtue, there are many duties of virtue" (DV 55 [395]).

When imperatives are understood in such a manner, it can be seen that they are distinct from practical principles. For they are statements which express the constraint on a non-holy will to adopt particular practical principles. Kant unfortunately introduces ambiguity into his terminology when he sometimes refers to imperatives themselves as practical principles, for example, when he calls a hypothetical imperative "an assortorical, practical principle" and a categorical imperative "an apodictical (practical) principle" (F 36-37 [415]).

A further point about moral imperatives is that they make *duty the incentive of the will* (cf. DV 16 [219]). We shall see that Kant apparently means by this that the maxim, e.g., "To tell the truth," is to be chosen because one has also chosen to select one's subordinate maxims by the principle of autonomy.

There are places where Kant also uses the term "law" ambiguously by calling imperatives laws (cf. F 44n. [420–421n.], SC 19, 42 [21, 41], and DV 20, 27 [221, 227]). And there is yet another sense of "law" suggested by other remarks: in the *Foundations* Kant says that "A maxim is the subjective principle of volition. The objective principle (i.e., that which would serve all rational beings also subjectively as a practical principle if reason had full power over the faculty of desire) is the practical law" (F 20n. [400n.]). Kant even goes so far as to distinguish examples of laws make the thought of duty for its own sake the sufficient motive of every dutiful action. (*DV* 52–53 [392–393])

Thus, the morally *perfect* human will actually *chooses* subordinate maxims, such as "To tell the truth," on the basis of the principle of autonomy; the morally *good* human will at least *tries* to fit its subordinate maxims to the principle of autonomy since it has *willed* the policy described in the principle of autonomy. The categorical imperative tells a man that his duty is to adopt the principle of autonomy as his supreme maxim, thus making this his supreme duty and one which must be fulfilled in order to fulfill any of the rest.

Kant therefore believes that a person does not have a *good will* merely because the person follows a specific categorical imperative, e.g., the imperative "Tell the truth," merely to the extent of adopting as his maxim "To tell the truth." A person has a good will only because he follows *the* categorical imperative, and adopts the principle of autonomy as a maxim. For this reason Kant says that "for the pure intellectual judgment of mankind, the rule excluding a mean between good and evil must remain fundamental . . ." (*R* 34n. [39n.]). Since ethical legislation has been said to command the principle of duty itself as the sufficient motive of the will, Kant also claims that no *action* fulfills any *moral obligation*, and in that sense is *morally right*, unless it is done ultimately from the principle of autonomy. We shall also consider below the well-known

---

in this third sense from maxims, thereby introducing an ambiguity into the use of "maxim" and specifying a more narrow sense of the term than he usually employs: "Practical principles . . . are subjective, or maxims, when the condition is regarded by the subject as valid only for his own will. They are objective, or practical laws, when the condition is recognized as objective, i.e., as valid for the will of every rational being" (*SC* 17 [19]). In this third sense laws do not *state that* a policy of action is necessary for they merely mention policies which *are* valid without saying that they are valid or necessary.

passages from the *Foundations of the Metaphysics of Morals* where Kant claims that no human action has moral value unless it is done from duty; thus, he believes that no man's *action* has moral *value* unless it proceeds ultimately from the adoption of the principle of autonomy as one's maxim.[6]

II

We can now consider four lines of argument suggested by Kant's remarks in defense of his doctrines concerning the categorical imperative. In order to simplify discussion of these arguments I shall first point out an equivocal use that Kant makes of a certain set of technical terms which appear in these arguments. These are the terms "object," "end," "purpose," and "matter" (or "material").

Kant is sometimes contrasted with utilitarians because he claims that the consequences of actions are irrelevant to the moral value of actions. Now he often seems to use the terms "object," "end," "purpose," and "matter" to apply to the consequences of actions as *distinct* from the actions themselves. For example, he says that a man may appear to act from the precept not to make a false promise, but at bottom may only be trying to avoid "some other evil" such as loss of credit, whereas to make a false promise is "of itself bad" (*F* 42 [419]). I am "truthful from duty" rather than "out of fear of disadvantageous consequences" when "the concept of the action itself contains a law for me" (*F* 22 [402]). Again, when I lie

[6] Kant does, however, suggest in a footnote to the second *Critique* that "Of every action which conforms to the law but does not occur for the sake of the law, one may say that it is morally good in letter but not in spirit (in intention)" (*SC* 75n. [72n.]). This seems to be the only momentary weakening on Kant's part of the strict doctrine that "it is not sufficient to that which should be [is said to be] morally good that it conform to the law; it must be done for the sake of the law" (*F* 6–7 [390]).

to avoid discredit, the law governing my action is given by "the object through its relation to the will" and in such a case "I should do something for the reason that I will something else. The moral, and therewith categorical imperative, on the other hand, says I should act this or that way even though I will nothing else" (F 67–68 [441]). When the object determines the will then "the will in these cases never determines itself directly by the conception of the action itself but only by the incentive which the foreseen result of the action incites in the will—that is, I ought to do something because I will something else" (F 71 [444]). ". . . In the case of an action performed from duty, no regard must be given to the interest in the object, but merely in the action itself and its principle in reason (i.e., the law)" (F 35n. [413–414n.]). I should not "search for an end which I might perhaps propose to achieve with my declaration" when my truthful avowal is demanded in court (R 4 [4]). A categorical imperative

> directly commands a certain conduct without making its condition some purpose to be reached by it. . . . It concerns not the material of the action and its intended result but the form and the principle from which it results. . . . the result being what it may. (F 38 [416])

> The categorical (unconditional) imperative views the action as objectively necessary and necessitates the agent to it immediately, by the mere thought of the action itself (i.e. of its form), and not mediately, by the thought of an end to be attained by the action. (DV 21 [222])

These passages, taken together with the fact that Kant speaks of an end, matter, and object of choice interchangeably (cf. DV 41, 55 [383, 395]), suggest that Kant indeed does believe that moral imperatives command actions regardless of their consequences, and regardless of any end, object, or matter related to those actions.

However, Kant also uses the terms "object," "end," "purpose," and "matter" more broadly. He uses them in such a way that even a morally valuable action itself may be called the object, end, purpose, or matter of the good will. This will is then said not to seek "any other end" (F 36, 37 [414, 415]) or "some [other] purpose [*irgend eine andere . . . Absicht*]" (F 38 [416]) in its morally valuable actions.

> . . . Ethics . . . provides a *matter* (an object of free choice), an end of pure reason which it presents also as an objectively necessary end, *i.e.*, an end which, so far as men are concerned, it is a duty to have . . . a material determining ground of choice beyond the formal one that Law contains. . . . (*DV* 38 [380–381])

Even in a single passage Kant uses "object" in the broad sense yet "matter" (and perhaps "end") in the narrow sense; for he says that the form of the relationship between wills in a business transaction can be contrasted with "the *matter* . . . of the will, that is, the end that a person intends to accomplish by means of the object that he wills; for example . . . profit from the transaction" (*MJ* 34 [230]). In fact the equivocal use of these terms permeates Kant's ethical writings[7] and a possible

---

[7] For example, Kant's observation that *every volition must have an end* (*object, matter*) sometimes appears to mean only that the volitions of agents with phenomenal selves must involve some phenomenal *content*, e.g., seeking the happiness of others. In this case the morally valuable course is to seek the happiness of others from respect for duty rather than merely from a sympathetic disposition (cf. *SC* 34–35 [34]). Yet at other times Kant takes this observation to mean that all men are forced by reason to conceive of the "inevitable consequences" of their "right conduct" as forming the final end which is happiness proportioned to obedience to duty (cf. *R* 4–5 [4–6]). Here the term "end" seems to be meant in the narrow sense, where right actions are distinct from ends, although in this very passage Kant both says that "morality requires no end for right conduct" and also speaks of "all such ends as we *ought* to have (duty)."

occurrence of an actual fallacy of equivocation based on these terms will appear below in some of Kant's arguments on behalf of his doctrines concerning the categorical imperative.

The first argument I shall consider attempts to show that every good human will and every will which fulfills a duty and every will which does a morally good action adopts the principle of autonomy. The second and third arguments try to show that if there is any imperative binding a human will, then the categorical imperative is one such imperative. The second and fourth arguments maintain that obedience to any imperative involves obedience to the categorical imperative by adopting the principle of autonomy as a principle of volition.

FIRST ARGUMENT

The first section of the *Foundations of the Metaphysics of Morals* contains the following argument. (Cf. F 12, 16, 19–21 [394, 397–398, 399–402].)

> (*a*) Any *good will* is *good* only because of its willing [i.e., its maxims].
>
> (*b*) The *moral import* of the *maxim* of a non-holy will, e.g., a human will, is due to the fact that the agent acts from duty rather than from inclination.
>
> (*c*) The *moral worth* of an *action* done by an agent with a non-holy will is due to the fact that the agent acts from duty rather than from inclination.
>
> (*d*) The moral worth of an action done from duty lies in the maxim determining the action rather than in the *purpose* to be achieved by the action.
>
> (*e*) Therefore, the moral value of an action done from duty is independent of any *objects of the faculty of desire* and is independent of the *realization* of the object of the *action*.
>
> (*f*) Therefore, the moral worth of an action done from duty

does not derive from the *effects* or *purposes* of the action regarded as *incentives* of the will. [Thus, the determining ground of the good human will is not an incentive concerning an effect or purpose of the action.]

(g) The only things that could determine a [non-holy, e.g., human] will are either the *material*, a posteriori incentive (a material principle) or the *formal*, a priori principle of volition.

(h) Therefore, when an action is done from duty, no *object of the will* determines the will and the will is determined by the maxim "To follow [*zu leisten*] the law even when that thwarts my inclinations."

(i) Therefore, when an action is done from duty, the [ultimate] principle of the will is not a particular law applicable to certain actions, and the determining ground of the will is not any particular law but is instead the conception of the law in itself.

(j) The only kind of law the conception of which could determine the will yet which is not a particular law is universal conformity of actions to law in general.

(k) Therefore, when the human will is good [and when it produces an action which is morally valuable and done from duty] the will has as its [ultimate] maxim the principle of autonomy: "Never to act in such a way that I could not also will that my [subordinate] maxim should be a universal law."[8]

The crucial problems about this argument can be uncovered by asking how Kant arrives at steps (e) and (f). Just before presenting premise (d) Kant discusses the difference

---

[8] Beck translates what Kant calls a "maxim" in step (h) as an imperative: "I ought to follow the law even when it thwarts my inclinations." To be sure, Kant does phrase the "principle" involved in (k) as "I should [*soll*] never act in such a way that I could not also will that my maxim should be a universal law." In view, however, of the distinction pointed out in note 5 above between imperatives and the principles they enjoin, I have stated a genuine principle in my rendering of Kant's argument instead of the imperative which Kant mentions.

between doing actions from direct or indirect inclinations vs. doing them from duty. Thus, it is natural to suppose that by speaking of *purposes* or *effects* in (d) and of objects of the *faculty of desire* (*Begehrungsvermögen*) in (e) he means to consider an object of *inclination* (*Neigung*). Then he would arrive at (e) and (f) by claiming that since an action done from duty derives its worth from its maxim, and since the maxim of an agent acting from duty disregards the agent's inclinations, then "From the preceding discussion it is clear that the purposes we may have for our actions and their effects as ends or incentives of the will cannot give the actions any unconditional and moral worth" (F 19 [400]). In addition, since the worth of the action is due to its maxim, the actual realization of the object of the action is also irrelevant to the action's worth.

Now this line of reasoning only excludes incentives of the will which are, as Kant goes on to call them, a posteriori incentives, that is, purposes which some wills *happen* to have but which every will need not have, e.g., an object of inclination. If there are ends which it is objectively, morally necessary to have we might be able to claim that these provide a priori incentives, and Kant has said nothing yet to rule out the possibility that the worth of an action derives from a maxim whose object, end, and purpose is such a morally necessary end. To preserve my life out of inclination, from an a posteriori incentive, is to have as my maxim "To preserve my life since I have an inclination to do so." To act from duty, however, might be to have as my maxim merely "To preserve my life (regardless of inclination)." Kant so far has not proved that the latter kind of maxim cannot be the ultimate maxim of a good will acting to preserve the agent's life, that is, cannot be the formal principle mentioned in (g) and the law mentioned in (h). Thus, Kant has not proved that the incentive which determines a good human will is never the conception of the action of preserving one's life, as distinct from the conception of the relation of this action to one's inclinations. Thus, if we interpret "object" and "purpose" in (e) and (f) so that we can see how those steps follow from what precedes, we do so at the expense of admitting that step (i) is a *non sequitur*. For Kant has not succeeded in ruling out a particular law such as "To preserve my life (regardless of inclination)" as the maxim determining a good human will when the will is responsible for the morally worthy action of preserving the agent's life.

We can save the argument from such a simple *non sequitur*, of course, by supposing instead that it involves a fallacy of equivocation on the terms "material" and "formal" in (g): step (g) actually follows from what precedes only when a principle such as "To preserve my life since I have an inclination to do so" is said to be "material" in the *narrow* sense, i.e., is said to present an action as leading to the *further goal* of satisfying an inclination; yet step (i) follows from (g) and the previous steps only when we take "material" in the *broad* sense, where any principle with *phenomenal content* may be said to have matter, e.g., where the matter is the preservation of one's life.

Kant's argument can be given a logically valid form, however, by interpreting the expressions "purpose" and "object" in a different way, namely, by taking them as referring to any object of the *will* in the broad sense of "object," that is, to any specific phenomenal content of a maxim and not necessarily to an object of inclination. Then, indeed, nothing is left in a maxim besides its form when all phenomenal content is left out. But what reason is there to suppose that steps (d) and (e) are *true* when the terms "purpose" and "object of the faculty of desire" are taken in this broad sense? No reason is given in the *Foundations*,[9] and there Kant simply presents (*a*), (*b*), (*c*), and (*d*) as parts of common-sense moral opinion.

One's hopes are raised by the early portions of the *Critique of Practical Reason*, for it looks as if Kant is offering an argument to show that no object of the will in the sense of any phenomenally characterized action can be the determining ground of a will acting from moral laws (cf. *SC* 19 ff. [21 ff]):

1) If the idea of an object or material of the *faculty of desire* determines the will, the determining ground of the choice is pleasure produced by the (idea of) the actual existence of the object.

2) That the (idea of) the actual existence of an object gives pleasure to an agent can be known only a posteriori.

3) Thus, the practical principle of such an agent cannot be known a priori to be necessary and lacks objective necessity.

4) Moral laws are capable of being known a priori to have objective necessity.

5) Therefore, if the idea of an object or material of the *faculty of desire* determines the will, the practical principle of the agent is not a moral law.[10]

---

[9] Kant does remark in the *Foundations* that the purpose of one's action could have been achieved without a human will, and that by contrast the conception of the law is already present in the agent acting from this conception (cf. *F* 20 [401]). But the most that this proves is that the worth of an action does not derive from the *realization* of its purpose; the *conception* of the purpose, however, can also already be present in the agent.

[10] There is some question here just what Kant means by speaking of something's *determining* the will. For in this early part of the *Critique* Kant speaks of practical principles and moral laws sometimes as principles of volition, e.g., "I will tell the truth," and sometimes as imperatives, e.g., "You should never make a deceitful promise." Thus, when he speaks of a determination of the will he may sometimes merely mean to consider the way in which a will, whether holy or non-holy, *adopts one policy rather than another* because of its principle of volition, and at other times he may be speaking of the *necessitation* or *constraint* which

Now Kant later says that the faculty of desire is called the will (cf. SC 57 [55]) and thinks that he has proved that no object of the *will* can be the determining ground of a will whose maxims are moral laws (cf. SC 26 [26–27]). This suggests that the above argument may be an attempt to rule out as the conception determining a moral will any conception of a phenomenally characterized action. In fact, Kant goes on to argue in the *Critique* much as he did in the *Foundations*: when every object of the will is eliminated as the determining ground of the will, nothing remains but the mere form of universal law; and the fundamental "law," i.e., imperative, of a pure practical reason—a reason which does not subserve the "lower faculty of desire"—is the categorical imperative.

If the argument at the start of the second *Critique* is indeed aimed at proving that no object of the will in the broad sense of "object" can be the determining ground of a will which adopts a moral maxim, then the argument depends on a dogmatic, metaphysical assumption about the will. It depends on the premise that any decision which appears to aim ultimately at some object, such as keeping a promise, or making money from a deceitful promise, must really aim ultimately at getting pleasure or avoiding pain. For Kant says elsewhere that "an incentive can determine the will to an action *only so far as the individual has incorporated it into his maxim* (has made it the general rule in accordance with which he will conduct himself) . . ." (R 19 [23–24]). Thus, premise (1) suggests that in the above examples one's maxim must be "To keep a promise

---

an imperative places on a non-holy will. Yet because the argument in this part of the second *Critique* can be made general enough to cover both holy and non-holy wills and because Kant speaks here of determining *grounds* of the will and later of a *cause* determining the will (cf. SC 34–35 [34]), I shall take Kant to be arguing that the principles of *volition* of a rational will are not objectively valid or necessary if the conception of the object is involved in the basis of the volition.

if that will get me pleasure (or prevent pain)" or "To make a deceitful promise when that will get me money provided that money in turn will get me pleasure (or prevent pain)." Kant's point would then be that such principles lack objective necessity and that the imperatives commanding them are not moral imperatives. But Kant would then be making the unsupported, dogmatic claim that the will, whether good or bad, can never determine itself to action *merely* by adopting a principle such as "To keep a promise (regardless of the pleasure or pain I get from doing so)" or such as "To make a deceitful promise when that will get me money."

Suppose we try to improve Kant's argument by avoiding this arbitrary assumption concerning pleasure and pain. For Theorem I of the *Critique* considers cases "when the *desire* for this object precedes the practical rule and is the condition under which the latter becomes a principle . . ." (*SC* 19 [21], my italics). It would be of little help merely to interpret "desire" here as referring to *inclination* and to admit that we have inclinations not directed toward pleasures and pains. For that would still leave us with the dogmatic claim that a will can determine itself to action by adopting, e.g., the principle "To tell the truth if I have an inclination to do so" but never merely by adopting the principle "To tell the truth (regardless of inclination)." We could, however, try taking "desire for this object" merely to mean *willing* this object. This omits reference to pleasure and pain and to inclination. Even so, all that Kant could plausibly argue is that when an object of the will *precedes* the choice or the practical principle, it does so as a further goal toward which the action is a means, so that the principle has the form "To do x since I will to get y." But this would still require us to take y as a willed object distinct from the action x. This would indeed prove that "To pay my debts since I will to improve my credit" is not objectively necessary and not a moral law. But it would fail to prove that "To pay my debts" is not a moral law which can be the ultimate determining principle of a will which ignores inclination. For paying one's debts can be made the object of the will *through* adopting "To pay my debts" as a maxim and in that case the object in no relevant sense *precedes* either the principle or its adoption. Thus, the argument in the *Critique* would still fail to show that morally valid maxims are independent of all objects of the will in the *broad* sense of "object." The strongest conclusion it could lead to is that the determining ground of a will which ignores inclination and which functions as a "higher faculty of desire" is not an object of the will in the *narrow* sense of "object," i.e., some goal beyond the action itself.

Thus we cannot use the argument given at the beginning of the second *Critique* to provide plausible support for premises (*d*) and (*e*) in the argument from the *Foundations* when the latter argument is taken in its valid form. In the final section of this paper I shall show that even the logically valid form of the argument is unsatisfactory, for premises (*d*) and (*e*) are not supported even by common sense when "purpose" and "object" are meant to cover any phenomenal content or aim of the will.

It is interesting to note that there is textual evidence which suggests that Kant himself did *not* intend the argument from the *Foundations* in the form we have seen to be valid. For he says in the course of his discussion that

> I can certainly have an inclination to the object as an effect of the proposed action, but I can never have respect for it precisely because it is a mere effect and not an activity of a will . . . an act from duty wholly excludes the influence of inclination and therewith every object of the will. . . . (*F* 19–20 [400])

Now since determining oneself to action by the conception of the action itself, e.g., according to the maxim "To pay my debts," involves an activity of the will independent of considerations of inclination, Kant does *not* seem to intend "object" in the broad sense necessary for his argument in the first section of the *Foundations* to have valid form. His own argument, in contrast to the valid one I have developed from his remarks, involves either a *non sequitur* or a fallacy of equivocation.

SECOND ARGUMENT

We might try using a passage from the second section of the *Foundations* to prove that the principle of autonomy is the ultimate maxim of any good human will and of any human will which acts from duty. After introducing the distinction between categorical and hypothetical imperatives, Kant decides to "inquire whether the mere concept of a categorical imperative does not also furnish the formula containing the proposition which alone can be a categorical imperative" (*F* 43–44 [420]). For a moment it looks as if he is seeking merely a recipe for constructing categorical imperatives, merely a characterization of their general structure—but the conclusion of his remark suggests that he is seeking a categorical imperative *itself*, and maintaining that there is only one such imperative. This is confirmed by his further remarks. He says that "If I think of a hypothetical imperative as such [*überhaupt*], I do not know what it will contain until the condition is stated [under which it is an imperative]" (*F* 44 [420]). He does not mean that he does not know the *general structure* of a hypothetical imperative for one need not know the condition sought in order to know this—the general structure is to enjoin and to constrain one to adopt a maxim whose content is the policy of doing an action aimed at gaining something one does (or may) desire. We need to know the condition, what the action is a means toward, only when we are interested in the actual *content*, and not merely the general structure, of a hypothetical imperative.

Kant has previously characterized a categorical imperative in the following way:

> (*a*) A categorical imperative presents an action as of itself objectively necessary without making any reference to any further purpose or other end. It concerns not the matter of the action and its intended result, but the form and the principle from which the action follows (cf. F 37–38 [415–416]).

He then goes on to argue in the passage previously considered (cf. F 44 [420–421]):

> (*b*) A categorical imperative contains only the unconditioned law and the necessity that the maxim accord with it.
>
> (*c*) Therefore, a categorical imperative represents as necessary conformity of the maxim of the action to the universality of a law as such.
>
> (*d*) Therefore, there is only one categorical imperative, which is: "Act only according to that maxim by which you can at the same time will that it should become a universal law."

Kant himself carries the argument no further at this point but it is easy to extend it as follows:

> [(*e*) Therefore, since imperatives constrain non-holy, e.g., human, wills to adopt principles, the categorical imperative constrains them to adopt the principle of autonomy: "To act only according to that maxim by which you can at the same time will that it should become universal law." Further, since there is but this one categorical imperative, every human will which fulfills a duty adopts the principle of autonomy.]

Step (*b*) seems a reasonable interpretation of what a categorical imperative is, but it merely describes the *general structure* of one; for it does not say what the law in question is, e.g., "To tell the truth." Such a description of the general structure of a categorical imperative is not itself a categorical imperative. It is therefore difficult to see how Kant can reach step (*d*).[11]

After arriving at (*d*) Kant says that all "imperatives of duty" can be derived from this one categorical imperative as a principle. But the most Kant has shown is the general structure of categorical imperatives. He has not shown by his argument that what he calls *the* categorical imperative is even *a* categorical imperative. Certainly he does not prove that there are no subordinate categorical imperatives, e.g., "Tell the truth." Thus we cannot successfully extend Kant's argument to reach conclusion (*e*), which depends on the assumption that there are no other categorical imperatives commanding distinct principles to be adopted by a will which fulfills some duty.

It would be wrong to suppose that Kant merely believes that an *absolutely* good human will must fulfill *all* its duties and obey *every* categorical imperative, thus adopting both the principles enjoined by subordinate imperatives and the principle of autonomy, and that *somewhat less good* human wills fulfill only some duties and obey only some subordinate imperatives. For Kant's insistence that good and bad men are to be judged on the basis of the single, supreme maxim of the will which governs all their choices and his insistence that for a good man this is the principle of autonomy rules out

[11] Without premise (*a*) Kant would make a mistake in reaching the conclusion in (*c*) that the law is universally valid or necessary. For the "necessity" mentioned in (*b*) that maxims conform to the law is only the *necessitation* imposed on non-holy wills to adopt the unconditioned law. But a mere unconditioned principle, e.g., "To lie," certainly need not be universally necessary. We can, of course, omit (*a*) if the term "law" in (*b*) entails that laws are universally valid, but then the reference in (*c*) to the universality of law is redundant.

the possibility that any good men act ultimately from a plurality of principles given by a plurality of subordinate categorical imperatives. If Kant were able to prove (1) that there is a categorical imperative commanding the principle of autonomy; (2) that there is but one supreme maxim of any human will; (3) that it must be possible for a will to fulfill all its duties; and (4) that the only principle which could govern all its choices and still lead to fulfilling all its duties is the principle of autonomy, then Kant might be able to show that a good human will has the principle of autonomy as its supreme maxim when it fulfills a duty. But in the second section of the *Foundations* Kant fails to *prove* that if there are imperatives governing men then one such imperative is the categorical imperative; and he never even tries to *prove* that the will has only one supreme maxim governing all its choices—after all, such a claim is another example of dogmatic metaphysics.

THIRD ARGUMENT

The third section of the *Foundations* claims that the principle of morality and the categorical imperative can be deduced from the concept of freedom. I shall not consider Kant's opinions as to whether we have grounds, in turn, for supposing that we are free. For his derivation of the principle of morality is itself unsatisfactory. Thus, he again fails to prove that if men have any duties, then one such duty is to obey the categorical imperative and to adopt the principle of autonomy.

Kant argues as follows (cf. *F* 73–74 [445–446]):

(*a*) Freedom of the will (of a rational being) is what enables the will to be causally effective independently of being determined by foreign causes. (The "negative" definition of freedom.)

(*b*) It follows from the concept of causality that there are immutable laws according to which that which is the effect must be established (*gesetzt werden muss*) given that which is the cause.

(*c*) Therefore, a free will is governed by such laws.

(*d*) Natural necessity is the property of the causality of an irrational being, whereby a foreign cause determines the being to its activity.

(*e*) Therefore, natural necessity is governed by the law: "Something else determines the efficient cause to its causality."

(*f*) Thus, a free will is one which is a law to itself in all its actions. (The "positive" definition of freedom.)

(*g*) The principle "The will is a law unto itself in all its actions" is the principle of autonomy: "To act according to no other maxim than that which can also have itself as a universal law for its object."[12]

At this point Kant seems to confuse the principle of autonomy, which he has just tried to derive, with the categorical imperative, claiming that "this is just the formula of the categorical imperative and the principle of morality" (*F* 74 [447]). But even a holy will is free in the sense Kant has been discussing, and since Kant believes that holy wills are not subject to obligations, it is necessary for Kant to argue further in order to prove that non-holy free wills are obligated to adopt this principle of autonomy. His further remarks suggest two ways of doing this (cf. *F* 82, 87–88 [453–454, 457–458]):

(*h*) As a mere member of the noumenal world all the actions of a being with a non-holy will would accord with the principle of autonomy. The noumenal world contains the ground of the phenomenal world and of the laws of the phenomenal world (e.g., the psychological laws concerning desires and inclinations) and thus the noumenal world is directly legislative for a desiring being whose noumenal will is free.

[12] Beck again mistranslates a principle as an imperative, rendering *zu handeln* as "I should act" instead of "To act."

(*h'*) Only as a member of the noumenal world is a being with a non-holy free will his proper self (and not merely an appearance of himself).

(*i*) Therefore, a being with a non-holy free will ought to obey the laws of the noumenal world and ought to conform to the principle of autonomy.

It may be that Kant thinks either (*g*) and (*h*) or (*g*) and (*h'*) are sufficient to yield (*i*). Let us concentrate, however, on the earlier part of the argument, since (*g*) itself is not derived in a satisfactory fashion.

In this argument Kant is not seeking laws which govern the way in which a noumenal cause produces a phenomenal appearance as an effect. He is not, for example, seeking laws which govern the way in which activity of the will produces phenomenal actions. He is rather concerned with the causes *of* the will's noumenal activity when the will exerts its causality through its activity. This is not clear from the start of the argument, for premise (*a*) merely denies that foreign causes determine the will's activity without stating that this activity is itself caused. But it is clear from the ensuing contrast between freedom and natural necessity: in the case of natural necessity the cause is itself active only because of the influence of a prior external cause, but in the case of freedom the cause of the will's activity is interior to the will.

Some defenders of the notion of free will might balk at this suggestion that the activity of a free will is itself caused, for the concept of spontaneity seems to concern an uncaused starting point for a causal chain. But Kant's position could be made more plausible by interpreting the expression "activity of the will" in a particular way. First, note that one way of stating practical principles is either in the form "I will do *x*" or in the form "I will do *x* if *y*." The point of the words "I will" is not to make a prediction, as one could be using "I shall."

The point is to indicate personal decision, the willing of a policy of action. Thus, we may try to distinguish the *willing* of a *policy* of action from the *activity* of the will which produces as a phenomenal effect a *particular* action satisfying that policy. For in order to decide to do a particular action of that sort in a particular set of phenomenal circumstances, the person might need not only to will the general policy of action but also to believe that the phenomenal situation in which the phenomenal self is located permits such an action, and to believe that certain phenomenal steps are involved in executing the action. Kant may take a practical principle to indicate that a cause, namely, the willing of a certain policy of action, is connected with an effect, namely, the activity of the will toward producing a particular action dictated by that policy.[13] Provided that this connection is necessary, such a principle would be in Kant's view a causal law. It would differ from causal laws in science, e.g., "Fire causes smoke," inasmuch as the cause and effect of which it speaks are noumenal.

On this interpretation, however, *all* practical principles leading to action when adopted are equally necessary, since *any* decision by a will possessing spontaneity will lead (when the agent has appropriate beliefs) to activity of the will aimed at the action mentioned in the principle. At best it would seem that (f) should only mean that the cause of a will's activity is not foreign to the will, e.g., the determining ground of a free will does not lie outside its maxims. But we cannot reach step (g) unless the following claim is true:

> (1) A nonuniversalizable principle is the maxim of the will only if a cause of the will's activity is either a noumenal event lying outside the will or else a phenomenal event.

---

[13] Further causally contributory conditions, e.g., beliefs about the phenomenal circumstances of the agent, might also be needed for this cause to produce the effect.

What reason would there be, however, for believing such a claim? It would not be enough, for example, to show that if a nonuniversalizable principle is adopted then gaining pleasure or satisfying inclination is part of the determining ground of the will. For the *conception* of this pleasure or satisfaction through which the will is determined is still intrinsic to practical reason and to the will rather than foreign to it (cf. *DV* 9 [212]).[14] Perhaps it would be necessary to modify Kant's "hedonism" in order to prove (1) and to claim that actual pleasure in the phenomenal self must be felt in order for the will to determine itself to activity through a nonuniversalizable maxim. But there would be no reason to believe such a dogmatic, metaphysical claim.

In Problem II of the second *Critique*, however, Kant does seem to argue in support of a premise similar to (1). He says that a free will must be independent of conditions belonging to the phenomenal world, and that the material of a principle, an object of a maxim, cannot be given except empirically; thus, such material is ruled out as a determining ground of a free will. Perhaps Kant means that since we only obtain the concept of lying, for example, from phenomenal experience, we must count that experience as part of the cause or one of the causes of the will's activity when the will attempts to produce such an action. But this would have the awkward and unacceptable con-

[14] Thus volition is not causally conditioned by anything external to it when the conception of this pleasure or satisfaction is used by the will to cause itself to act—for this reason Silber's defense of Kant is inadequate. (Cf. J. R. Silber, "The Copernican Revolution in Ethics: the Good Re-examined," *Kant-Studien* 51 [1959/60], pp. 85–101.) If the fact that *beliefs* about the agent's phenomenal circumstances contribute toward producing activity of the will directed at an individual action falling under some policy is enough to show that there are foreign causes of the will's activity, then it is difficult to see how *any* principle of the will can ever spontaneously produce activity of the will directed toward phenomenal action. For any principle leading to phenomenal action would seem to involve connection with such beliefs.

sequence of also ruling out truth-telling and promise-keeping as possible actions of a free will.[15] It is possible that Kant is here confusing the claim that the *necessitation* of a hypothetical *imperative* depends on the existence of phenomenal desires with the claim that the *content* of a particular practical *principle* is in some sense "empirically given." In any case, there seems to be no clear reason to suppose that the will mentioned in (f) cannot be determined by adoption of a maxim whose content is specified by empirical concepts. Thus, premise (1) lacks adequate support.

At best Kant could plausibly claim, as he does elsewhere, that "laws" which are not universalizable are ones lacking *objective necessity to be adopted*. But the necessity at issue in (b) is, on the present interpretation, only the necessity connecting a decision (*once the decision occurs*) to pursue a policy of action with activity of the will directed toward a particular action satisfying the policy.

Suppose, however, that Kant does believe that a free will is an absurdity (*Unding*) unless there is a cause even for the adoption of a policy of action, e.g., for adopting a maxim such as "To tell the truth." If so, then he apparently thinks that the concept of causality dictates that every event even in the noumenal world has a cause. In this case, the regress of noumenal causes goes on interminably, and the principle of autonomy is not, as Kant claims, the ultimate or supreme maxim of a moral will—for there is no *ultimate* maxim. It would certainly be arbitrary for Kant to stop supposing further causes once the regress reaches the principle of autonomy.[16]

---

[15] For Kant does not suggest that the concepts of truth-telling or promise-keeping can be obtained merely by analyzing the nonempirical concept of universalizability.

[16] I can see no reason to suppose that the principle of autonomy has special causal status in this regress merely because it *systematizes* all lower-order principles.

Finally, even if Kant can narrow down the "laws" of which step (*c*) speaks to universalizable maxims such as "To tell the truth," he still will not be able to reach the conclusion that the will *adopts* the principle of autonomy without further premises. For the most he has shown is that in adopting principles such as "To tell the truth" the will acts *according to* the principle of autonomy, just as fire and smoke act according to the principle "Every event has a cause." Kant needs further arguments to prove that the only way the will can act *from* a principle such as "To tell the truth" is by acting *from* the principle of autonomy as a *maxim*.

FOURTH ARGUMENT

We shall explore one further attempt to prove that the principle of autonomy is adopted by any human will fulfilling any moral obligation. Let us see if it is plausible for Kant to argue as follows:

(*a*) If a human will obeys a morally obligating imperative then *pure reason of itself* determines the will.

(*b*) If pure reason of itself determines the will then the ultimate maxim of the will is the principle of autonomy.

(*c*) Therefore, if a human will obeys a morally obligating imperative then its ultimate maxim is the principle of autonomy.

Premise (*a*) is suggested by a set of remarks at the beginning of the second *Critique*: Kant says that categorical imperatives present laws which determine the will independently of conditions only contingently related to the will (cf. *SC* 18 [20]); he also contrasts the case in which pure reason as empirically conditioned determines the will with the case in which pure reason of itself determines the will (cf. *SC* 15 [16]).

Kant advances premise (*b*) at another point in the second *Critique* when he claims that pure reason of itself determines the will only when the will is determined by the mere form of the practical rule (cf. SC 23–24 [24–25]). Since reason here determines the will, the conception of the universally valid form of the subordinate maxim is connected with the will through adoption of a practical principle, the principle of acting from maxims which have universally valid form.

Now what is meant by saying that pure reason of itself determines the will? The contrast with the case in which empirically conditioned reason determines the will suggests that Kant may merely mean that pure reason of itself determines the will when the principle of volition is not dependent on or conditioned by the satisfaction of inclination or additional volitions. If this is what he means, then Kant fails to provide any adequate support for premise (b); for we have seen that none of his other arguments succeed in showing that the will is never determined merely by adopting the maxim "To tell the truth" when it is determined independent of inclination and independent of additional volitions.

But perhaps we should pay attention to the fact that in the *Foundations* Kant speaks of "the idea of a reason which determines the will by a priori grounds" and says that a law of the determination of the will "holds not merely for men but for all rational beings as such; . . . it must be valid with absolute necessity . . ." (F 28 [408]). Such laws "are established a priori" (F 29 [409]). Thus, Kant may mean that when pure reason of itself determines the will then the principle of the will can also be known a priori to be objectively valid or necessary; he may even wish to say that the person not only can but does know a priori that his principle is valid or necessary. There are two problems with such an interpretation: First, even if a man *knows* that "To tell the truth" is valid, the ultimate principle of his *volition* may merely be "To tell the truth." Even if he only knows that "To tell the truth" is valid by checking it for universalizability, that does not prove that he adopts the principle of autonomy as a principle of *volition*.[17] Secondly, this interpretation ignores the fact that in the first *Critique* Kant characterized *pure* reason not as reason which supplies every principle of a priori knowledge, but as reason insofar as it supplies only principles of *absolutely* or *pure* a priori knowledge (cf. FC 58 [42–43]), and he defined pure modes of a priori knowledge as those excluding not only empirical grounds but even empirical *concepts* (cf. FC 43 [28]). Although it is not clear that Kant was consistent in his use of "pure" in the first *Critique*, this does suggest a further possible interpretation of what it is for pure reason of itself to determine the will.

Kant may mean that when pure reason of itself determines the will not only is the principle of volition unconditioned and valid or necessary a priori but it is an absolutely or pure a priori principle, i.e., a principle involving no empirical concepts. Now since "To tell the truth" does involve a concept which can be learned only from experience, viz., the concept

[17] For this reason, Kant's rejection of moral-sense theories and of the possibility of defining good and evil objects of the will independently of the concept of duty are insufficient to prove that a will which obeys some moral imperative also adopts the principle of autonomy. He rejects moral-sense theories because they *derive* the *notion* of duty from a phenomenal feeling and merely make it serve "refined inclinations" (cf. SC 40–41 [38–39]). The law, he claims, can only be thought by reason and is not an object of sensation; and, as noted in the *Lectures on Ethics*, a feeling cannot belong both to our rational and sensuous nature (cf. LE 37). Yet we may note that the will's being determined by the conception of truth-telling when its maxim is "To tell the truth" has nothing to do with such phenomenal feelings. Kant claims that the concept of *good* is either derivable from a practical law or else is "the concept of something whose existence promises pleasure and thus determines the causality of the subject (the faculty of desire) to produce it" (SC 60 [58]). Yet this does not prevent the practical law from being a particular law such as "To tell the truth" or, in another sense of the term "law," from being an imperative such as "You ought to tell the truth." Our question is whether Kant proves that one obeys such an imperative and fulfills a moral obligation only if one adopts the principle of autonomy as one's ultimate maxim.

of truth-telling, this would not be the principle of a will determined by pure reason of itself—thus Kant would finally be on his way toward proving that the only principle of determination for such a will is the principle of autonomy. Indeed, Kant says in the *Foundations* that it is of the utmost importance to derive the *concepts and laws* of morals from pure reason (cf. *F* 32 [411]). Kant might then claim that when pure reason of itself determines the will, the will adopts the principle of autonomy as its principle of volition, and that if the will then goes further and adopts some specific subordinate maxim on the basis of the principle of autonomy, that further step is not the work of pure reason but is the effect of the volition resulting from the influence of pure reason (and perhaps also the effect in part of judgment's applying the principle of autonomy to a particular maxim).

It is worth noting that such a defense of premise (*b*) will *not* follow merely from emphasizing a different sense in which Kant speaks of "pure" reason. In the *Critique of Judgment* Kant says that pure understanding, pure judgment, and pure reason "are called pure because they are legislative *a priori*" (*TC* 15 [179]). Now to say that practical reason legislates a priori could mean any one or a combination of the following:

1) A man's reason *could* make him aware that certain practical principles are a priori objectively valid or necessary.

2) A man's reason actually *does* make him *aware* that certain practical principles are a priori objectively valid or necessary.

3) A man's reason *makes it true* that certain practical principles are *objectively valid or necessary.*[18]

---

[18] I doubt that Kant believes reason to be legislative in this sense, however, for he says that if the legislator of a law not only is author of the obligation (necessitation) which accompanies the law but also is author of the law, then the law is merely contingent and arbitrary. (Cf. *DV* 27 [227].)

4) There are certain practical principles which are objectively necessary and a man's reason *makes it true* that he is *constrained, necessitated,* to adopt them.

5), 6) A man's reason could (does) make him *aware* that he is constrained, necessitated, to adopt certain practical principles.

Now whichever combination of these claims Kant might mean by saying that reason is legislative a priori, since he does *not* speak of this as *pure* a priori legislation, there is nothing to prevent the practical principles in question from being principles such as "To tell the truth" rather than the principle of autonomy. Thus Kant is unsuccessful when he tries to use this sense of "pure" reason in support of premise (*b*):

> pure reason can be practical only if the maxim of every action is subjected to the condition that it qualifies as a universal law. For as pure reason applied to the power of choice without regard to the object of choice, inasmuch as it is a power of principles (here of practical principles—hence inasmuch as it is a legislative power) it can make only the form of the maxim, its fitness for universal law, into the first principle and determining ground of choice, since the matter of the law is excluded. (*DV* 10 [213–214])

Here Kant fails to show why "To tell the truth" must be eliminated as a principle providing the determining ground of choice. If, however, he means to speak in this passage of "pure" reason as reason legislating *pure* a priori principles, then this argument returns us to the sense of "pure" reason specified in the first *Critique*.

Now if we do take pure reason in the sense of the first *Critique*, as reason providing a priori principles without empirical concepts, we must ask whether premise (*a*) is acceptable. Why can I not obey the imperative "One ought to tell the truth" or "Tell the truth" merely by adopting as the principle of my volition "To tell the truth"? Why must I also adopt the principle of autonomy? It would seem that the former is sufficient if the translation of "One ought to tell the truth" or "Tell the truth" is: "A non-holy will is constrained to adopt the objectively necessary principle 'To tell the truth' as a maxim." Perhaps Kant thinks that the correct translation of this imperative can only be: "A non-holy will is constrained to adopt the objectively necessary principle 'To act only from universalizable maxims' as the principle of volition whereby the principle 'To tell the truth' is made a maxim of the will." I shall consider whether this analysis accords with common sense in the final section of this paper.

Notice that Kant must establish that every imperative makes reference to the principle of autonomy as a principle of volition before he can successfully support premise (a) by use of certain other arguments found in the second *Critique*. Beck has pointed out[19] that in the second *Critique* Kant flatly claims that consciousness of the moral law is the sole apodictically certain fact of pure reason, which needs no justifying grounds yet which has the "credential" of giving a positive content to the negative concept of causality developed in the first *Critique*. The moral law "defines that which speculative philosophy had to leave undefined. That is, it defines the law for a causality the concept of which was only negative in speculative philosophy, and for the first time it gives objective reality to this concept" (*SC* 49 [47]). But we have already seen when discussing Kant's remarks about freedom in the third section of the *Foundations* that Kant fails to prove that a free will never has as its ultimate maxim "To tell the truth" when it obeys the particular categorical imperative "One ought to tell the truth" or "Tell the truth," i.e., "One is constrained or ob-

[19] Cf. L. W. Beck, *A Commentary on Kant's Critique of Practical Reason* (Chicago: University of Chicago Press, 1960), ch. 10.

ligated to adopt the objectively necessary principle 'To tell
the truth' as a principle of volition." Why cannot this be a
categorical imperative and be seen to be true as a fact of pure
reason? We could be said to see that it is true (1) by testing
it intellectually against the principle of autonomy, where the
latter principle is viewed not as a principle of *volition* but as
stating that universalizability is an adequate test for the moral
validity of maxims, and (2) by being aware of our self-con-
straint to adopt the principle "To tell the truth." This would
show that every human reason tells the person that universalizability is the test for valid maxims and also constrains his
will to adopt specific principles which it sees to be necessary.
This seems to be all that we need require in order to admit that,
as Beck puts it, "Only a law which is given by reason itself to
reason itself could be known a priori by pure reason and be a
fact for pure reason."[20] To be sure, Kant says that the difference between rational and empirical grounds of determination
of the will is shown to a man by the peculiar feeling of respect
which he has toward the law (cf. *SC* 95 [92]). But he also says
that when a man cultivates his talents he gives us the example
of a law and this awakens our respect for the law (cf. *F* 20–
21n. [401n.]). Why must this be a law mentioning the principle of autonomy as a principle of volition rather than merely
the principle "To cultivate my talents."

III

Having seen that Kant's arguments in support of certain of his
doctrines concerning the categorical imperative are unsatisfactory, we must now consider whether these doctrines agree with
present-day common-sense moral opinion and whether there

[20] Cf. *Ibid.*, p. 169, and *Studies in the Philosophy of Kant* (New York:
Bobbs-Merrill, 1965), p. 211.

is some way of deriving the categorical imperative which Kant overlooked.

I am not asking whether Kant was correct in his estimation of the climate of moral opinion in the Germany or Europe of his day. The question is whether we now have any initial reason to give credence to a moral theory which Kant failed to substantiate through arguments. In setting forth our present opinions I shall be no more or less tendentious than Kant was when he attempted to estimate the opinion of his contemporaries.

When he maintains that ethical legislation makes duty the incentive of the will Kant departs from common sense. If a man tells the truth, for example, when it is his duty to do so yet does the action merely for the sake of something he desires and independent considerations of moral obligation, then we would, I believe, still admit that his *action fulfilled his obligation* and was morally *right*. We do not in this sense contrast the "legality" of the action with its morality (cf. *DV* 25, 52 [225, 392]).

I doubt that there is any prevailing common opinion as to whether an action is *good* to the extent that it accords with duty and regardless of whether it was done because it was right. In this respect Kant's doctrine about the moral *value* of actions at least receives no clear support from common-sense moral opinion. Certainly we do generally value an action more *highly* and also consider the *agent* more *praiseworthy* if one of the agent's reasons for doing it was that it was the right thing to do. Even so, Kant goes too far in supposing we commonly think that an agent deserves no credit unless he acts from the principle of autonomy. The most Kant has seen is that whatever other reasons we might have for calling a man or an action good, one case we would take to be a *paradigm case*, a perfect example, of a good action is one in which the action is done in part from duty. Further, a case which we would take to be a paradigm case of a good man is that of a man who, among other things, intends always to do what is right and to fulfill his obligations, and who also has this as one of his motives when he conforms to particular duties and obligations. It is only in this sense that we agree that the moral worth of an action or of an agent does not derive from his acting in accord with his inclinations and that (at least sometimes) an "absolutely good" human will acts from duty.

It is also true that one paradigm case of someone's acting *as a moral (vs. nonmoral) agent*, acting in a way that *expresses* his moral status—be it good or bad—is a person's acting in part because he wanted (desired, intended, etc.) to do what he thought was right or, alternatively, acting in spite of the fact that he thought he was doing what was wrong.

Now telling the truth, for example, *because* we know it is our duty is certainly doing more than merely adopting the maxim "To tell the truth." For the latter could be adopted by a creature completely lacking the moral concepts of right and wrong. As Kant says in the *Lectures on Ethics*, an action done from duty is done "on account of the inner character of the act itself" (*LE* 22). But this does not mean on account of its character merely under a description of its phenomenal content, e.g., "truth-telling." Rather, "an action should arise from the impulsive ground of its own goodness" (*LE* 65). That is, the action should be done because it can be described as "right." One's ultimate maxim in this case is "To do what is right," and the subordinate maxim is really, e.g., "To tell the truth provided that it is right to do so." Thus, there is a plausible supposition *similar* to but not identical with steps (*d*) and (*e*) in the valid form of the argument previously discussed from the first section of the *Foundations* (p. 264 above). This is the claim that the moral worth of an action done from duty does not derive *entirely* from its being determined by the conception of a principle specifying an object of the will or specifying a purpose of the action. This is plausible provided that we think of the object or purpose (in the narrow sense) as specified in the principle under a description such as "truth-telling" rather than by a phrase already implying rightness, e.g., "action done because it is right." Then the most that Kant can plausibly claim is that *part* of the worth of a moral agent and of his action *may* derive from his acting from principles such as "To tell the truth provided that it is right" where these maxims are chosen because one also adopts as a maxim "To do what is right," and because one believes that truth-telling is right.

Perhaps we also commonly think that one paradigm case of a good man is that of a man who, among other things, *knows* the *test* for right and wrong and *wills* to apply it always. I doubt, however, that we believe that a man is not morally good *at all* if he merely does what he thinks is right without knowing how his action fits the supreme test of what is right.[21]

Whether Kant's own criterion of universalizability is a sufficient *test* of moral *maxims* is too large an issue to discuss here. If this test could be shown adequate, then Kant might finally be able to derive the categorical imperative as a genuine moral imperative by means of a moral argument which he never did explicitly utilize. He could argue as follows: the standard for moral maxims is universalizability; the principle of autonomy is itself universalizable; therefore (assuming that

[21] I doubt that many of us consider actions done *only* from, say, love to be *more* valuable than those done, say, from a motive of love and a motive of respect for duty, when each motive is strong enough to produce the action in the absence of the other motive. On the other hand, we need not suppose that a man who acts from love would always be a *better* man if he acted from duty in addition. The best example with which to teach someone what a good man may be like, however, is one in which the man acts from both motives.

moral imperatives *do* apply to men), there is a moral imperative constraining men to adopt the principle of autonomy. Indeed, Kant does attempt a moral proof which concludes that *consciousness that* one's act is *dutiful* is itself a duty: "It is a basic moral principle, which requires no proof, that *one ought to hazard nothing that may be wrong. . . .* Hence the *consciousness* that an action *which I intend to perform* is right, is unconditioned duty" (*R* 173–174 [185–186], Kant's italics). To argue plausibly, however, that one must *resolve* to do nothing wrong in the sense of resolving to apply the *principle of autonomy*, Kant would need to advance a further argument, possibly of the sort I have just suggested. Even so, he would only have proved that *one* of our duties is to adopt the principle of autonomy. He would not have shown that such obedience to *the* categorical imperative is required for any will to be good or for any action to be right or good. For there is no reason to suppose that the categorical imperative can properly be used to impose such strict requirements.

University of Pennsylvania

Pepita Haezrahi / The concept

of man as end-in-himself

"Now I say man and generally every rational being exists as an end and must never be treated as a means alone."[1] Thus Kant's proud assertion. We might be inclined to sympathise prompted by some obscure feeling of its sublimity, did not Kant fall back from this emotional vantage to a particularly unsatisfactory piece of reasoning in lieu of proof.

"This position," writes Kant, "that humanity and every intelligent being is an end in itself is not established by my observation or experience, as is seen, first, from the generality by which we have extended it to every rational being whatso-

Reprinted from KANT-STUDIEN, *Band 53, Heft 2 (1961/62), pp. 209–224, by permission of the editors.*

[1] Kant, *Grundlegung zur Metaphysik der Sitten*, zweiter Abschnitt [author's trans.; cf. p. 52 above].

ever; and second because humanity was exhibited not as a subjective end of mankind (i.e. not as an object which it stood in their option to pursue or decline) but as their objective end, which whatever other ends mankind may have, does as a law constitute the supreme limiting condition of such subjective ends and which must consequently take its rise from reason a priori. . . ."[2]

And in proof he advances: "rational nature exists as an end in itself. Man necessarily thinks of his own existence in this way; thus far it is a subjective principle of human actions." But "Also every other rational being thinks of his existence by means of the same rational ground which holds also for myself," and therefore the above (i.e. "rational nature exists as an end in itself") "is at the same time an objective principle from which, as a supreme practical ground, it must be possible to derive all laws of the will."[3] This argument, it seems to me, begs the question at the crucial point. In order to substantiate this contention, it must be remembered that for Kant (at this point of his critical philosophy) the concept of human dignity is defined in the moral domain only. I regard myself as possessing dignity, as being of infinite value, solely on the ground and to the extent to which I also regard myself as capable of moral action, i.e. as a rational being whose will is capable of determining itself in accordance with and for the sake of the moral law. The certainty which characterises my direct and immediate experience of my moral responsibilities assures me that the view I have of myself as possessing dignity is fully justified. Supposing that we concede the plausibility of an argument, based on analogy and inductive reasoning, which from the fact that I regard myself as possessed of dignity on certain grounds draws the conclusion that other rational beings when

2 Kant, *ibid.*
3 Kant, *ibid.* [changed to Beck's trans., pp. 53–54 above].

regarding themselves so (i.e. as possessed by dignity) will probably do so on the same grounds, in other words, that the same complex of circumstances and conditions which assures me of the certainty of my own freedom and moral responsibility, assures other rational beings of *their* freedom and *their* responsibility. Yet, as we must stress, no point in this argument necessarily implies an assurance for men of each other's freedom and moral capacity. In other words, the inductive assumption, or even an established fact that each rational being regards himself as possessed of dignity, on the same ground and for the same reasons that each other rational being regards himself as possessed of dignity, does not involve a logical necessity for rational beings to regard *each other* as possessed of dignity. This, however, is the decisive test for a general recognition by rational beings of the universal application of the dignity of man.

More explicitly: (*a*) The proposition "all men qua men are possessed of dignity" cannot be deduced from the concept (of human-dignity) itself since universal validity in the distributive sense is not an essential qualification of the concept and therefore not implied in it. Hence, (*b*) the complex and synthetic concept "the objective universality of the dignity of man" is not a self-evident concept, i.e. immediately perceived by reason. Therefore, (*c*) the validity of the synthesis it performs is in need of proof. This proof, I submit, Kant's formalistic argument fails to supply.[4]

[4] It may be interesting to point out that Professor Paton was very much aware of the dubious nature of Kant's professed proof for the objective validity of man-as-an-end-in-himself, and the in consequence necessary universal acknowledgment of man's status as an end. But he tried to patch things up by offering another possible deduction pieced together like a jigsaw puzzle from different loci in Kant's ethical writings. The end of the good will, he argues, cannot be less perfect than the will. Let us therefore look for something that is not less perfect than the good will.

In Kant's defence it must be said that he treated the whole matter rather casually. He did not in fact intend to convince anyone by this argument, since he did not think that any man, in his capacity of rational agent, would need to be convinced by what his own Reason would tell him most plainly should he but stop to reason. All one needed to do was to make men stop in the pursuit of their desires—and make them reason. This is done by the Categorical Imperative. In his argument, Kant only meant to retrace what happens when men *do* stop to reason. That is, Kant thought he was merely formulating in precise terms what men think in their own slovenly way, when they declare: "Other men are human beings too." According to Kant, the moment someone sets up a Categorical Imperative for himself and submits to it, he is governed by Reason. And being governed by Reason, when Reason is no longer the servant of his desires but their master, he imposes certain limitations on himself. He asks himself whether he could wish other people to act in the way in which he is just proposing to act. By doing this he already assumes other men to be possessed of rationality, of free will, in short, of a will which can be determined by the moral law. So that when he decides that a certain maxim will not do, he implies at the same time that other people, did they but stop and think, would reject it too. He acts against the background of a moral universe.

There are for instance ends which are also duties, like performing moral actions for the sake of duty (*Metaphysik der Sitten*, *Tugendlehre*, Einleitung, III, IV). But products of moral actions are not absolutely good, and morally good actions are not absolutely good, such supreme goodness belonging only to the will (*Kritik der praktischen Vernunft* [Akademie ed., p. 62; Abbott trans., p. 182]). Now since the end cannot be less perfect than the will, therefore only rational agents as far as they are possessed of a will itself capable of being a good will actuated by the idea of the law, can be the Ends of a Categorical Imperative (viz. H. J. Paton, *The Categorical Imperative*, pp. 166–172).

On this view Reason is common to all men.[5] When not forced into the service of one man's particular desires, correctly reasoned conclusions are valid for all, and would be reached by all who considered the same problem. If one man becomes aware that rational beings are ends-in-themselves, by representing to himself the moral law, this awareness being rational is implicitly valid for all men and accessible to all men. It is therefore enough if men stop to reason, to make them realise that other men are ends-in-themselves. The main difficulty for Kant lies in making men also *act* by the light of their reason. It never occurred to Kant that men could, on rational grounds, refuse to treat other men as ends.

To our generation however this possibility *has* occurred, indeed the question has been brought home to us with great emphasis. We can no longer afford to be casual about it but must seek a more stringent answer to the question: How can a universal application of the concept of man-as-an-end-in-himself be rationally vindicated?

Let us briefly trace this concept in the different phases of the development of Kant's ethical thought. In common with most of Kant's other basic ideas this concept originated in

[5] In this argument Kant most closely follows the Stoic doctrine as expounded by Marcus Aurelius, in *Eis Heavton*, Book IV, ch. 4: "If the faculty to reason is common to us (i.e. all human beings) then Reason itself, by and through which we are rational, must be our common possession. If that be so, then also the Reason which prescribes what ought and what ought not to be done is common (to all human beings). If that be so, then the law too is common (i.e. valid for all human beings). If that be so, then we are citizens. If that be so, we take part in some commonwealth. If that be so, the Universe itself must be in a way, a commonwealth. For in what other commonwealth, could anyone claim, that the whole of the human race take part as citizens? Thence, then, from this commonwealth in which we all have part, we hold our very faculty of reasoning, and our rationality, and our being subjects to laws; or whence (else could we hold it)?"

what I have termed on another occasion the "humanitarian superstitions" of the eighteenth century, and is moreover strongly coloured by Rousseau's version of these ideas. Now according to Rousseau the intrinsic worth of a human being qua human being, which for short we shall term the dignity of man, is part of man's innate nature. By an innate qualification of their nature human beings are endowed with freedom of will and hence are capable of virtue.[6]

Man's innate capacity of virtue[7] is, objectively speaking, the reason for the worth and dignity of human beings. Subjectively it is recognised by a corresponding sentiment, itself innate in human nature: the natural love of man for humanity.

In his pre-critical writings Kant followed Rousseau very closely: "True virtue," he writes, "can be grown only on principles; the more universal these principles the nobler and more elevated the virtue. These principles are not speculative rules of reason, but the awareness of a feeling which dwells in every human heart and which is more than mere pity and helpfulness. I think this sentiment is best described as a feeling for the Beauty and Dignity of human nature [*Das Gefühl von der Schönheit und Würde der menschlichen Natur*]."[8]

To be capable of virtue, according to Kant, one must possess this feeling. The feeling, however, is innate and therefore

---

[6] "La liberté morale . . . seul rend l'homme vraiment maître de lui, car l'impulsion du seul appetit est esclavage et l'obéissance à la loi qu'on se presente est liberté . . . la vertu n'est que la liberté morale." Rousseau, *Lettres sur la vertu et le bonheur.*

[7] It is only a capacity for "virtue," i.e. to be pursued in the face of objection, for according to Rousseau, the actual natural goodness of man has been vitiated by the impositions of culture, and needs to be reinstated by perseverance in merely virtuous actions "until perfect artificiality becomes nature again." *Ibid.*

[8] Kant, *Beobachtungen über das Gefühl des Schönen und Erhabenen* (1764) [Akademie ed., II, 217].

universal. "Beauty and Dignity" are also innate qualities of human nature as such. But in distinction from Rousseau, Kant holds that this "Beauty and Dignity" are grounded primarily in the rational quality of human nature. Kant also holds, that what we call the "Beauty and Dignity of Human Nature" refers to and comprises more than the sole capacity for moral virtue, namely capacities for scientific research, philosophical speculation, artistic creation, religious inspiration, etc. At this particular point in Kant's philosophical evolution neither the concept of the "dignity of man" nor its (assumed) universal validity present any difficulty. Both are contained in the definition as an inherent, innate part of human nature indissolubly bound up with the rational qualities in their various activities and modifications (in the Arts, Sciences, Philosophy, etc.) which thus provide the main *raison d'être* of human dignity. The universal validity (in its distributive sense) of human dignity, on the other hand, is vindicated on the basis of a universal participation of human beings in the rational, this being by definition an essential quality of human nature.

Later, in his critical writings, Kant had to change his ground for reasons of method. In view of the requirements of the transcendental method of deduction,[9] Kant had to abandon his former view of moral virtue as grounded in an innate natural sentiment. In accordance with his new method Kant grounded moral virtue, which he now calls the good will, in

---

[9] Transferring the problem of objectivity from the *Critique of Pure Reason* to Ethics, Kant formulates his question thus: "Whether in Ethics too there might not be a pervading lawfulness, which does not depend on the material content, or the material differences and variations of what is willed, but determined solely by the manner in which it is willed, i.e. the particular modality of the will itself which thereby provides this lawfulness with objectivity in the transcendental sense of the word, i.e. provides a ground for the necessary and universal validity of ethical values." Ernst Cassirer, *Kants Leben und Lehre* [Berlin: B. Cassirer, 1918], p. 266.

its determination by the categorical imperative, that is in the determination of will by reason.[10] The possibility of a will determined by reason, he declared from the *presupposed* possibility of freedom. On the other hand, he viewed Human Nature as split in two parts, one irrational and sensual, and one rational part. Inner worth and dignity are made conditional on the domination and determination of the irrational part by the rational, that is, ultimately on the freedom of the human will which enables man to determine himself in accordance with the dictates of his reason and regardless of his sensual desires and impulses. In short, the dignity of man is made to depend on the ability of man to perform moral actions[11] and bear moral responsibilities, that is, in the last instance, on the freedom of the will.

In this new framework, the demonstration of the objective reality of the dignity of man, and the vindication of its objective universality are rendered extremely difficult, perhaps impossible altogether. For on closer inspection Kant's deduction is seen to move in a circle: He presupposes the freedom of the human will as a necessary condition for the possibility, i.e. existence and reality of moral obligation and responsibility, and then attributes dignity to men because they have free will, i.e. are morally responsible. Now a categorical judgement cannot be deduced from two hypothetical judgements. The objective reality of the dignity of man cannot be deduced from the hypothetical reality of freedom, much less can the universality of its application be so deduced. But nothing less than such *objective reality* is demanded by Kant for this concept. Nor, to judge from the way in which he first introduced

[10] Thus receding further away from Rousseau by grounding both virtue and its recognition in reason.

[11] Thus oddly enough re-approaching Rousseau, by relating Human Dignity solely to the moral sphere.

this concept *Nun aber sage ich*—"Now I say man and every reasonable agent *exists as an* end in himself . . . ,"[12] or to judge from the vital function and crucial importance of this concept for Kant's system of ethics, could he admit or less.

Nor is it any help that there exists in fact one point at which we can break through the circle of Kant's deduction and touch reality, namely the point reached in our immediate moral experiences as a datum of so vivid a certainty that it excludes all doubt. "A higher certainty than that which assures us of our moral self, our autonomous personality, is not conceivable."[13] But this experience is as we have seen of necessity limited to my own person. It can therefore assure me of my own freedom, my own moral responsibility, and therefore of my own dignity and worth, but not of the dignity of others. It is, however, the *dignity of others that is in question* if I am to limit my own freedom out of a respect for theirs.

Moreover the *dignity of others* must not be demonstrated solely from my sense of moral responsibility and obligation and from my voluntary self-limitation, for then it would be dependent entirely on my pleasure whom I wished to honour in this way, and who were to be the recipients of a dignity conferred by me. This is a possibility Kant most certainly would have rejected as detrimental to the moral rightness of an action. From a Kantian point of view it is most unsatisfactory and unacceptable that man should acquire moral dignity by being treated *as though* he possessed it. From a Kantian point of view, man must be treated as being possessed of moral dignity because he *is* so possessed. A corroborating reason for this position derives from Kant's view that moral

[12] Kant, *Grundlegung zur Metaphysik der Sitten*, zweiter Abschnitt [p. 52 above].

[13] Kant, *Kritik der praktischen Vernunft*, Teil I, Kap. 5.

worth and dignity cannot be acquired by an outside grant but must be acquired by inner effort.

Some sort of objective justification and vindication is therefore desperately needed at this point if the autonomy and the very meaning of ethics in Kant's sense is to be saved.

Kindred problems have been faced, to name but a few, by Rousseau in the idea of "la volonté générale," by J. S. Mill in his idea of "the general happiness," and Sartre in his proposition "l'acte individuel engage toute l'humanité." A brief survey of the respective arguments and their respective solutions might conceivably be of some help in indicating how our solution may be found.

Taking Rousseau first, we find that he has the easiest stand. "Les engagements qui nous lient au corps social ne sont obligatoires que parce-qu'ils sont mutuels; et leur nature est telle qu'en les remplissant on ne peut travailler pour autrui sans travailler pour soi. Pourquoi la volonté générale est-elle toujours droite, et pourquoi tous veulent-ils constamment le bonheur de chaqu'un d'eux si ce n'est parce qu'il n'y a per-sonne que ne s'approprie cet nom chaqu'un et qui ne songe a lui même en votant pour tous? Ce qui prouve que l'égalité de droit et la notion de justice qu'elle produit derivent de la préférence que chaqu'un se donne et par conséquence de la nature de l'homme."[14] Men, according to this argument, re-spect each other's persons and attribute dignity to each other, because this is the only *practical* way to pursue their own ends in comparative safety and security. By a voluntary self-limi-tation, they secure a similar self-limitation in others, indeed the one is the condition of the other. "Ils ne sont obligatoires que parce qu'ils sont mutuels"; and this self-limitation in retro-spect confers rights and privileges and dignity on the members

[14] J. J. Rousseau, *Le Contrat Social*, 11, 6.

of the *contrat social*. In other words, this dignity depends on the willingness, or the enforced willingness to self-limitation (enforced by the very circumstances of human existence and its natural dangers). But if there should be a man, or a group of men whose *préférence* for themselves need not, thanks to accidental circumstances, be limited in order to assure its own success (for instance the near extermination of the red races in North America); then there is no power in the world which can force those men to attribute dignity to the others, and therefore these others will not possess dignity. Rousseau's argument does not safeguard the objective universality of the dignity of man. It provides for a comparative generality inside closed societies only, more or less in the sense of Lindsay, "other people's behavior is necessarily an assumed background to ours . . . different social atmospheres compel us to act differently. . . . If one knows that people are willing to co-operate one acts differently even if one's purpose is not allowed to alter. . . . Moral rules . . . are no use unless they are generally kept and form an *effective* moral code, i.e. most men are ready to keep them and enforce their keeping. . . ."[15]

Rousseau's argument is mainly valuable as a reminder that we must not allow the dignity of man to be reduced to a conditional status for fear of finding our system of ethics disintegrate into relative and ephemeral moral codes. For the objectivity and autonomy of ethics—and without such objectivity and autonomy, whatever else it would be it would no longer be ethics—is indissolubly bound up with the absolute validity of the dignity of man and unrestricted universality of its attribution.

J. S. Mill's famous argument on general happiness runs: "The sole evidence it is possible to produce that anything is desirable is that people do actually desire it. . . . No reason can

[15] A. D. Lindsay, "*The Two Moralities*," pp. 21–22.

be given why the general happiness is desirable except that each person so far as he believes it to be attainable desires his own happiness. This however being a fact we have not only all the proof which the case admits of, but all which it is possible to require that happiness is good; that each person's happiness is a good to that person and the general happiness, therefore a good to the aggregate of all persons."[16] If analysed this argument proves a mine of problems each of which has had its day as a *cause célèbre* of philosophical disputation. The only points which need concern us here are (*a*) the argument (given the relationship what is desired is desirable, what is desirable is good and therefore what is desired is good) from the goodness of each person's happiness for himself to the goodness of general happiness for the aggregate of persons and (*b*) the argument from the fact that each person actually desires his own happiness, to the alleged fact that general happiness is desired by all (i.e. desirable to all). It has often been pointed out that the validity of Mill's argument hinges on the definition of general happiness. If the general happiness is a sum of particular happinesses, then each individual desires it to exactly that degree to which his own happiness is involved. Thus, if, for instance, I desire to regain my coat from a cloakroom in which hang many other coats desired by many other people, it is possible to define the concepts of all the coats, all the people, and all the desires of all the people for all their coats. Now my desire for my coat, though definable as part of the general desire for all the coats in the cloakroom is neither increased nor diminished nor affected in any other way by being part of a general desire. Nor is my coat affected in any way by hanging together with other coats. But if to regain my coat I have to queue up so as to avoid a scramble in which all coats including mine are liable to be damaged,

[16] J. S. Mill, *Utilitarianism*, ch. 4.

then my desire is no longer a mere item in the sum total of all desires but enters into some co-ordinated system with them limiting its own intensity and accommodating itself to all the others somewhat in the manner described by Rousseau in the *contrat social*. My desire is now modified in its activity by the collective desire of which it is a part, but it still is a desire for my own coat and for nothing else, though my coat gains a relative safety from damage. I can however envisage the possibility that my desire for my coat enters into some combination with the other people's desires for their coats. Thus, by joining in with other people, I am able to pay an attendant to guard it whilst I'm away, brush it, and mend it, a thing beyond my means if I were on my own. My desire forms a collective system with all other desires, by which my coat is actually benefited. Still my desire is centered on my own coat, and if through this organic relationship other people's coats benefit as well as my own, this is as far as I am concerned of secondary importance, a mere accidental by-product of the situation. In other words, though my happiness be an organic part of the general happiness, i.e. increased, modified, even changed in its content by the whole of which it is a part, and though I be a tireless worker for the improvement and enrichment of general happiness, I am basically concerned only with my own happiness, and with general happiness only insofar as it is the precondition of my own. At no point in the rational argument leading from my own happiness to general happiness had I any reason to entertain a disinterested regard for other people's happiness. At no point was I confronted by a rationally necessitated demand (arising from the argument itself) to desire general happiness for itself and regardless of my own. In other words, at no point was I given the opportunity to exercise the generosity which is Mill's ultimate intention.

We must therefore conclude that the fact that general

happiness is desired by all people, or even the proposition that it ought to be desired by all people, are not sufficient to cover Mill's ethical meaning. To it must be added a demand that it be desired for its own sake, for the sake of the regard I have for other people, and regardless of any satisfaction that might accrue to me in the process. This must be so if I am to put the consideration of general happiness above the consideration for my own in case of conflict—as Mill taught. This demand however is implied in none of the concepts which appear in the original argument (my happiness, general happiness, my person, the aggregate of persons, good for me, good for all, etc.), nor in the relations defined to hold between them. From the given fact of my desire for my happiness for its own sake, the process of reason can at the outside lead me to a concept of general happiness as the ultimate warrant and supreme condition of my own happiness. It can never furnish me with the idea of general happiness as being desirable for its own sake, nor confront me with a demand to desire it for its own sake. This demand is not justified by the preceding argument, nor indeed definable without a certain forcing of the concepts with which Mill operates. It must therefore be regarded as an intruder from some other domain, a heterogeneous eruption which, from the point of view of the argument, gratuitously breaks up the cohesion of the argument. Besides, in the given context, this demand defeats its own ends for if all people acted on the maxim that one ought to desire and pursue general happiness at the expense of one's own happiness, nobody would be happy at any time, and general gloom and misery the sole effect. To sum up, we may say that a pursuit of Mill's argument in vindication of the idea of general happiness as a *moral* duty has shown that the moral obligation so defined (i.e. a regard for other people's happiness and, a fortiori, a regard for their persons) cannot be deduced from the explicit tenets of Mill's utilitarian system of ethics. On the contrary this idea having been, as it were, injected into the system by some heterogeneous force and being antagonistic to the general tenor of his philosophical theory disrupts its inner cohesion.

The profit of this lesson for our study for the Kantian theory is this: Though the idea of the unconditional regard we owe to other people's persons as the core of all our moral obligations is not as an idea incompatible with the general tenor of the Kantian theory of ethics, analogy from Mill's argument brings home the suspicion that in Kant's case too, the idea in question may have been injected into the system by the eruptive and nonrational force of some intuition, rather than being the rationally demonstrable deduction from rationally valid concepts Kant took it to be. In short, what Kant had taken to be a simple case of *intellectus quaerens intellectum* is really another case of an *intellectus quaerens fidem*, and as such likely to be disappointed in its quest.

Let us see what we can learn from Sartre's argument in vindication of his proposition, "l'acte individuel engage toute l'humanité," which runs thus: To choose is to affirm the value of that which we choose, because it is always the good that we choose. Nothing can be good for us without being good for everybody. Hence to choose for oneself is to choose for everybody.

Sartre interprets both the proposition and its proof in two different senses, a metaphysical sense and a moral sense. I intend to show that the two do not accord and that the moral interpretation rests on a supplementary intuition of the intrinsic worth of human beings, which is alien to the basic metaphysical tenor of Sartre's existentialist thought and superimposed on it. Moreover the argument (quoted above) which could just pass in its metaphysical setting becomes plainly fallacious if a moral interpretation is attempted.

To expound the first interpretation of Sartre's argument we must briefly sketch in its metaphysical background. Sartre's fundamental tenet is that God does not exist. Since God does not exist, man's freedom is absolute and he can never escape it. No objective truth, no moral principle, no religious conviction, no intrinsic value exist apart from man's choosing to believe in them. Thus man is responsible for the truth he believes in as well as for providing the proofs in its favour. Man is responsible for his very experiences, since the respective significance and interpretation of experiences are determined by the selection he makes. Man thus selects the manner of being he chooses to become. In consequence freedom is not simply an attribute of man, but his very essence (*la liberté est l'étoffe de son être*), and any action, thought, impulse, which denies this freedom is an act of bad faith. Any attempt to appeal to a moral principle, an intrinsic value, a religious conviction, when faced with a choice, is an action smacking of insincerity, cowardice, and *mauvais-foi*. It is a deplorable and moreover *futile* attempt to evade and shift one's responsibilities. Whatever man chooses to do or to be, he must choose in the consciousness of his absolute liberty and full responsibility. This is the only possible *right* choice (*la choix au nom de la liberté*) and in choosing to choose so, man sets it up as an objectively right principle of action. Thus in choosing the right way for himself, he *ipso facto* chooses the right way for others. Man is compelled (by the logical necessity of his metaphysical situation) to choose the freedom of others when he chooses his own. It is factually impossible for man to pursue his own liberty without pursuing at the same time the liberty of others.

Two unavoidable consequences follow from this metaphysical theory. The first, which need not concern us further for the moment, is that seen against this stark metaphysical background the implications of "l'acte individuel engage toute l'humanité" become truly terrifying. For it means that man, in whatever he chooses to feel, think, or do, moulds the whole of humanity in his own image. The second, which is of the greatest importance for us, is that the regard for the liberty (i.e. the persons, as liberty is the essence of the human person) of others is a necessary result of a regard for my own person and therefore an automatic not a voluntarily sought consequence of this regard. As such it is morally irrelevant. The only *moral* duty, which can be defined within the bounds of Sartre's metaphysical assumptions, is a duty to oneself.[17]

This however does not suit Sartre's purpose at all. He intends to establish a moral code where such a code ought to be established, namely in the relation between one man and another, in the intrasubjective sphere. Sartre proceeds to do this in the following manner: He asserts that the sole datum which can be immediately and directly experienced is the reflective consciousness expressed in the declaration *cogito ergo sum*. At the same time, through this same primary experience I gain an intuitive knowledge of the existence of *l'autre:* "Je découvre l'autre comme une liberté *posée* en face de moi qui ne pense, qui ne veut *que pour ou contre moi.*" However we may regard this affirmation of a primary and intuitive perception of the "other," and the assertion that this intuition is part of the very first *cogito*,[18] it is enough for our purpose that Sartre admits it to be the yield of a primary intuition wholly unconnected with the preceding considerations of his metaphysical theories.

[17] In this connection it is of no consequence whether choosing for oneself implies also choosing for others, since it is one's own salvation one works out, and in which one is primarily interested. The salvation of others is an inevitable, though not undesirable corollary to one's own.

[18] Descartes affirmed that in this experience and through it the I gains knowledge of the existence of God. Both affirmations however seem the expression of some separate intuition, separate from the perception of the I, that is, rather than inferences from the primary datum of the *cogito*.

The point we wish to make is that the yield of this intuition is not only wholly unconnected with the above theories, but directly contradictory to them, and indeed overthrows them at every point. For the astonishing thing about this suddenly revealed "other" is that he is not identical nor indistinguishable from the I; nor is he compelled to live in harmony with the I. He is free to choose for or against the I. Therefore the I must be free (from the point of view of the other) to choose for or against the other. That is, what the I chooses for itself (for itself it chooses only the good), it does not necessarily choose for the other. In other words, "To choose for oneself is to choose for others" is a moral injunction, not a law of human nature (i.e. metaphysical human nature). Therefore the proposition "l'acte individuel engage toute l'humanité" must be classified *as a moral injunction*[19] to regard all one's actions "as though" they were obligatory for all mankind, and not as a statement that they are. Hence the metaphysical and the moral interpretations of Sartre's theory of choice, action, and responsibility, are mutually exclusive.

The disturbance occurs at the very point where the intuitive perception of the other as a free and therefore dangerous being breaks the train of the argument. The "other" is no longer something which I mould in my own image every time I make a choice; he is a person for himself, who makes his own choice irrespective of and uninfluenced by the choice I make for him. *Il veut pour ou contre moi.* He therefore possesses the dignity of a free person, and as such I ought to respect him even as he ought to respect me. That is, we both ought to choose to respect each other's persons though we are not by virtue of our very nature *compelled* to do so. Thus and thus only *moral* decisions and acts can be defined.

[19] Equivalent to Kant's categorical imperative: Act only on that maxim which is also fit to become a universal law of nature.

Let us illustrate this point by re-examining Sartre's proposition, "l'acte individuel engage toute l'humanité," and the argument which is supposed to vindicate it. The first step of his argument—to choose for oneself is to affirm the value of that which one chooses—is factually correct and moreover a self-evident proposition if only value be defined loosely enough, i.e. not restricted to moral value. Similarly we can accept the second step, that it is always the good which we choose,[20] if the concept of the good be also defined loosely enough to cover all possible values. The third step, "nothing can be good for us without being good for all," on the other hand seems highly questionable. There is no reason on earth why something should not be good for me, or why I should forego something that seems good to me simply because it may not be good for everybody.

Moreover, it seems to me that most of one's desires and purposes insofar as they have not yet been subjected to the categorical imperative and adjusted to the requirements of the moral law[21] represent primarily choices for us against others. If our wills are directed toward concrete ends, toward material possessions, it is the exclusive rights in these possessions which we covet most.[22] Even in the pursuit of spiritual ends and rational achievements where exclusiveness of possession has no real meaning, since the same spiritual content can be pursued, attained, and its possession enjoyed by many men

[20] Viz. "Nihil appetimus nisi sub ratione boni, nihil aversamur nisi sub ratione mali."

[21] I.e. subsequently cut to the moral measure.

[22] The more desires for material things accord and agree with each other, the fiercer their battle against each other, viz., the pun attributed to Francis I and cited by Kant: "was mein Bruder Karl will, das will auch ich (nämlich Mailand)." The bigger the difference in what we desire, the greater our chance of not getting in each other's way. But differences in what is desired entail a mutual negation of the value of what is chosen.

at the same time without loss to its inner richness, exclusiveness of possession is nevertheless highly valued. In the latter case, the value of exclusiveness refers to the personality of him who possesses rather than to what is possessed. We are wont to cherish the belief in the exceptionality of our persons and our pursuits,[23] and this alone is reason enough to make any choice for ourselves at the same time a choice against others.

In consequence it seems fairly safe to conclude that the act of "choosing for oneself" does not *de facto* involve an act of "choosing for all." On the other hand considered as a moral exhortation "choose for all what you would choose for yourself!" appears highly unsatisfactory, since not I but they must

---

[23] I think this is why we are both pleased and displeased if we chance upon people whose ideas and pursuits completely resemble our own. However great our joy in finding kindred souls, a joy which is nourished chiefly by the praise implied in such agreement, the annoyance at finding our most cherished "exceptionalities" duplicated is far greater, for such duplication devalues our exceptionality: unless of course one marries the duplicator and continues to be exceptional à deux. Compare Goethe's "Lebt man denn wenn andere leben" *(West-östlicher Divan)* and Thomas Mann, who also ends by quoting this line of Goethe's: "From Switzerland came the two volumes of Hermann Hesse's 'Das Glasperlenspiel.' In far Montagnola my friend had achieved his difficult and beautiful novel, of which until this moment I had known but the introduction. . . . I often said of this introduction that its style was so near to me 'als wär's ein Stück von mir.' Enabled to take in the whole in one comprehensive view, I felt almost terrified to see how similar it was to what had occupied me so intensely these last years. The same idea of a fictional biographer, and the same overtones of parody, which this form permits. The same emphasis on music. The same criticism of our age and our culture though more dreamy and utopian than my own . . . still, there were similarities enough—more than enough, and the entry I made in my diary: 'to be reminded that one is not alone in the world is always annoying,' bluntly expresses this facet of my feeling. It is but another version of Goethe's: 'Lebt man denn wenn Andre leben?' " Th. Mann, *Die Entstehung des Dr. Faustus* (Amsterdam: Bermann-Fischer, 1949), p. 68.

choose for themselves what they consider of value and goodness. Even the injunction to "make the freedom of others your end at the same time that you make your own freedom your end" (freedom in the sense Sartre gave to the word) proves vain simply because such a pursuit would be self-contradictory and meaningless inside Sartre's theory. For if the right choice for man is the choice made in the full consciousness of his absolute liberty and accepting full responsibility for it, the liberty of another man which I make my own end is not his choice, and therefore cannot represent a right use of his essential liberty. In other words other people's liberty (in the metaphysical sense) cannot be an end for my will for I cannot bestow liberty on other people. Moreover, any attempt on my part to do so would be tantamount to a denial of their liberty. But the liberty of others cannot be denied at all since it is according to Sartre a reality perceived by an immediate and decisive act of intuitive perception. The intuitive perception of the "other" as an independent entity, endowed with the power "to choose for or against me," faces each one of us with a demand to respect the liberty of the other on a plane of mutual engagements. This is, however, tantamount to a demand, that men should respect the persons of all other men.

Once again we watch the impetuous idea of the dignity of man qua man, injected into a recalcitrant and incompatible system of thought by the force of some irrational intuition, play havoc with the consistency and coherence of that system.

Summing up what we have learned from the case of Kant, Rousseau, Mill, Sartre, we can say that what looked at first blush like rationally arguable demonstrations of the dignity-of-man-in-others—by inductive reasoning from the data of one's own experience,[24] have proved but a barrage of words designed to hide the mental jump performed under their cover.

[24] That is in Kant and Mill, *not* in Sartre.

This mental jump is occasioned by the intrusion of a logically always gratuitous,[25] at times inimical idea[26] into the argument. With its appearance previously used concepts acquire a new meaning, and a new validity. But as the words[27] denoting such concepts are usually not replaced by others or qualified by an epithet to evidence the inner change in content, the fallacy of seeming to prove what has really been accepted[28] without proof (namely the intrusive idea) is made possible.

Let us now try to examine this intrusive and troublesome idea of the "infinite worth of the human person" on its own merits and apart from these diverse systems. Let us agree to give it the form of a proposition couched in Kantian terms: "All men qua men are endowed with dignity" and examine possible proofs for its validity.

Then in the first place we must say that this proposition is not an analytic proposition as Kant attempted to show. For from the bare concept of man, only his rationality can be deduced with any certainty as to its universal validity. But the quality of rationality does not entail (by logical necessity) the quality of moral goodness nor does it entail the possession of dignity. The proposition "all men qua men are endowed with dignity" must therefore be a synthetic proposition.

It is however not a synthetic proposition a posteriori for the following reasons: (1) I can experience only my own dignity as a moral being, since I can be certain only of my own freedom and my own capability of moral action. (2) Since morality lies in the manner of willing, and since it is beyond my

[25] In Kant and Sartre.

[26] In Mill.

[27] I.e. "general happiness" in Mill's, *liberté* in Sartre's argument.

[28] I use "accepted" rather than "assumed," because intuitions and postulates, if based on intuition, possess a greater compelling power than assumptions.

power to see into the hidden motives of another man, I can never actually be certain that they perform moral actions and are capable of performing moral actions. (3) I am on the other hand continually faced with the sight of people who disregard the moral law and who therefore definitely do *not* perform moral actions. (4) Any judgement from myself upon others is therefore not warranted by experience. But even if it were so justified inductive reasoning could never supply sufficient certainty for the objective and absolute necessity of this synthesis. We must however have sufficient certainty, nay absolute certainty in this matter.

The proposition "all men qua men are endowed with dignity" if it be at all objectively necessary, must therefore be an a priori synthetic proposition.

Now it seems to me that if any rational necessity can be said to exist for the synthesis in question, it is not of the same kind of rational necessity as the rational necessity in which the synthesis between will and freedom finds its justification. There is no necessity to conceive all men as *eo ipso* endowed with dignity, similar to the necessity to think of the will as being free. In other words, the extension of the attribute of dignity to all men qua men (i.e. to conceive of dignity as a prerogative natural to all men) is not a category of reason. But perhaps a rational justification for the a priori synthesis between man as such and dignity can be found in some middle term, in which as pre-condition common to both, both could be grounded? Now if such a term could be found, the composite concept of the dignity of all men would derive from this term, and therefore be dependent on this term. It would be a conditioned, a hypothetical synthesis. This would lead to Ethics itself (as a discipline) being dependent on the same middle term. Ethics would thus be reduced to a heteronomy dictated by that term. Therefore all attempts to vindicate the proposition "all men qua men are endowed with dignity" by the authority of the scriptures, a metaphysical doctrine inclusive of a teleological view of the universe, or man's biological qualification, must be repudiated as damaging to the unconditional validity of human dignity as such, and by implication, to the autonomy of ethics. All attempts to vindicate the proposition "all men qua men . . ." by individual and outstanding[29] qualities must be repudiated as pernicious to the universal attribution of human dignity. All attempts to vindicate the proposition "all men qua men . . ." by a mutual agreement to accord each other this dignity (a *contrat social*) must be repudiated as damaging to the reality of dignity.

Finally the necessity of performing the synthesis between "human being" and "dignity" is not grounded in an emotional compulsion[30] innate in all human hearts. As a matter of fact,

---

[29] As Kant did by making dignity dependent on moral capacity.

[30] Viz. Rousseau's view, and also Kant's view in his precritical writings, especially in *Beobachtungen über das Gefühl des Schönen und Erhabenen*, quoted above. Kant's latter occasional loose references to the heart as the seat of morality, must not be interpreted to mean that he had given up the view that morality is exclusively grounded in reason. He uses the term "heart" to cover those decisions prompted by *reason* and *common sense* but not fully understood in their theoretical demonstration. At no time does he oppose heart (the irrational) to reason (the rational). He opposes heart (rational reason, *Eingebung des natürlichen Verstandes*) to mind (of which at times in speculative deliberation one can make unsound and incorrect use). I believe passages like the one on Herr Garve ought to be interpreted in this sense: "Hr Garve's remarks (about the difference which I define between the discipline that teaches us how to become happy and that which teaches us how to be worthy of happiness) are: 'For my part I must confess that though I can understand this division of ideas with my *head* I cannot find this division in my *heart*. I cannot even comprehend how anyone can be sure that he had isolated his desire for happiness to such a degree, that his actions were indeed done for duty's sake only.' . . . In spite of Hr Garve's confession that he does not find the division (or rather separation) aforementioned in his *heart* I do not hesitate to contradict him and defend his heart against his head. He, the upright man has

very few people actually *feel* that all people are endowed with dignity. Mostly the innate emotional regard for other people's persons embraces a restricted and definite group (who are thought of as endowed with dignity in virtue of their class, profession, nationality, etc.). Almost always the purely emotional respect for other people's persons excludes certain groups on more or less defensible rational reasons, or on irrational, sometimes even unconscious grounds.

The synthetic proposition "All men-qua-men are possessed of dignity" is therefore incapable of any proof whatsoever, including the transcendental proof for the objective necessity of categories. Since it is also very rarely the object of an intuition, in the usual sense of intuition, it can only be classified as a *postulate* which because of the uniqueness of its nature and position can only be described by comparison. Like the postulate of freedom it is wholly implied in the given datum of moral experience and represents the ultimate reason for this experience. In another sense it resembles the postulate of the existence of God in its (i.e. the latter's) structural relationship to religious experience, for it can be taken for the effective real cause of moral experience as well as for its ultimate reason (formal cause). That means that moral experience, though it is our only means of discovering this postulate, is not to be treated as though it were the cause or the ground of the postulate. On the contrary, the postulate is to be treated as though it were the cause and the ground of moral experience, on the justification that moral experience can be explained completely

---

indeed found (this division) in his heart (i.e. in the determination of his will), but he could not adjust it in his head to the usual explanations according to psychological principles (which are all of a physical causal nature) so as to understand what cannot be understood or explained, namely the possibility of a categorical imperative and in order to speculate on this imperative. . . ." Kant, *Über den Gemeinspruch: Das mag in der Theorie richtig sein, taugt aber nicht für die Praxis* (1793), Part II.

only by this postulate. (Note the close analogy to the postulate of the existence of God in religious experience.) In short, the postulate is to be treated not like a postulate. It is to be treated in all respects and to all purposes, like a statement of fact, the statement of an ultimate, irreducible, unquestionable fact. Now it so happens that the irreducible and unquestionable fact the postulate is supposed to state is not a very probable fact. It is indeed "a fact" denied and invalidated by the greater part of our experience and knowledge. It therefore resembles those tenets of our convictions of which it can be truthfully said: *credo quia absurdum*. An act of faith, and a gratuitous act of faith at that, is needed for its acceptance. Moreover it has a peculiar quality of its own, the power of challenging the will. Its challenge is that the will by electing to treat the postulate as though it were a statement of fact, will in the end prevail by creating the fact, whose statement it was supposed to be.

To sum up: the postulate that all men qua men are endowed with dignity fulfils the following four simultaneous functions:

(*a*) It functions as a necessary hypothesis without which moral experience would be neither possible nor explicable.

(*b*) It is a statement of fact (i.e. a statement of existence) and as such is the real and efficacious cause of moral experience.

(*c*) It is an affirmation of faith in the face of clear evidence to the contrary.

(*d*) It is a challenge to our wills, i.e. a regulative idea.

Since it fulfils all those functions simultaneously, each of the four propositions correctly defines one facet of its nature.[31] All facets play definite and decisive rôles in moral theory and

---

[31] It is interesting to note that Kant explicitly uses *b* first part, *c*, *d*, but never *a*, and would probably reject *b* part two, for reasons of method.

practice, so their separate description might not prove altogether useless.

The significance of Kant's assertion, "Now I say that man exists as an end in himself," must not be obscured or diminished by would-be and impossible proofs of its validity. It should rather be gauged in the sense of Rudolf Otto's perceptive if somewhat sentimental annotation: "It is with great inner emotion that we look upon this eruption of a deep and independent intuition, for we are privileged to witness the birth of the mightiest and most significant of all ideas that were ever pronounced in the domain of ethical enjuiry: The idea of a concrete, existent value-in-and-for-itself, an idea moreover which reason can accept and respect."[32]

Cambridge University

[32] Rudolf Otto, Notes to Kant's *Grundlegung zur Metaphysik der Sitten* (Gotha: L. Klotz, 1930), p. 199.